THE WHICH? GUIDE TO THE INTERNET

About the author

SINCE working for a decade in the software industry Richard Wentk has been a freelance writer, computer trainer and consultant, with a particular interest in making computer technology accessible to non-technical people. He now works mostly over the Internet from his home in Wiltshire.

Acknowledgements

The author would like to thank Lisa Maturo, Sara Edlington, Jesa Macbeth, and everyone who contributed to the case histories.

THE WHICH? GUIDE
TO THE INTERNET

RICHARD WENTK

CONSUMERS' ASSOCIATION

Which? Books are commissioned and researched by
Consumers' Association and published by
Which? Ltd, 2 Marylebone Road, London NW1 4DF
Email address: books@which.net

Distributed by The Penguin Group:
Penguin Books Ltd, 27 Wrights Lane, London W8 5TZ

First edition September 1997
Copyright © 1997 Which? Ltd

British Library Cataloguing-in-Publication Data
A catalogue record for this book is available from the British Library

ISBN 0 85202 683 8

For a full list of Which? books, please write to Which? Books,
Castlemead, Gascoyne Way, Hertford X, SG14 1LH
or access our web site at http://www.which.net/

Cover design by Ridgeway Associates
Cover photograph by Mehau Kulyk/Science Photo Library
Typographic design by Paul Saunders

Typeset by Business ColorPrint, Welshpool, Powys, Wales
Printed and bound in Great Britain by Clays Ltd, St Ives plc

CONTENTS

INTRODUCTION

THE INTERNET is one of the most surprising technical innovations of the century. In essence it is very simple; it is a resilient computer network which makes it easier for people across the globe to communicate with each other. But its practical and social implications have yet to be fathomed, and it is growing and evolving at such a rate that it is impossible to predict what it will be like even ten years or so into the twenty-first century.

The statistics speak for themselves. According to surveys by Datamonitor and Intelliquest, there were 635,000 Internet users in the UK in 1995. By the end of 1996 this number had grown to 2.5 million. Indeed, the number of users both in the UK and worldwide seems set to continue doubling every year until at least the start of the twenty-first century. At the time of writing, over 50 million people worldwide use the Internet every day, exchanging a volume of information that dwarfs the contents of the world's largest libraries.

The Internet is currently in a state of transition. Originally designed as an experimental testbed for computer communication systems that would continue to function after a nuclear attack, it has moved away from being the preserve of the military and academics and is now open to everyone. It can be used for a relatively modest fee, and this has brought it within the reach of schools, colleges, offices, people working from home and anyone else who wants easy access to information and lightning-fast communications. For some people it has become a vital part of their work, while for others it is an alternative to TV, radio and the newspapers, with the added benefit of two-way instead of

one-way communication. The change in the Internet's population is forcing it to grow and develop into a more accessible and
less technology-oriented medium.

But for all that, it remains a mystery to many people. Even with
recent technological advances it is still more complex and harder
to use than it might be – although this is changing rapidly as
various business organisations realise that a fortune is to be made
from cheap, easy and fast Internet facilities for the home. Socially,
it has been trivialised and sensationalised by the popular press as
the exclusive preserve of child pornographers and other social
inadequates. While the Internet inevitably mirrors the seedy
aspects of life, the reality of most of what goes on on-line is
somewhat less sensational and a good deal more useful. For a
typical home user, its advantages are obvious: speed, accessibility
and a chance to make contact with millions of people, some of
whom are likely to become friends.

This book aims to demystify the Internet and explains in plain
English what it can and cannot be used for. In the pages that
follow, you will find explanations of the most widely used
Internet jargon words and ideas, advice on how to get the best
from the various services it offers and examples of how to fit in
with other Internet users, making it seem as if you are an 'old
hand'. Also included are outline descriptions of how to choose
between competing services and software packages, practical
explanations of how to achieve basic tasks, and details of useful
advanced skills for more experienced users. Whether you are
planning to use the Internet for fun, for profit, for exploration or
simply out of curiosity, this book will provide everything you
need to get the very best from the time and money you spend
on-line.

CHAPTER 1

WHAT CAN THE INTERNET DO FOR ME?

THE INTERNET is the perfect tool for exchanging information and is a natural progression from the telephone and the fax machine. The telephone is a very good way of getting the sound of your voice from one place to another and the fax machine can send an electronic copy of a printed page around the world. However, both are limited because they deal with only one kind of information.

When connected to the Internet, a computer can do everything the telephone and the fax can do as well as a variety of other tasks: exchanging text, documents, sounds, music, photographs, drawings, plans, video clips and even computer software. It can make copies of the same information available to thousands of people at once, or change the way that the information is presented, depending on who is looking at it. It is also possible to use the Internet to find information about people, companies, topics and organisations.

The Internet is a library, a notice board, a messaging system, a shop front, a debating society, a social club, an archive, a newspaper and a personal assistant, all at once. However, its potential is still being explored, and new applications, for example, on-line shopping, are continually being developed for it.

Its uses tend to fall into two groups: communicating with like-minded people; and discovering and sharing information about almost any subject. The three tools offered on the Internet to do this are electronic mail, the newsgroup system, and the World Wide Web. Individually, each has its merits, but the Internet's power is most obvious when they are all used together. To get a better idea of what this means it is helpful to take a closer look at each one.

Electronic mail (email)

Email is the electronic equivalent of traditional paper mail: you type a message into your computer, specify an address, then send it to the Internet. Within a few seconds, or perhaps a few minutes at most, unless the Internet is suffering from technical trouble, the message will arrive at its destination.

Email compares favourably with the telephone, the fax and the traditional memo and letter. Unlike a telephone call, an email message does not require instant attention but remains unread until the recipient chooses to look at it. He or she can then reply to the message immediately, wait until later or simply ignore it.

This flexibility makes it an excellent medium for many kinds of business and social interactions. It is also more convenient to use than a fax as the text is sent directly, without the need for it to be printed out and run through a fax machine. In addition, emails do not have the grainy, rough quality that makes faxed letters and memos so difficult to read.

Email messages are cheaper to send than both faxes and letter post, and they are less likely to get lost in a busy office. While paper faxes and letters can pile up on desks and be misfiled, email messages can remain filed electronically inside a computer. This makes it possible to arrange the information in various useful ways – for example, by listing all the messages from one person, or by finding all those that mention a given word or phrase. Of course, you need to be organised yourself to make the most of this filing facility.

Because of these advantages, people who use email tend to do so for everything that does not require a formal letter or a personal conversation; this ranges from friendly social chatter to various business-related exchanges, such as price lists, negotiations, questions, and so on. Its only major drawback is that it can be slightly unwieldy for pictures and diagrams, but since most messages consist only of text, this is not usually a problem.

CASE HISTORY – Juliette

Juliette Wilson is a freelance journalist and has found that email has changed the way she works, and communicates with friends.

'I work from home, and the best thing about email is that I can now send in work without using a fax, a floppy disk or a print-out. Email is quicker and cheaper, and it means I can bounce corrections back and forth to an editor if he or she doesn't like something and wants it changed. I've also found it's a good way to get information from abroad. I've even done whole email interviews with people I've never met face-to-face: instead, I've sent them a list of questions, and they've sent me the answers.

'It's great for socialising as well. A lot of my friends have email now, and recently we worked out how to set up a mailing list so that if one of us sends a message we all see it. We spend a lot of time gossiping and making stupid jokes on it, which livens up the day no end when you work from home. When we want to go out as a group we've found it's a great way to arrange the details. Trying to co-ordinate 20 people by phone for a concert or a theatre date can be a nightmare, but with email it seems to be much simpler and more relaxed.'

Newsgroups

In spite of its name, the newsgroup system, also known as Usenet, has nothing to do with news. Instead, it offers tens of thousands of discussion areas where people can 'chat' sociably, exchange views and information, and – in some cases – annoy each other mercilessly.

Newsgroups are like public bulletin-board systems. When you send a message – this is known as 'posting' – to a discussion area, everyone else who reads that area will see it. If someone replies, everyone will see the reply as well. In this way a conversation develops with participants all over the world.

Newsgroups are used for entertainment, debate and getting answers to questions. The list of subject areas covered is vast and includes a dazzling array of useful and not-so-useful subjects: fish-breeding, scuba diving, various computer topics, humour, discussions about different cultures, and even a support group for pizza delivery drivers. (Quirky subjects like this are not unusual on the Internet.) While some groups are inane or contain information of dubious legality, others are more serious and professional. The latter groups are useful places in which to find answers to questions about the subjects they are dedicated to.

Many newsgroups have a document called an FAQ – a Frequently Asked Questions list – which is posted regularly to it. FAQs were invented for the benefit of long-standing group members, who objected to having to answer the same questions each time anyone new joined the group. Over time many FAQs have become a summary of the wisdom of each group. At the very least they define its culture and explain what kind of messages and questions are and are not appropriate. At best they offer a surprisingly detailed summary of what is known about a particular subject. Even though these summaries are prepared by amateurs, the information they contain can be more useful than that available in bookstores and libraries.

The groups themselves are arranged either by subject matter or by geography. Some UK cities, such as London, Oxford and Birmingham, have their own newsgroups, and these are used for casual chat and discussions about local issues. The UK also has its own collection of national groups, which include professional, religious and hobbyist interests. A handful are used for job offers and job applications and non-commercial buying and selling; they work rather like the popular free classified newspapers that are widely available in the UK's larger cities.

However, most groups are international in scope, making them a truly global resource. But sometimes as the readership increases, the quality of information goes down. The main problem with the newsgroup system is 'noise' – a technical term for messages that are either annoying or irrelevant. 'Spam', the newsgroup world's equivalent of junk mail, is a big part of the noise problem. Spam is advertising that is sent to as many groups as possible, irrespective of whether it is appropriate to them. It is a blatant attempt to use the newsgroup system as a mass-mailing tool, and it causes major annoyance to everyone who uses it. Fortunately, there are ways to deal with spam and other undesirable messages which can make the experience of Usenet more pleasant and useful. For more information on filtering messages and newsgroups in general, see Chapter 5.

CASE HISTORY – Paul

In the autumn of 1996 Paul Johnson, a computer consultant, was diagnosed with stomach cancer. He was already familiar with the Internet but was still surprised at how much information and support was available on-line.

'I started by looking at a newsgroup called alt.support.cancer, which turned out to have a lot of really useful information. You never know with newsgroups whether or not they're going to be full of rubbish, but this one certainly wasn't. It put me in touch with other people in the same boat who were asking the same kinds of questions and dealing with the same issues that I was.

'The great thing about this was that it pointed me in the direction of other resources. Some of these were on-line – such as web pages to do with self-help, diet and so on – and some were in "real life" ['real life' is the Internet term for everything that does not happen on the Internet]. There are even a couple of doctors who regularly post help and suggestions. As a result of the contacts I made on the group I found a local cancer support group, which has been amazingly helpful.

'People assume that the Internet is full of computer experts and porn merchants, and that's it. But it's just not true. Some of the things people were posting to the newsgroup were actually very personal, and very moving – the kind of thing you'd find it hard to express to a friend or partner, never mind an anonymous audience. But that doesn't seem to stop people. Because of this you can get a really strong sense of community even though you never physically meet. It is strange, and I can see it wouldn't suit everyone, but when it works it can work really well.'

The World Wide Web

The World Wide Web, often shortened to 'the Web', was invented in the early 1990s by British physicist Tim Berners-Lee. He created it to help him keep track of the various pieces of loosely related information he was keeping in his computer. Since its introduction, the World Wide Web has taken the Internet by storm. It is rather like an electronic magazine or noticeboard with contributions from millions of people. Articles contain 'links' – special highlighted words or phrases – which can be clicked on with a mouse and lead to related subject matter. This can contain links of its own, and so on, indefinitely.

If you are creating web articles of your own (see Appendix 4), it is possible to add links to information in someone else's articles; this is one reason why the Web is such a rich source of information on so many topics. Each article, or collection of articles, is called a 'web site' – usually shortened to 'site'. As an example, imagine someone who has created a site devoted to mountaineering. Apart from personal anecdotes and photographs, they can include links to information about mountaineering that has already been written by other people. These links can add more details, offer a different perspective, explain technical terms and include yet more links to various mountaineering resources such as magazines, shops and discussion groups. This web of connections makes the original article much more informative and useful than if it had been standing alone. Where a book author has to use pointers such as 'For more information on this subject see this magazine, and that book', anyone using the Web can integrate these cross-references so all the information is immediately accessible.

The Web's great strength is that it is open to everyone, and anyone can put up information. No one has to pay a subscription or impress an editor in order to be published, and no central organisation says what is or is not appropriate. The technical skills required are modest, and people who would normally turn pale at the thought of programming a computer have created web sites with very little effort. The costs can be modest too. Private users who are not developing commercial sites can usually put their information up for free.

Because of these attributes you will find information about absolutely everything on the Web: summaries of academic research; press releases, brochures and advertising from large companies; sites created by hobbyists who want to share their enthusiasms with the world; random diary pages written and posted by ordinary people just for the sake of it, and so on. The quantity and the variety of the information available is breathtaking, for example, fan pages dedicated to cult TV shows, information about sports, poetry, art, stock market quotes, DIY, and so on.

Apart from entertainment and informative articles, the Web offers access to unprecedented amounts of raw information. You can find up-to-the-minute news stories and weather reports, details of cheap flights from the major travel services, and even free software.

For some businesses it is an effective way to generate new sales. Because web pages can be read by anyone anywhere in the world, the limitations of local trade no longer apply. Any business that takes credit cards can now reach an international audience for a relatively small outlay.

CASE HISTORY – Elizabeth

Elizabeth Clear runs a Victorian art and poster shop in Glastonbury, Somerset. Web-based advertising transformed her business, almost overnight.

'We were approached by someone in 1996 to see if we would like to contribute to a web site for local traders that would be called The Isle of Avalon. To start with we were concerned about the price, but we compared it with the Yellow Pages *and it was much cheaper, which was a good start. But we decided to do a little research first.*

'The first thing we asked the organiser to do was search the Web for keywords to do with our business – pre-Raphaelite, Victorian, Romantic, and so on. Apart from a few museums and university papers he found nothing. That was when we realised we were in with a chance of doing something new.

'We began by putting up a straight catalogue – just a list really, with a logo that my partner designed. Then we started adding images. Now we have a montage of our bestsellers, which gets a lot of attention.

'We had maybe a thousand email enquiries last year. Some are silly – you get people writing to you and saying things like "Burne-Jones did a painting with two people in it – have you got it?" – but some are orders, which we ship right away. We also get a lot of phone calls from

abroad. And because the business is mail order — we can put a poster in a cardboard tube and send it anywhere in no time — it works very well. We go out of our way to be very helpful, so we're starting to become known as the place to get these prints. We're dropping the Yellow Pages *and also all our newspaper advertising. Advertising on the Web is much cheaper and better value for money. And the other advantage is that we can make changes immediately — we tell the site manager what we want, and he can do it more or less on the spot.'*

Is the Internet for me?

If you are an academic, a technology consultant, a teleworker or a journalist, the benefits of the Internet are obvious: low-cost access to unlimited quantities of information and the ability to exchange both work and comments with colleagues and employers are the main attractions. But the Internet is also starting to become an indispensable tool for other professionals. Doctors, lawyers and engineers can take advantage of a number of on-line databases and other sources of information which are more convenient and accessible than those available at a large library. Information found on Internet sites is a useful complement to information available in paper form.

Small businesses can use the Web to advertise their services for a negligible amount of money. Considering that a single advertisement in a magazine can cost hundreds, or perhaps thousands, of pounds, a web site that can be seen by an equivalent number of people, takes about two weeks to design and costs perhaps £50 a month to maintain is obviously good value for money. Other advantages exist too: unlike an advertisement in a magazine or newspaper, a web site can maintain a record of the people who see it. This makes it easier to keep in touch with them and build a profile of potential customers.

Email also has obvious advantages for professional users. Although sending plans and diagrams can be expensive compared with a text-only email, it is still quicker, simpler and cheaper than using a courier service or a fax machine, especially if the recipient lives abroad.

In short, anyone who needs to send information from place to place quickly and cheaply or is looking for a convenient source of research material will benefit from being on the Internet. For someone who already has a computer the costs involved are very reasonable, and a trial period is well worth the time and money. Someone who does not have a computer can still try out the Internet first for a small outlay (see Chapter 2), and it is worth doing this to get an accurate idea of what the benefits might be.

For anyone else (other than the sorts of people mentioned above), the Internet is not particularly useful except for the fact that it is a good way for people with similar interests to get in touch with each other. People who already have a busy social life may not feel it is worth taking the time to do this, and the Internet will have little to offer them apart from occasional distraction. Although the Internet is likely to become part of everyone's life over the next few years, for now there is no pressing reason why someone who belongs in this category should get on-line.

Children will find that using the Internet is a wonderful way of doing research for homework. (Some material on the Internet is definitely not suitable for children, but there are ways to stop children from reading it, and these are discussed in more detail in Chapter 8.) As an educational resource the World Wide Web is unparalleled, although newsgroups are perhaps too harsh an environment for all children to feel comfortable in. Children with an inquisitive nature may find that the Web is the best toy they have ever had, although it is unlikely to make much difference to their academic achievements unless used in a structured way. Finally, they can play computer games against real opponents over the Internet.

It is important to be aware that the Internet has drawbacks, the most obvious being that it is still to some extent an experimental system. Problems occur fairly regularly – not often enough to cause most people any serious loss of money or information, but frequently enough to be irritating. To a large degree, the number of problems you encounter depends on which company you choose for your connection, although it is probably fair to say that almost all have had, or will have, some kind of technical teething trouble.

The Internet has nothing at all in common with traditional media, which present a very professional, formal front; instead, informality rules, and therefore the tone is often very different. It has a very obvious culture all of its own, and this does not appeal to everyone. Some of the more colourful newsgroups, for example, can sometimes be verbal equivalents of a pub brawl; people speak their minds without holding back. Anyone who does not have an open mind may find some of the content or the exchanges shocking or offensive, and it is important to be aware of this possibility.

In many ways the Internet is like a foreign country. The inhabitants mostly speak English but their customs and traditions are completely different from those most of us are used to. Almost everyone goes through a process of acclimatisation before they feel comfortable with the new environment.

At heart the Internet is simply a tool that makes communication easier with everyone else on it – without exception. Everything that people do, from the most exalted activity to the most debased, is represented on-line in an accessible way, thereby creating an environment that some people find very difficult. Some people find that email and other forms of electronic communication are simply detached and unreal.

CASE HISTORY – Aboodi

Aboodi Shaby is an alternative health practitioner living in Wiltshire. He was initially interested in the Net but did not find enough to sustain his long-term interest.

'For me the appeal of the Net was about finding interesting ideas and home pages of alternative things, and it was fun for a while to surf around, look at various sites and try things out. For example, I found some interesting Islamic chants and appealing artworks that I wouldn't have been able to discover any other way. But the novelty wore off very quickly. I felt it was a bit like hanging around a big bookshop – a nice way to spend a couple of afternoons, but not the sort of thing I'd want to do permanently.

'One of the problems was that technically I didn't really know how to go about finding people with the same interests. And besides it seemed a

bit strange trying to meet people on-line. I think I prefer to meet human beings face to face rather than through the Net. Rather like a telephone chat line, the encounter simply doesn't feel very real.

'For me it would be nice to have the opportunity to play around on someone's modem in the same way that it's nice to channel-hop on someone's cable TV system once in a while. But that doesn't mean I would want to take out a subscription. Really I'd be happiest if I could use it in a local library once in a while instead of from home — that would be the ideal for me.'

Putting it all together

Although email, the Web and newsgroups are very useful individually, the true power of the Internet becomes clear when they are used together. Experienced Internet users are already finding that the range of tasks they can use the Internet for is steadily increasing, and for some people it has already become indispensable.

CASE HISTORY – Paul

Paul Cooper is a journalist who has been using the Internet since 1994. His experience is typical of more dedicated Net users.

'I think almost everyone starts off feeling baffled and bewildered. It's not just the technology. The Internet is a strange thing and it has lots of strange people with strange ideas using it. Quite a few seem to be — how can I put this? — a few slices of bread short of a sandwich. Others are more normal, but may not be the kind of people you'd associate with in real life. So it takes a while to get used to suddenly having all these strangers in your home, all doing their best to make it a more colourful place.

'But eventually you settle down and start using the thing properly. This is where it sneaks up on you — for the first few months you think you're dabbling with it, then you wake up one day and suddenly it's very hard to do without.

'Take my work, which is science journalism. I can look on the Net and get the latest stories before they appear anywhere — before anyone

sees them in print or hears about them from radio and TV. And I can backtrack too – there are archives I can look through, and libraries I can raid. So I can follow a story through, put a news story into some kind of context, make connections between related stories, or even follow someone's career. Before, it used to be much harder.

'Socially – well, I've met a few people in person, even been to a couple of Internet parties, although to be honest they had too many people who talked only about computers for me to really enjoy them. Last Christmas I had cards from Cornwall, the States, Australia and even Brazil, all from people I exchange email with but have never met. This summer I've arranged a flat-swap with someone from New Zealand. She gets to see London, we get to see Wellington. No hotel bills for either of us. Obviously email has saved me a lot in international calls, too.

'But it's useful in all kinds of unexpected ways. I've arranged CD swaps with people in other countries (they can get CDs I can't and vice versa), found cheap flights for a weekend in Barcelona, bought software, magazines and books from the States, checked rail timetables and ordered flowers for my girlfriend. Really, the only thing stopping everyone from using it is that it's still too complicated – I had to get a friend to help me set it up – and too expensive. Not everyone can afford £1,000 or so for a decent computer. I think once the price comes down it will be just like the phone and the TV and the radio – everyone will use it without thinking twice. Although I do sometimes waste time on it – it's frighteningly easy to do that – I wouldn't give it up for anything now.'

CHAPTER 2

Getting a connection

To access the Internet, home and small-business users need five things: a modern telephone connection with a socket, a computer, an optional extra for the computer called a modem, a subscription to an Internet service and suitable software.

Alternative ways of getting on-line are through educational establishments and workplaces. All universities have an Internet connection, as do an increasing number of schools. Access for students is usually free, although it may be restricted in some ways: for example, some newsgroups may not be available.

A similar situation often applies in the workplace. Many companies and institutions now offer Internet access to their employees, although again the service may be limited. Some companies ban newsgroups altogether because they feel they are a possible source of distraction. Sometimes only an email service is provided.

Of course, universities and companies do not make their connections available for public use, but in some ways home users are in a better position because they can pick and choose between the different service providers. If they find that one is not good enough they can try another.

Counting the cost

While 'professional' connections are free for employees and students (although they are paid for by the companies and universities), home users have to pay two costs. Depending on which company you buy your Internet connection service from, the first is either a flat fee which buys unlimited time, or a 'pay as you go' charge where you pay more the longer you use the service.

The second is the telephone charges, as connections to the Internet are still made over the telephone lines. (Some subscribers with cable connections are able to make free telephone calls at off-peak times, so users with this system will not always have to pay this second cost.) Fortunately, most Internet services have arranged for calls to be charged at the local rate, or in a very few cases at a rate very close to it. This helps make the costs quite reasonable – for example, at weekends local calls with BT cost a penny a minute. However, if someone is on-line a lot, they will need to budget to cover these additional costs. These can vary from £5 to £10 a month for light use (10 minutes per day outside office hours) to perhaps £50 a month for people who use the Internet during the day for work purposes.

Internet access providers and on-line services

Although it is usual to talk about 'the Internet' as if it were a single entity, in fact two rather different kinds of services are available: one type offered by Internet access providers (IAPs), and the other by on-line services. Both have strengths and weaknesses. The biggest difference is that IAPs provide only a 'raw' connection to the Internet, while on-line services provide other services as well. As a rule of thumb, on-line services are ideal for anyone who wants to use the Internet with the minimum of effort and technological complexity, while IAPs are for those who appreciate direct access to the facilities it offers and are prepared to spend more time learning to use them. It is useful to know about the main differences before deciding which is the right sort for you.

Internet access providers (IAPs)

IAPs offer two things: a connection to the Internet; and a package of suitable software which lets you use the facilities the connection offers. These facilities typically include one or more

How your connection to an Internet access provider (IAP) works

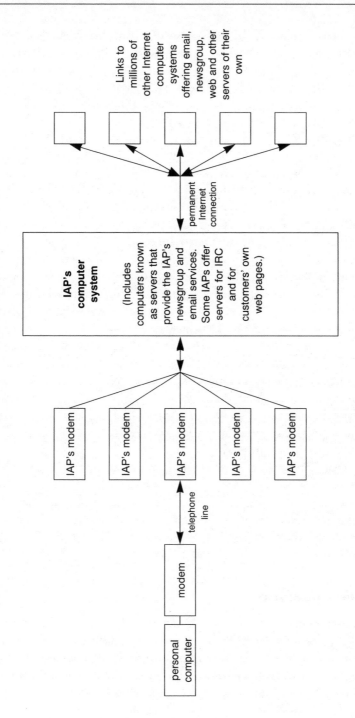

Links to millions of other Internet computer systems offering email, newsgroup, web and other servers of their own

permanent Internet connection

IAP's computer system

(Includes computers known as servers that provide the IAP's newsgroup and email services. Some IAPs offer servers for IRC and for customers' own web pages.)

IAP's modem
IAP's modem
IAP's modem
IAP's modem
IAP's modem

telephone line

modem

personal computer

23

personal email addresses, access to the newsgroup network (Usenet), and access to the World Wide Web. (As part of the deal many providers also include 'space on the Web' at no extra cost; this is used to publish your own web pages, see Appendix 4.)

It is important to note that these facilities can be extended with extra software. A raw Internet connection can be used in many different ways, and the software that an IAP supplies is really just a starting point. Many people find they use this software for a while, and when they are more experienced they change to other software which suits their needs more closely. This can be bought commercially or copied from the Internet itself. Some IAPs skimp on software, which means you may be denied certain more advanced Internet facilities (such as those mentioned in Chapter 3) or forced to use email and newsgroups in an expensive and inefficient way. The easiest way to tell if this is the case is to check if you are being offered anything more than a 'web browser'. If not, you will almost certainly not be getting the best from your connection.

The costs of using an IAP's services can be very reasonable – typically a flat fee of between £4 and £10 a month – and in return subscribers get unlimited access. This means they can spend as much time using the Internet as they want without worrying about extra charges from the IAP – although of course this does not include telephone costs, which are charged in the usual way. (See Appendix 1.)

IAPs range from small local services that have a few hundred users, to large country-wide networks with tens of thousands of customers. They all offer more or less the same facilities. The biggest differences are in the quality of the service – in terms of its speed, overall reliability, the level of help, and the quality of the software they offer – and the cost.

On-line services

On-line services – the best known are America Online (AOL), Prodigy and CompuServe – offer a very different experience to that available from an Internet access provider. They are more like electronic magazines, which offer a connection to the Internet as a sideline.

How your connection to an on-line service provider works

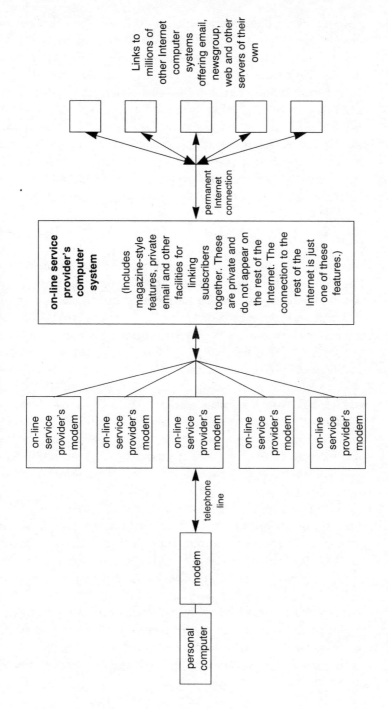

Links to millions of other Internet computer systems offering email, newsgroup, web and other servers of their own

permanent Internet connection

on-line service provider's computer system

(Includes magazine-style features, private email and other facilities for linking subscribers together. These are private and do not appear on the rest of the Internet. The connection to the rest of the Internet is just one of these features.)

on-line service provider's modem

on-line service provider's modem

on-line service provider's modem

on-line service provider's modem

on-line service provider's modem

telephone line

modem

personal computer

If you subscribe to an on-line service, you effectively get two services in one. The first gives you access to magazine- and TV-style features on a wide range of subjects, the ability to exchange messages and chat electronically with other subscribers, and a chance to read and contribute to various discussion areas. These facilities are available only to other members of the same service, and are hidden from the rest of the Internet. The other part of the service is a link to the Internet, which offers the usual newsgroup, web and email facilities. On an on-line service this connection is no more important than any of the other features and facilities – it appears as one option among many others.

Which is best for me?

For beginners, on-line services offer a number of advantages. The first is that they smooth the way to an introductory experience of on-line life by supplying software that is very easy to install and use. This software is proprietary, and you do not have the option of changing it for something better; except in a few special cases other Internet software will not work with an on-line service (see page 229).

The second benefit is that on-line services provide immediate starting points for exploration; newcomers do not feel lost and unsure as to what their options are. Connecting to the Internet via an IAP for the first time can be daunting because there is no obvious way to find interesting information. Connecting to an on-line service is usually much more straightforward because an index appears on-screen listing all the different options.

The third advantage is that these on-line services attempt to make information easier to find by leading you to it and gathering details about similar subjects together. Having these prepared for you saves you from having to search for them for yourself. However, it can limit less adventurous users, who may be less likely to explore the other information on the rest of the Internet as a result.

The main disadvantage of on-line services is their cost. A small monthly payment covers a certain number of 'free' hours. Any further time over and above this is charged as extra, often at a fairly hefty rate. This can make it hard to budget for these services effectively, and naturally, the services are designed to entice customers to spend as much time on-line as possible.

For light use, say, a few hours a month, this pricing system offers better value than a connection with an IAP. According to AOL, its subscribers spend an average of about seven hours a month on-line, and with AOL's current pricing scheme this costs less than the £11 a month charged by a typical IAP. But beware, with heavier use it can be surprisingly easy to run up a huge monthly bill when using an on-line service. If and when these services start to offer a flat-rate pricing system – something already offered by AOL in the USA and introduced in the UK in the summer of 1997 – they will become very good value. Until then, their extra costs need to considered carefully.

Other, subtle, disadvantages of on-line services are obvious to more experienced users. Although the software offered by on-line services is simple to use, it is sometimes not quite compatible with the rest of the Internet. This means that some information, particularly on the Web, will not appear as it should. In extreme

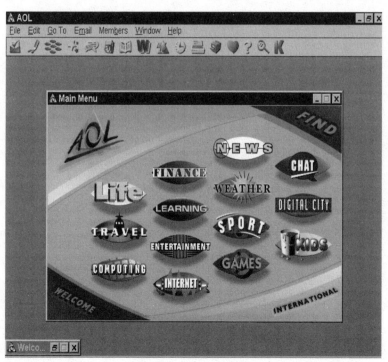

cases it will not be possible to read it at all. Although certain on-line services are moving towards allowing their subscribers the option of using other software – in effect, offering the same kind of general-purpose connection offered by an IAP – getting it to work can be an awkward process. All the on-line services are working to remedy this, but in the meantime the access they offer to the Internet can be slightly flawed compared with that available from an IAP.

Another point to consider is a cultural one. There is the common perception among established Internet users that some on-line services are more respectable than others (see page 105). If you attempt to join in a discussion in a newsgroup while using one of these less popular on-line services you will have to contend with prejudice, making it difficult to persuade others to take your views seriously.

Finally, the community offered by on-line services may not suit everyone. 'Live chat' – where groups of people type messages that immediately appear on each other's screens – is a popular feature on on-line services, but in practice much of it can be trite and uninteresting. Although the same can be said of some parts of the Internet, the latter offers a much wider variety of choices – some of still lower but others of much higher quality.

A practical comparison

For a better idea of what the differences are between IAPs and on-line services, it is useful to look at one particular example – how news is presented by both.

All the on-line services offer news features that are very similar to those in electronic newspapers, with headlines and background stories. They are always easy to find and concentrate on the same subject matter you might expect from a national daily newspaper, although because of the international nature of the Internet, foreign coverage is usually better. But the stories are much shorter than their equivalents in a daily newspaper, and you will not find the editorial depth you may be used to.

Searching for news on the Internet is a completely different experience. If you want news, you have to search the Web to find it for yourself. This can take a fair amount of time initially because you will need to do some exploring to find the sources of news that interest you. But once you have done this, you can return to these sources very quickly.

This approach gives you much more control over which news you read, when you read it and the amount of background and other detail you want. It also gives you a much broader selection of possible sources. On the Web you can find electronic versions of UK and foreign newspapers, direct connections to various press agencies and newswire services, various technical journals and publications, electronic versions of popular magazines, electronic magazines that have never been in print, and so on. The level of editorial comment varies from none at all to the same as that in a traditional newspaper. One advantage of the Internet is that the web versions of some magazines and newspapers publish readers' comments as soon as they are received. This gives the medium an immediacy that cannot be matched anywhere else.

29

It is the difference in depth, effort and detail that most obviously separates on-line services from the Internet as a whole. With an on-line service you will get easy access information that is known to be interesting and useful, but your ability to explore it in detail is relatively limited. On the Internet the volume and diversity of information can be overwhelming initially, but with a little practice you can find almost anything you want. You can then start to create a personalised library of high-quality news and information services to suit your individual needs.

In short, if you have an enquiring and open mind, and can appreciate the attraction of getting information that is hard to find elsewhere, then a direct connection to the Internet via an IAP is ideal for you. It is also a better choice if you plan to spend a large amount of time on-line.

However, if you prefer to get information with the minimum of effort or if you are more interested in socialising and making new friends, and do not intend to use the Internet a great deal, you will almost certainly find that an on-line service will suit you better.

CASE HISTORY – Michael

Michael Jeffries is in his final year at a sixth-form college. He is studying sciences and is a keen amateur astronomer. When looking for information on his hobby he found that the depth of material available on the Internet was far greater than that offered by an on-line service.

'College has its own Internet link, and at home my Dad has an AOL account, so I've had time to look at both. The good thing about the astronomy areas on-line is that AOL has links to the astronomy information available on the Internet. The different AOL-specific discussion areas are actually pretty interesting too. There's a lot to get you started, and it's very easy to use.

'But once you start looking around the Internet for real you realise just how much more there is. There are hundreds of web pages, including ones put up by NASA with details of all their latest missions, the latest pictures from the Hubble Space Telescope, and so on. And the astronomy and science newsgroups have a much wider range of readers than AOL has, and professional astronomers contribute too, which is really good.

'If I was just dabbling or looking for people ·to chat to then AOL would be fine. But I think people who are more serious about a subject or keen on something obscure or unusual will need to spend a lot of time on the Internet to get what they want.'

Other options

Not all services fall neatly into these two categories. Some attempt to use the Web to simulate an on-line service, but without the need for special software (you access it like you would any other web site). Others offer more obscure Internet-related services which use Internet technology in an unusual way. These are discussed below.

Combined services

Which? Online, VirginNet and the Microsoft Network (MSN) are examples of combined services. Although they offer all the usual Internet facilities and use Internet technology, they also maintain a private web site with information that is available only to paying customers. With the exception of MSN, which is a very large site that is much more like a true on-line service, the private (paid for) area tends to be smaller than that offered by a genuine on-line service, and the information is usually more tightly focused. These services are some of the newest to appear on the Internet, and to some extent they are still experimental. Both the content and the way the information is presented are still evolving and are therefore not standardised. Although slightly more expensive than other options, they can be good value if you find the information they offer unusually interesting or useful.

Intranets

Intranets are only notionally related to the rest of the Internet. An Intranet is an internal computer network used within an organisation, which offers the employees the same facilities as those available on the Internet – email, newsgroups and something similar to the World Wide Web – but is not available to the general public. Intranets do usually allow limited access to the Internet, although the Intranet itself is designed to be for and about the company. They are useful for smoothing communication across a company and can remove the need for the countless reams of paper traditionally used for office administration. Unless you work for a company with an Intranet, or are considering setting one up, you will not get a chance to use one.

Bulletin boards

Socially, bulletin board services (BBSs) are the Internet's immediate ancestor. Although they use much simpler and cruder technology, they were the source of the first public experiments with facilities similar to email and Usenet. Unlike the Internet, which was designed by and for computer professionals, academics and military users, BBSs have always been the preserve of the amateur and open to the general public.

The various BBS networks communicate with each other over telephone lines; they do not have access to the high-speed links that are the backbone of the Internet. Information is passed from computer to computer during the night. It can often take days to get a reply to an email even if the recipient writes a response as soon as it arrives.

The attraction of BBSs is that they are small and local, the users can be quite sociable, and access is usually free. Some even offer a kind of email link to the Internet, although again it is not as instantaneous as that offered by an IAP or on-line service.

With the growth of interest in the Internet it is likely that BBSs will soon become marginalised as a specialised hobby, rather like amateur radio or CB. In the meantime they continue to attract younger users who cannot afford a true Internet connection, and anyone else who likes the idea of socialising with other users locally. However, because of their limitations they cannot be recommended except for those on the very tightest of budgets.

Try before you buy?

The easiest way to discover what the Internet can do for you is to try it for yourself. Fortunately, a number of low-cost trial options are open to everyone. Some of these do not even require a home computer.

Many large county-libraries offer Internet access on a pay-as-you-go basis. You simply pay a few pounds an hour for the time you are on-line. This fee sometimes includes a single email address and perhaps even space for your own web site.

Similar services are available at cybercafés — futuristic teashops with a collection of Internet-ready computers — as well as a small number of restaurants and pubs. If you live in or near one of the UK's major cities you should be able to find one locally.

Although these facilities provide a good insight into the Internet, it is important to be aware of their drawbacks. The first is that they assume everyone has a basic level of computer literacy. If you have never used a computer before it is wise to learn the basics — including mouse control and how to use the windowing system used on modern computers — somewhere else. Ideally, this should be a place where you can experiment at your own pace, for example, at a friend's house. Otherwise, you can waste a frustrating initial couple of hours working out how to use the computer, while the seconds tick away, instead of exploring the on-line world. Even if you are already computer-literate, make sure someone is on-hand to answer questions and help you learn the basic techniques, so that your time is used as effectively as possible.

Another disadvantage of these facilities is that you will be forced to use one particular brand of software. Since some software that works well for the World Wide Web may not be quite so convenient for email, you may be left with a false impression about the ease of use – or otherwise – of the Internet as a whole. It is also worth remembering that the software you use in one of these places has already been set up for you. You should allow for the fact that setting up an equivalent connection at home will not be as straightforward as sitting down at the computer and turning it on in a cybercafé.

Finally, you will be able to explore only the Internet itself. You will not be able to try out any of the major on-line services this way, and so will not be able to get a clear picture of the different kinds of facilities they offer or whether or not they will be better suited to your personal requirements.

CASE HISTORY – Felicity

Felicity Green is a graphic designer who is suspicious of computers. However, she found that using the Internet connection at her local library was a good way of keeping in touch with her friends overseas and exploring.

'I'm really not keen on computers – I think they're incredibly badly designed and much harder to use than they should be, and I usually get totally frustrated with them. But a lot of my friends were starting to get on-line, and one in particular moved out of the UK to America. She was moving around a lot so there wasn't any other practical way to keep in touch.

'To be honest, even though it was all set up for me, I didn't find it easy to use to start with. I was learning the basics and aware that time was ticking away and my bill was running up. It's not expensive here at £3 an hour, but it's still nerve-wracking when I'm paying for the time spent on-line.

'Eventually I got the hang of it. And actually I found the Web delightful – there are hundreds of art and design resources on there that I would never have heard of otherwise. Email wasn't quite so straightforward, but that's because the library here doesn't supply proper software – just a web browser, which is fine for the Web but very clumsy for email. Still, I've managed to keep in touch with my friend and have even found some new people with similar interests to "talk" to. It can be strange having a conversation with someone on the other side of the world who I've never even met, but it does seem to work.

'The best thing is that this library offers people web space of their own. So I learned how to use that, put up a kind of electronic CV with a list of my work, some samples, and something about me. Apart from getting occasional passing comments from people who have seen the site and liked it, it's even got me some new work.'

Trying out on-line services

Almost all the on-line services publicise their products by offering free trials. These are made available on the front cover of computer and Internet magazines. To take advantage of a free trial offer you need a recent computer and a modem. If you already have these then experimenting with free trials is an excellent way to explore the different on-line services. If you do not have your own equipment, the only way to try an on-line service is to ask a friend who is already using one to let you try it for a few hours.

A typical free trial takes the form of a CD-ROM (offers on floppy disk are now extremely rare), which supplies the special software needed to use the service. You will also be credited with a certain amount of 'free time' on-line. This amount varies enormously – some companies have offered as much as 99 free hours, which is equivalent to over a year's average use.

Once you have installed the software and made a connection you will be asked to give your credit-card details. Although you may think you are running a trial account, once you give these details to all intents and purposes you have joined the service. When your free time has run out, money will be debited from your account unless you give notice that you no longer wish to stay on-line. In some cases this can be given only in writing. So it is important to keep track of the time you use and to remember to cancel if you decide the service is not what you are looking for. All of them include some kind of on-line accounting system which shows you how much time and money you have spent, and it is a good idea to locate this first so you can keep track of your expenditure and not run up a huge bill.

Trying out combined services

Combined services also tend to offer free-trial accounts. These can be a good way of learning about the Internet at home without paying by the hour for it – although of course this is only possible if you already have a PC and a modem. This type of trial gives you a taste of the Internet proper, although with some services it can be less than clear where the Internet ends and the private subscription-only information starts. In general, however, what you will see is the Internet as it is in real life and not the simplified, modified or stylised version that the main on-line services tend to present.

Some combined services have less aggressive marketing policies than the on-line ones, and will assume that you do not want to continue with your subscription after a free trial unless you tell them otherwise. They are ideal for testing the water, especially since the main Internet providers do not – as a rule – offer free trials themselves.

Trying out IAPs

Although IAPs do not offer free trials, experimenting with one of their services is not necessarily an expensive experience. Apart from the monthly subscription, some – but by no means all – IAPs ask for an initial 'set-up' fee. This covers the cost of the administration needed to create your account and includes your personal email address. The set-up fees are usually moderate – between £5 and £30, depending on what the IAP wishes to charge. If you already have a computer and a modem at home it can be worth trying out one or two IAPs for a month or so to see if they suit you. Unfortunately this is not possible with all IAPs; some specify a minimum contract period.

One problem with attempting this, is that it can be very difficult to set up certain computers (especially those which use the Windows 95 system) to work with more than one IAP at the same time. Even if you delete one IAP's software, it may still leave traces, which can prevent software from another IAP from working properly. This can cause problems if you try two trials one after the other or at the same time, or if you use one IAP and want to try a different one to see if their service is better. These are not the kind of difficulties that can be solved by a beginner – if you have these problems, your IAP should be able to sort them out for you.

IAP SERVICES PROVIDE:

- raw connection to the Internet
- email address or addresses (can be accessed from a different IAP, even in a different country – for example, a cybercafé abroad)
- access to the IAP's newsgroup computer
- (sometimes) free personal web space
- 'free' software. Other software can be used instead quite easily.

ON-LINE SERVICES PROVIDE:

- access to magazine-style features with related articles, user contributions, live chat, and links to the Web
- email address or addresses (can be accessed from abroad if the on-line service has a suitable telephone number – cannot be accessed from a cybercafé or via an IAP)
- access to Internet features (newsgroups, the Web) but sometimes with technical limitations
- (sometimes) free personal web space
- 'free' software, proprietary to the service. Other software can be used only with difficulty, if at all.

CHAPTER 3

COMMUNICATING WITH OTHERS

THE INTERNET is highly successful at bringing people together. Although traditional mail is popular and still very widely used, compared with the Internet's ability to transfer messages almost instantly at negligible cost, it is slow and old-fashioned.

While email is the most popular tool for keeping in touch on the Internet, other facilities are also available: IRC, on-line chat, mailing lists, Talk and Instant Messages, WebPhones and video links. Some of these are still at an experimental stage, but all enable the user to communicate with other Internet users around the world at relatively low cost.

Email

For many people, email is the main reason why they use the Internet. The ability to send messages around the world almost instantly has obvious attractions for both business and private use.

A large number of companies now have internal email systems which make it easy for employees to send information from any computer to any other within the organisation. In a business setting, email is ideal for arranging meetings, sending memos, agreeing agendas, and even sending presentations and reports. Although many offices still like to use printed documents, email can minimise much of the administration required to keep information flowing smoothly.

For example, a memo sent by email is quicker and more convenient than a paper memo which needs to be either written or typed and then photocopied and delivered by hand. Email memos can also be sent between buildings on the same site, or even between different sites, much more quickly.

Some companies have found that email facilities can help deal with internal political problems and morale. Senior managers have found that they are suddenly more accessible, and an exchange of ideas and views in both directions, which is facilitated by email, can benefit the company enormously. Future Publishing, one of the UK's largest publishers of computer and other magazines, uses its internal email system to create a 'forum'. Each month an employee is asked to host the forum. Staff send him or her email questions, he or she then edits them to make them anonymous and passes them to the Managing Director, who posts public replies through email.

Home users can use email to keep in touch with friends and family, both in the UK and abroad, make new friends and join some of the Internet's equivalents of various clubs and organisations. Home shopping and banking services rely almost entirely on email, and so, in many ways, it is the most important service on the Internet.

CASE HISTORY – Anne

Anne Simpson is a lawyer who has been experimenting with email. Although she finds it more immediate and useful than some other forms of communication, she also finds it something of a distraction.

'There are two partners and four solicitors here, and we do a moderate amount of work with clients overseas. Email has been very useful for that – we've been able to do things like send over draft contracts to our South African office. It was much cheaper than faxing them, and they had no problems with reading them at the other end, which isn't always true of faxes.

'One drawback is the way that email arrives straight on my desk – or rather, in my computer. There's no secretary to field emails in the way that my secretary fields telephone calls and some of the post. This can be a distraction at times. I do admit, though, that it is much harder to filter email through someone else as most of it really is for my attention, and some of it really is urgent.

'It's also not as immediate as a fax. We use a dial-up connection to the Internet, which means in-coming mail stays on our IAP's computer until our computer dials in automatically – at the moment it does this three times a day. A permanent Internet connection would cost thousands, and we just couldn't justify that at the moment. So I've tended to use email for messages that are important but not absolutely crucial. If something has to go through quickly I'll still send a fax or call the person.

'But despite that, it's been useful. We also use it internally. If I have a question for someone here I can email them, and it doesn't interrupt the flow of my work the way making a call would. It wasn't hugely expensive to set up, so on the whole I'd say it's been a good thing.'

Email in practice

Email is very easy to use. The hardest part is setting up your connection to the Internet. Less good IAPs expect you to type in

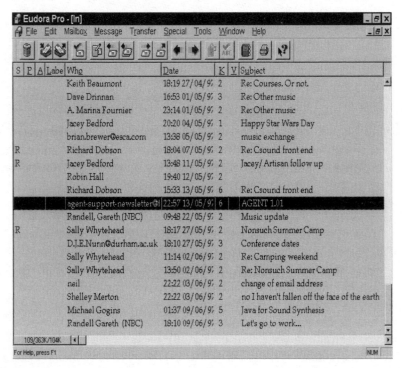

a series of technical details before you can make a connection. (The IAP will send you an information sheet listing them; they include the Internet addresses of the computers the IAP uses for email and all the others on their network which are needed to create and maintain any kind of Internet connection.) But the better ones provide software which does it all for you; in fact this part of the setting-up process is hidden from you completely. Because of this it is a good idea to ask just how much help you can expect to get when you attempt to install the software for the first time.

Email can be used in two ways. 'On-line' email is written and sent while you are connected to the Internet. 'Off-line' email is written before you make a connection, then all the messages you have prepared are sent in bulk when you connect. At the same time, any messages that are waiting for you are quickly copied to your computer. You should use the off-line option wherever possible as it saves you money and allows you to write and read email at a much more leisurely pace. Whether or not you have the option to do this depends on the software supplied by your IAP. Almost all software includes off-line facilities, although sometimes it is not obvious how to use them.

Once everything is installed, the only information you need in order to send someone an email is his or her address. This appears as a collection of words separated by dots, with an '@' (at) sign – for example, *someone@which.co.uk* You must write the address exactly as shown; include all the punctuation and do not put in any extra spaces, otherwise the address will not work. When giving this address verbally it is pronounced 'someone at which dot co dot uk'. Once you have typed in the address in the area marked 'To:' in your software, and added a subject to the subject line, you can add as much or as little text as you like. This text is known as the 'body' of the message.

If you are replying to someone else's message their address will appear in the 'To:' area automatically, so you do not have to type it in again. The subject they specified will also appear in the 'Subject:' area, usually with a 'Re:' in front of it – for example, 'Re: My cheque'. When replying it is usual for software to include a copy of the sender's text preceded by quote marks – which are typically '>'s. This saves you having to re-type the parts of the message that you want to respond to, and also makes it clear which parts are written by you and which by the original sender. To make email more conversational, it is common practice to edit some of the quoted text and reply to each paragraph in turn, leaving a gap to make it clearer and easier to read.

For example:
```
From: ras@angel.i-way.co.uk
To: jw@skydancer.com
Subject: An email example
>Here is an example of quoted text.
>
>There can be lots of quoted paragraphs. Each is marked
>with the quote mark to show that it was written by
>someone else.

And here is the reply section. It doesn't have quote
marks.

>Here is some more quoted text in a different
>paragraph.

And here is another reply to it. It's usual to break up
conversations like this.
```

Paragraphs can be quoted more than once. If someone replies and quotes your quote the results can look like this:

```
>>Something I said originally, with two quotes because it
>>has been through the quoting process twice — once when
>>the other person replied and again when I quoted their
>>reply.

>The other person's reply to my message

My reply to their reply doesn't have any quote marks,
because this is a fresh reply.
```

It is common practice to limit the number of quoted quotes, otherwise a message can become hard to read. Often there is enough context in the most recent reply to make it clear what the conversation is about.

Email on the Internet and on on-line services

There are small but significant differences between the email facilities that on-line services offer their members and those available on the rest of the Internet. On the Internet, email is a text-only system. In other words, an email is simply a list of words. All the other attributes that appear in a printed letter – the size and style of the lettering, the page layout, and so on – are not included. Although this seems limiting, it guarantees that a message will be readable on any computer system no matter which software it uses. Text is the 'lowest common denominator', and a text-only message will always get through.

Because on-line services supply their own software, they can be slightly more creative. Most offer email which can include extras such as **BOLD**, *italic* or underlined text, or letters that appear in different sizes or colours. It is also easier to add non-text information such as diagrams and charts to an email and be sure that it will be readable at the other end. (This process, known as sending an attachment, is described in more detail on page 44.)

Perhaps the most significant difference is that emails sent between members of the same on-line service are more secure. While the information is passing over the Internet it can be tapped, because it is effectively available for public scrutiny. As a result Internet email is not at all secure and can in theory be read by any third party (see Chapter 8). Fortunately the skills and equipment needed to read email without the sender's knowledge are well beyond those available to home users, and with millions of messages sent every day very little goes astray. But in theory, if you use Internet email to order something with a credit card, a third party might be able to intercept your order, copy your card details and then use the card without you knowing.

On-line services offer a much higher level of security. According to the staff of America Online, nobody can read anyone's mail – not even the system's administrators, who usually have the ability to monitor anything that happens within their computer networks. This security gives on-line services a commercial advantage over the Internet. Many companies use one of these services simply because it is a secure way to do business with their customers. However, this extra security only applies as long as the email is being sent to someone else using the same service. If it is sent to an Internet address it is just as vulnerable as any other message. There are ways to improve the security of Internet email, but many of these are hard to use or have other disadvantages (see Chapter 8).

The other difference between on-line services and IAPs is that some on-line services allow you to unsend email (if you have changed your mind about posting it) and also check whether or not the recipient has read your message. Although the Internet has an optional 'receipt' scheme, which sends a message back to you telling you that someone has read your message, it is quite cumbersome. Receipts appear as long lines of computer gibberish which are hard to make sense of. If you use the receipt option you will get one of these messages for every email you send. You are unlikely to find this useful in practice. Receipts can also wreak havoc if you send the same email to a group of people. Instead of one receipt you will receive a large number, and again this is more of an annoyance than a useful option. On-line services offer a simpler facility which shows you much more clearly when a message has been read.

Attachments

The word 'attachment' is used to describe any information that cannot be sent as text. This includes photographs, diagrams, illustrations, and so on. With modern software, attachments are easy to use; you simply create an email message, tell the package which information you want 'attached' to it and then send it in the usual way. Messages with attachments are much longer than standard text messages, so it can take a while for them to be sent.

At the other end, the attached information can be 'detached' and saved for later, viewed, listened to or whatever is appropriate (an attachment may contain software). This is also a straightforward process – often the information appears 'inside' the email, and the email software understands what to do with it automatically.

Originally, Internet users had to add attachments by hand. This involved running the information through software that converted it into a special format, cutting and pasting the resulting gibberish into an email, and then sending it. The process was reversed at the other end. This was time-consuming and laborious, so a system called MIME (Multipurpose Internet Mail Extensions) was developed. MIME is now a standard feature of most email software and is used to hide the conversion process. Any software that uses the MIME system makes it possible for the user to send attachments with very little effort.

However, attachments do still have problems. The first of these is a size restriction. Some of the older computers on the Internet can work only with small email messages – larger messages are mangled or marked undeliverable and sent back ('bounced'). Because of this, very large attachments sometimes have to be split into smaller chunks. Each of these is sent in a separate message.

Unfortunately, it is not possible to know whether or not a message needs to be split before you send it. In fact, it is usually easier to try to send it all at once and resort to splitting it only if it does not get through.

Recent software can deal with split messages quite easily. When sending a large attachment, it usually asks if you want to split it into multiple parts. When receiving one, the different parts are glued together automatically, and a single big message appears in your in-tray.

As some older software cannot do this, it is useful to know how attachments work, and also how to send them in parts and glue them back together. This process is described in more detail in Chapter 7.

The final problem with attachments is caused by a common misunderstanding: beginners sometimes forget that information in one form on their computer may not work on a different kind of computer. For example, many programs that work with Windows 95 do not produce information that can be read on an Apple Macintosh, and *vice versa*.

Windows 95 and Microsoft's Office software are particular culprits in this respect. They have email features that hide away the attachment process completely, making it seem as if you can send any kind of document to anyone. In fact you can use these features to send information only to someone else who is using Windows 95. These systems work very well in an office where everyone has the same software, but on the Internet, where people use thousands of different computer systems, they do not work at all and can lead to unreadable messages which appear as long streams of computer-generated gibberish. For Internet use it is better to use email software that handles attachments in the usual way.

CASE HISTORY – Martin

Martin Brown composes music for television and video productions. He has experimented with sending in sketches and short demo pieces by attachment, and is looking forward to the day when it will be possible to send in a complete piece of music.

'I was recently talking to someone at one of the satellite TV companies who wanted me to write some demos for them for their next season. This music is the kind that is played in the background when the station logo appears. It never needs to be more than about a minute long.

'Normally we supply music on special tapes called DATs, which are about half the size of ordinary cassettes but have CD recording quality. The problem with DATs is getting them to your client. Since I live in a village in the middle of nowhere this is a problem. Usually I don't have time to fight my way through the traffic in London to drop off a tape. Instead I use a courier service, which gets the tape there the next day before midday. If someone is in a real hurry I'll send it to arrive the same day, although this costs a small fortune.

'I'd been using my Internet connection for a while, then one day it occurred to me – I could send the music as an attachment. For fun I sent the producer some demos via email so he could listen to them on his PC.

'The idea almost worked. A minute of mono sound at reasonable quality is rather huge – over 5Mb – and this takes over an hour to send. I could have lowered the quality but I wanted to try out the real thing to see how well it worked.

'In spite of the size they got through easily, although it took most of the morning to send them. It was much cheaper than using a same-day courier, but I still wouldn't do it again until I get a faster connection.

There are other ways to compress the information, although some of the sound quality may be lost. The next step is to experiment with those, and they may be fine for TV sound.

'But anyway, it's reassuring to know that I'll be able to send in work this way within the next few years. It will make a big difference to what I do – although I doubt the courier company will be quite so happy.'

Automated email services

One of the more novel differences between email and conventional mail is that you can send email to a computer as well as to a person. Certain kinds of computers have been programmed to respond to email in a useful way. These fall into three main categories – autoresponders, email/fax gateways, and mailing list maintainers.

Autoresponders

An autoresponder sends a 'canned' reply to a request for information. For example, *Wired* magazine has an autoresponder that sends out submission guidelines for prospective authors. To use it an author sends an email message to the *Wired* computer network address, and the guidelines are sent back automatically. This is the simplest form of autoresponder. When it receives a message, it looks for a return address and throws away everything else in the message.

More advanced autoresponders look for certain words in the subject line of an email, and compose their response accordingly. For example, Demon Internet offers pre-written help articles on a number of subjects. Whenever someone sends an email request for help to Demon, they receive a list of these articles, together with 'request words' for each one. Sending an email with a request word tells the autoresponder to reply with a copy of the relevant article.

As with other computers that respond to email automatically, autoresponders are very literal minded. They do not understand English at all and will respond only to certain words or phrases. When using any of these automated systems it is important to follow the instructions exactly – otherwise the computer will not

47

respond as it should, and you will get an error message instead of the information you want.

Email/fax messages

It is now possible to send a fax to someone by sending an email to a special kind of address (given below). The email is directed to a computer which is connected to a telephone line and a fax modem that uses special software. When it receives your email, the computer converts the text into pages of fax information, dials out using the number you specify in the email address and sends the fax in the usual way.

This service is free, although it is still experimental. The only drawback is that sometimes the recipient gets a cover sheet which advertises the services of your IAP – but this can be a small price to pay for a fax that is sent abroad almost instantly at minimal cost.

These services are very easy to use. Demon Internet is one company that provides an email/fax gateway for its customers. To use it you send a message to an address of the form:

remote-printer.<any_name>@<faxnumber>.iddd.tpc.int (The details within the angle brackets change depending on where you would like the fax to be sent – the others should be typed exactly as shown.) The fax number must be an international number, including the standard international prefix for a country (for example, 1 for the USA, 44 for the UK, and so on) but does not include the special codes used to call abroad, for example, '00' which is used to dial any international number from the UK.

Within the UK, the usual '0' at the front of the number is replaced by '44'. For example, to send a fax to Fred Someone on 0171-123 4567 you would send an email to:

remote-printer.Fred_Someone@441711234567.iddd.tpc.int

Note that the first and second parts of the name are separated by an underscore ('_') character rather than a dash ('-'). It is possible to include attachments of certain kinds with the faxes, and these will be printed in the usual way. Other kinds of attachments will be ignored. For more information about this service see page 244.

Mailing lists

Mailing lists are used for exchanging email with a group of people instead of with a single person. Most email software includes 'cc' (carbon copy) and 'bcc' (blind carbon copy) options which make it possible to send the same message to more than one person at once. Mailing lists automate this process and remove any need to keep track of everyone's email address by hand.

A computer with a special email address serves as a 'post office'. A message sent to this address is copied to everyone in the group automatically. A computer program on this computer also administers the list and adds and removes people from it when they request it to. This is done without any human intervention, although all lists have a manager – called a moderator – who makes sure the computer does its job properly and steps in if problems occur.

Busy lists can attract a flood of messages, so most have a 'digest' option, which turns a collection of messages into a single long one. This is compiled and sent at a fixed time every day, or whenever the volume of contributions reaches a certain level. Most people prefer the convenience offered by the digest option, even though it makes a list less spontaneous. List members have to wait until they receive the digest and then wait again until their replies appear in the next one. Even though all the messages arrive at once it is still standard practice to treat each one individually, and to send any replies in separate messages. This is less confusing for the list's readers, and also makes the comments and conversations shorter and more manageable.

It is possible to find mailing lists devoted to almost any subject. They are usually much more pleasant and informative than newsgroups (see Chapter 5), and the people who frequent lists seem to be more mature and less argumentative. Every list has stages when someone on it is provocative or controversial, but these usually pass fairly quickly. List managers can generally be relied upon to step in to urge people back towards the main subject of the list, or occasionally to defuse arguments and restore order. Most moderators are fairly polite and mature, and some even supply guidelines for what is and is not acceptable to the list

– for example, it is usually acceptable to disagree with someone's point of view, but not to indulge in name calling. As a result, lists offer some of the most tightly knit and supportive communities available on-line. They are usually open to everyone, and are almost always free. Only a very tiny minority restrict their membership or charge for their services, and you are very unlikely to come across these.

CASE HISTORY – Kyle

Kyle Hamilton is a Californian member of the Amarok mailing list, which is run by and for fans of the musician Mike Oldfield. Apart from finding the list a very sociable place, he also gets other benefits from it.

'Amarok has subscribers from everywhere. Ann-Marie, the moderator, is Australian, and the regular posters include people from Spain, England, Germany, Portugal, Denmark, Poland, and a few other countries. Only about ten per cent of the people on the list post messages. Most seem happy just lurking – reading the list but not contributing to it.

'It is quite friendly, especially compared with newsgroups. People tend not to give each other a hard time, although we have had a few disagreements. We talk about all sorts of things. Even within the list you can tell there are different groups – people who are more into Mike's guitar playing, or his folk or rock connections.

'I've found I can get friends on the list to send me CDs. Payment is a problem, because it can cost more than the CD is worth to wire the money over. Instead we usually arrange CD swaps. They'll send me Mike's latest, and I'll find something for them they can't get over there. It is strange doing this with people I've never met, and maybe never will. But some of these people have become real friends. And it's always good to find someone who shares an interest – even if they do all live on different continents from each other.'

Finding and joining a list
Compared with other Internet resources, mailing lists can be hard to find. They are not widely advertised, so you will usually need to take an indirect approach when looking for them.

Unfortunately, there is no one central directory that lists them all, although attempts are being made to remedy this.

You can find them by using web search engines (see Chapter 4), by reading newsgroups or by word of mouth. If all else fails and you cannot find something suitable, it is relatively easy to start a mailing list yourself. Most IAPs can provide the facilities to do this. For more information see pages 241–2.

When you find a list, you should make a note of three things: the name and address of the moderator, the subscription address for the list, and any special instructions about how to join. The latter specify the information you need to send to the computer that administers the list so that it knows who you are and which list you want to join.

Joining a list

To join a list, you have to send an email to the list's 'post-office' address. The form and content of this message vary from list to list, but you should have found some instructions with its other details. At the very least you should know the email address of the moderator, who can explain what you need to do.

It is important to follow these instructions carefully as mailing lists are administered automatically and the software – the two most common programs are called Majordomo and ListServ – works literally. Adding extra words, questions or comments to a subscription message is pointless because these programs do not understand English. They can understand only messages that appear in a certain form. A typical example of a subscription message might be: *subscribe whatever-the-name-of-the-list-is*.

Possible variations include adding your email address before or after the name of the list, and adding an option such as 'digest' at the end. Sometimes you need to include the required text in the subject header of the message, and sometimes in the body. Occasionally you will need to add punctuation marks at various points, or send a confirmation message within a certain time period.

Whatever the details are, as long as you follow them *to the letter* you should have no problems. If what you are doing does not seem to work, you can ask the moderator for help. As a last resort he or she can also subscribe you by hand.

Once you have subscribed, you will immediately receive an email message welcoming you to the list and explaining how to cancel your subscription – a process known as unsubscribing. Keep a copy of this message somewhere safe. If you decide the list is not for you, it is a lot quicker, and also a lot less embarrassing, to be able to follow these instructions without having to send an email to the moderator asking how to do it.

List etiquette

It is a good idea to unsubscribe from any lists when you go on holiday. Otherwise you might find hundreds or even thousands of unread messages waiting for you when you get back. You should also unsubscribe from any lists when you change your IAP or email address. This is common courtesy, but also avoids the situation where email that should have reached you is returned to the list with an error message. The email will then be sent back to you, and everyone else, again, then returned to the list again, and so on indefinitely, until the moderator steps in to clear up the mess.

Moderators' opinions carry a lot of weight on mailing lists, but fortunately very few take advantage of this in a negative way. Apart from personal contributions, most content themselves with occasional comments that steer the conversation away from obscure topics of no interest to most members back towards the subject of the list. This is known as staying 'on topic'. Drifting off topic is not a heinous crime, and some drift is often essential to maintain interest, but too much is a bad thing.

Unless you have a very good reason for doing so, and know for certain that it will not cause any problems, you should never try to send an attachment to a mailing list. You should also avoid advertising goods and services, preaching – religious, political, or otherwise – and sending extremely long replies. Advertising and preaching will irritate list members, and long messages will usually be ignored because most people will not take the time to read them.

You should also be tactful and polite with other list members. Although moderators do not often remove people from a list for bad behaviour, they will do so if sorely provoked. Vigorous debate is acceptable, but being rude about other list members is not – no matter how justified it may be.

One problem with lists is that if you save all the messages for posterity, they will take up a great deal of your computer's filing space. You should get into the habit of deleting messages that are not particularly interesting and saving only those which you feel you may want to refer to again. Some lists are archived on the World Wide Web, so there is no reason to keep personal copies of messages from these. You can search the archive for a specific piece of information whenever you want. It is a good idea to find out if a list is archived on the Web before you start posting messages to it. Information on the Web can be read by anyone, and you may find your comments have inadvertently reached a much wider audience than you originally intended.

Instant communications

For those who prefer a more immediate form of contact, the Internet offers a selection of 'live' options – Internet Relay Chat (IRC), on-line chat, Instant Messages and Talk. These all link your keyboard and screen with those of one or more people. When you type a message, it appears immediately on the recipient's screen, and *vice versa*. Unlike email messages, in which the text is carefully composed, these 'conversations' are instant and spontaneous, and similar to a chat-line or telephone call.

IRC

Internet Relay Chat (IRC) is an Internet facility that works internationally, so you can chat to anyone anywhere in the world. Chats are organised into 'channels', for example '#uk', which is used by UK residents and those around the world who enjoy chatting to them. There are thousands of channels covering a huge range of interests.

To use IRC you need special software, because the software supplied by most IAPs does not include this feature. You also need to be connected to an IRC server (a special computer that provides a local link to the IRC system). Some software includes

53

a list of servers you can choose from, although it can sometimes be out of date or include private or academic servers that do not allow public access. Often the easiest way to find one is to work through the list by trial and error.

Once you find a server, you will be asked to choose a nickname. Most people on IRC use silly nicknames, so you might want to do the same to make sure you fit in with the IRC culture. Names that alternate upper- and lower-case letters are popular, as is anything that sounds colourful and informal: 'Skoob', 'Iwetec' and 'wEbGgRl' are all typical examples.

When you have decided on a nickname, you can join a conversation by selecting a channel with an interesting name. Most software shows a list of people using the channel, so everyone else will know you are listening even if you do not type anything. This is known as 'lurking'. If you cannot find a suitable channel you can create one of your own by typing in a name that does not exist and setting a subject. If the name is interesting enough, someone will eventually come across it and start a conversation with you.

Conversations appear as a list of messages on your screen. Each person's words are preceded by his or her name. As new messages appear the old ones disappear. Some software keeps a record of an entire IRC session so you can look at the conversation later in full. With older software, messages simply disappear altogether. If the software (and you) can cope, you can have as many simultaneous conversations as you like. Virtuoso IRC users can be in as many as ten channels at the same time, although attempting to keep track of everything that everyone said while doing this is something of a challenge.

IRC messages do not have to be public. If you want to have a private conversation with someone, you can either create a channel of your own and 'hide' it so it does not appear on any lists, and then invite the person into the channel, or you can use a feature of IRC which allows you to type messages to another person directly. All these features are explained in the help facility supplied with the IRC software.

Even at its best IRC is quite badly flawed. One problem is the length of time it takes for messages to make their way around the world. At peak times it can take up to a minute for a message to appear, making conversation very difficult. It can sometimes take a few minutes just for someone to say 'Hello' to everyone when he or she joins a channel. The world of IRC can also be very strange for anyone who is not used to it. The chat is largely trivial, and some people are happy to talk just for the sake of it.

Another drawback is that conversations can be hopelessly disjointed because people arrive, leave and interrupt each other continuously. Compared with the relatively lucid flow of a conversation on a mailing list, the result is chaotic. It is impossible to create a situation in which one person talks while everyone else listens. As soon as someone attempts this, someone else will arrive and change the mood with a trivial question such as 'Hi – so what's happening tonight?'.

IRC has its own social code:

- The creator of a channel, known as the operator, has special privileges, such as being able to throw people off the channel if he or she does not like them.
- One way to welcome someone on to a channel is to make them an operator too, so they have the same privileges. Operators typically have '@' signs in front of their names. (These are not to be confused with the '@' sign that appears in an email address. Although it is the same character, its meaning and usage are completely different.)
- Confusingly, some 'people' are not people at all – they are actually computer programs, which add their own comments according to how they have been programmed. These are known as 'bots'. Only the foolish or the naive ever mistake a bot for a real person. (This does happen sometimes – it is not unheard of for bots with female names to be asked out for the evening. Or worse.)

Apart from chat, IRC also includes a facility that can be used to find out more about somebody. 'Who' and 'Whois' list the details of other participants – such as their location and their email address – either for individuals or for everyone using the channel at the time. This is useful if you decide you want to email someone after a chat to continue the conversation.

IRC seems to be the preserve of younger Internet users, or at least those with a younger attitude. Conversations do not generally become serious or profound, so if you are looking for more intellectual stimulation and satisfying debates then mailing lists, or even newsgroups, will have more to offer you.

However, some people do find IRC compulsive. It is a part of the Internet that everyone should try at least once. And it can be an excellent way to make new friends.

CASE HISTORY – Sylvia

Sylvia Engle is an IRC enthusiast and uses it nearly every evening to keep in touch with a selection of friends from around the world.

'I know I'm wasting time really. But I'm lucky because I get free after-hours calls from my cable company, instead of paying money to BT. So I can spend as much time on-line as I like and it doesn't cost me a penny. I wouldn't use it so much otherwise – all that time on-line would soon get very expensive.

'I started out of curiosity. There were a lot of channels that seemed to be full of dubious activities, and I avoided those because I'm not into that sort of thing. Although, from what I've seen, there are a lot of people who are.

'I mostly enjoy straight gossip. It's just like talking to friends on the phone, except that you're typing instead. If you always use the same channels you soon get recognised and people say "Hi" when you sign on.

'To be honest it's quite studenty. A lot of 18-year-olds sit in university computer rooms around the world typing to each other. So I wouldn't say it's a good place for deep conversations about the meaning of life. There's a lot of flirting, a lot of sparring and sometimes a lot of put-downs. But if someone annoys you, you can try another channel.

'One strange thing is, you can use any nickname you like. I sometimes use "Skoob" because it looks male. If you try an instant sex change people treat you differently. It's really weird – it's something that a lot of people do. On IRC, you never know who you're talking to really – but that's all part of the fun.'

On-line chat

On-line services have their own version of IRC. This is built into the special software provided by the service and does not require any further setting up. It is also likely to be much easier to use than 'true' IRC – the options are much less confusing, and a lot of the features that might confuse newcomers are either absent or very well disguised.

On-line services offer chat in 'rooms'. These are similar to channels, except that they are usually linked to other information on the same subject, such as message areas, lists of web pages, short magazine-style articles, and so on. At the very least, the chat rooms are organised into categories. (This system is less confusing than that of the IRC, whose list of channels arranged in alphabetical order can seem endless.) Apart from the 'official' rooms, which are created by the on-line service itself, members can create 'private' rooms of their own. As with IRC, they can be hidden so that conversations in them are by invitation only.

Other advantages of on-line chat include much shorter delays (most messages appear instantly, even when they have come from across the Atlantic), and the list of messages on-screen is generally much clearer and neater. The main attraction is that chat makes it easy for people to find others with similar interests. People do occasionally make good friends through chat and will sometimes use it to ask for practical or emotional support. But this can be difficult in the more public rooms, which are used by anyone and everyone.

Finally, chat makes it possible for people to talk to experts and celebrities in special staged events – rather like a press conference with participants from all over the world, except that everyone is equipped with a keyboard and screen.

Unfortunately, many of the criticisms of IRC also apply to chat rooms. In reality, chat is a way to kill time, and it is certainly difficult to have an interesting debate.

CASE HISTORY – Chris

Chris Binns tried out the chat rooms on AOL but was not too impressed with what he found.

'Originally, I used CompuServe but it was starting to cost too much, so I thought I'd try AOL through one of its free trials. Chat on

CompuServe isn't too bad – not world-class maybe, but a lot of the people seem quite grown-up. AOL can be rather different.

'I have an interest in alternative philosophies and ways of looking at the world, and eventually I found a room devoted to metaphysics. The chat there seemed typical of a lot of chat. A large number of people would come in announcing themselves, sometimes just saying "So what's happening?", others would make a big dramatic entrance just so everyone knew they'd arrived. It was really wearing after a while. It really breaks up the flow of the conversation and makes it hard to follow.

'But even when it did flow I wasn't very impressed. Many people would say "So what's metaphysics, then?". I know it's not exactly a common interest, but answering the question for the hundredth time wasn't a good way to keep the conversation interesting. People would also cause trouble and disrupt the room by typing rubbish or being argumentative just to get attention. They'd come in and say "This room is really stupid" or something like that. Then everyone would be lured into being rude back to them, even though there's an "ignore" feature that kills annoying people's messages so you never see them.

'I eventually decided not to bother with the public chat rooms. It's so easy to waste time and money on them. I did find some slightly better chat rooms that were off the beaten track. The most interesting ones are not so easily found. But I still don't use them very often.'

Talk and Instant Messages

Talk is similar to IRC except that it is a one-to-one Internet service where the conversation is private and limited to two people. It is quite rare and is most widely available on academic and business computers that use the Unix system. Talk software for home computers is hard to find as it is not included as a standard feature in any of the popular Internet software packages. In addition, both people need to have the software before it is possible to have a conversation, and this limits its usefulness.

Although IRC is usually used by groups, its one-to-one facility is often used instead. The main difference between Talk and IRC is that Talk can be used to interrupt someone at work, but IRC cannot. Talk is more spontaneous, whereas IRC requires two people to make an appointment with each other when they want a chat.

On-line services offer a similar system, called Instant Message (IM) or some equivalent. To send an IM you specify the person you want to talk to and type a message. A window appears instantly on his or her screen with your text in it. That person can type underneath it and send a reply to you. It is an effective, if slightly slow, way to have a long-distance conversation with someone. Of course, if the recipient does not want to chat, he or she can ignore you or block your messages completely.

Although these systems are usually used for gossip and idle chatter, they do have their uses. Even though they are slow, they are still much cheaper than an international telephone call. While no one would use them to have a business discussion, they can be ideal for talking about holiday arrangements and making plans with friends and relatives in another country.

IMs are ideal for introducing yourself to someone on-line. If you are in a chat room and like what someone has said, sending them an instant message is an ideal way to strike up a more private conversation. IM names are the same as chat names, so it is obvious who to send the message to.

CASE HISTORY – Sean

Although IRC and IMs are generally used for entertainment, they also have more serious uses. In April 1997 Sean Redden, a 12-year-old from Texas, was using IRC when he saw a message that said 'Hello – help me!'.

'Most people on the channel thought someone was play-acting, but Sean took the message seriously. He discovered they were being sent by Tarija Latinen, a 20-year-old business student in Finland who was suffering from a serious asthma attack after being locked into the computer room by accident. Sean called in his mother who immediately rang the Texan emergency services. Guided by messages from Sean, they in turn contacted the Finnish emergency services. Eventually they were able to track down the student and send an ambulance.

'At this point Tarija's sign-on disappeared, and everyone – including Sean – was worried that it had been a hoax after all. In fact she had been taken to hospital, and Sean's intervention had saved her life.'

WebPhones

Because the Internet can be used to send any sort of information, it can be coaxed into behaving like a telephone connection. To do this you need special software and a computer that has a microphone and speakers or headphones. The computer must have a two-way – known as a 'full-duplex' – sound facility, so that it can make sound while recording the sound of your voice through the microphone. The sound in most PCs does not have this option, although it is possible to buy a better soundcard and install it at reasonable cost. Dedicated users can now buy true WebPhones that look and work like a telephone handset and plug into the computer.

WebPhone software takes the sound from the microphone and converts it into a form that can be sent over the Internet. If the person at the other end has a similar system, and if he or she is expecting you to call, it is possible to have a normal telephone conversation in this way.

The big advantage of this system is that it is possible to talk to anyone in the world for the price of a local call. One disadvantage is that the speech quality depends on the speed of your connection to the Internet, and also to some extent on the amount of Internet traffic between you and the person at the other end. The kind of slow connections available to home users tend to result in low-quality speech which has a lot of gaps.

The other drawback is that unless you happen to be connected to the Internet when a call comes in, there is no indication to show that the WebPhone is 'ringing'. So conversations have to be arranged beforehand. This is less of a problem in the USA, where local calls are free (or very cheap), and Internet users can leave their machines connected permanently. But in the UK, where this is not an option for home users, the lack of spontaneity is irritating.

Once this is solved and the connection speed improved, WebPhones are likely to become very popular indeed. They are already being used by some businesses which can afford a permanent connection. As speeds increase, it is likely that the present long-distance telephone rates will become obsolete as more and more people use the Internet instead of the telephone network to make long-distance and international calls.

Video links

The idea of a video phone that shows an image of someone while they talk has been in existence since at least the 1950s. But it has now become a real possibility on the Internet – although as with WebPhones, this facility is best thought of as experimental until connection speeds improve.

A number of companies offer video facilities over the Internet. These use a small camera, which perches on top of your computer's screen, and special software which compresses the video information so that it can be sent over the Internet as quickly as possible. The image from the camera is small and not very detailed, but good enough to make it possible to see who is talking.

One of the most popular systems is known as CU-SeeMe. CU-SeeMe software can be tried for free, and even if you do not have a camera you can watch people who do. At the moment the system is rather crude when used over a slow link – instead of smooth video, the images are jerky and tend to break up completely. But businesses with faster links can use it quite successfully.

CHAPTER **4**

FINDING INFORMATION

THE MOST popular medium for electronic publishing is the World Wide Web, and although the technology that drives it was finalised only in the early 1990s, it has already taken the world by·storm. As far as most people are concerned, the World Wide Web *is* the Internet. References to it have started to appear in advertising and other media, and the Web is set to become as important as television, radio and traditional print publishing.

A large part of the Web's appeal is that it is extremely easy to use, whereas many other facilities on the Internet, such as those described in Chapter 7, require moderate to advanced technical skills and knowledge. Complete newcomers can learn how to use the Web in ten minutes or less, and it takes only another ten minutes to learn how to use its search facilities (see page 66). Understanding how to publish your own material on the Web takes longer, but the countless examples of web sites produced by people with limited computer experience demonstrate that this is also relatively straightforward (see Appendix 4).

A web publisher creates a set of pages which contain text, images and perhaps sounds, animations or video clips. These are posted on the Web and remain there until the publisher decides to change them. To see the pages on a web site, users need to view them with a special piece of software called a 'browser', which is either free or available for a relatively small outlay. Both IAPs and on-line services include one of these in the introductory packages they send out when you become one of their customers.

The biggest difference between web pages and more traditional forms of publishing is that web pages can contain 'links'. A link appears as an underlined word or phrase, or part of an image. If you click on one with a mouse it leads you to a new page, and this can be anywhere on the Web (publishers are not limited to creating links only to their own pages). Following links is like following a train of thought: for example, a page created by a bungee-jumping enthusiast may contain links to pages about other dangerous sports, which in turn may be connected to the pages of an insurance company, and so on. This process is known as 'browsing' or 'surfing' the Web.

Because they always give you the option of jumping to related information, links provide an environment which appears to respond directly to your interests. Browsers keep a note of the links you choose as you visit various pages. This facility enables you to backtrack easily if you find you have followed a large number of links and want to return to a page several stages further back.

Another strength of the Web is that its pages do not have to be fixed in the way that printed pages are. This means that they can include forms for visitors to fill in – popular examples include product orders and 'visitors' books' – and links to email addresses and other Internet facilities. Pages can be set up to change automatically according to the time of day or the time of year and to display a counter that shows the number of people that have visited the page. Some sites also include a search facility to help you find your way to information more quickly.

Using the Web

To find a page, you need to know its address. Web addresses are known as URLs (Uniform Resource Locator) and typically look something like this:

http://www.somename.some-extension/someword/etc1/etc2

To view this page, you simply type the URL into the 'address' line in your browser. The browser then finds the page for you, copies the information to your computer and displays it on the screen. Once the page has appeared you can either follow its links to other pages or type in a new URL to see a completely different page. Some URLs include characters such as the tilde '~' or long strings of numbers. It is important to type in a URL exactly as it appears, adding no extra spaces, and including all the punctuation – no matter how strange it looks.

What is on the Web?

In terms of content, web pages divide neatly into two groups. The first group includes pages of business and professional information, created by organisations, magazines and newspapers, small and large businesses, schools and universities, towns and cities, government offices, and so on. These pages often have advertising or free information which is related to the organisation that maintains them; some have both.

A typical example is Railtrack's site *(www.railtrack.co.uk)*. These pages include the usual corporate public relations material but also feature an electronic train timetable. Visitors to these pages can type in a starting station, a destination and a preferred travelling time, and the timetable will then calculate and display the best route.

Another good example is the site maintained by *New Scientist* magazine *(http://www.newscientist.com)*. Instead of simply repeating the information already provided in the paper version, these pages include a searchable archive of features and back issues, additional background information, and other facilities such as job advertisements.

The editors of some magazines create pages where their readers can offer instant feedback and comments about the articles. Jesse Berst is a technology journalist and consultant who writes for Ziff-Davis, publisher of a range of computer magazines in the UK and the USA. In his regular column he includes emails that he has received from his readers. Although they sometimes disagree with his point of view, he includes their messages because the disparate comments make for a much livelier and more informative source of information than is usually possible in print.

The other group includes private and hobby pages which are maintained by amateurs who have created them for fun. These people either have a burning interest and want to share it, or simply want to tell everyone something about themselves. The pages vary hugely in both quality and content; some are extremely inept, while others are very impressive and professional. The range of content is vast, and often the sites include links to rich sources of background information that could take hours or days of research in a library.

CASE HISTORY – Simon

DJ Optik – real name Simon James – works in various dance music clubs and pubs around the country. He uses the Web to keep track of the latest news and also to order records and other items that would be impossible to obtain locally.

'One of the main sites I look at is called Hyperreal – http://www.hyperreal.com *It has a complete list of everything to do with dance culture. One of the best things about it is that there is a huge list of links to other music and dance sites. The dance scene isn't just about the music, it's about the culture – the clothes, the news, the people and the attitude. By following the links I can see what's happening in the dance scene throughout the world, browse through a clothes store's site in San Francisco, order records from Australia, or find out what's happening at a local club. Hyperreal is maintained by volunteers, so no one makes any money from it. And it's bigger than most sites. There's a lot of interest in dance music which doesn't get covered in any other way.'*

The Web does have other uses, some of which are quite unusual, for example, 'WebCams' – video cameras which produce an image that can be seen over the Web. One of the earliest was created to show whether a coffee machine in a Cambridge college was full or empty, so that students did not need to make the journey down the hall to find out in person. Since then hundreds of WebCams have appeared in all kinds of locations: it is now possible to check the surf off the coast of California, watch various people around the world while they work in their offices, examine the state of the sun as viewed from Australia, check skiing conditions in a Swiss resort, and look out over the frozen wastes of the Antarctic. The site at *http://wct.images.com* maintains a list of active WebCams, so you can see which ones are likely to be worth looking at.

Finding the information you want

There are three ways to use the Web. The first is to follow links to wherever your interests take you. Although doing this can be entertaining, it is not a particularly reliable way of finding specific information, and it is very easy to run up a huge bill this way. A typical surfing session can easily take an hour or two, so regular random browsing is not recommended unless you can afford it.

The second approach is to find URLs in magazines and other media. Many have web directories that list the best sites dealing with a particular topic. Although these lists are useful, sites do appear and disappear without warning, and this means that the directories can become out of date very quickly. Nevertheless, they do provide useful jumping-off points for further exploration.

The third and best way to find information is to use the Web's own search facilities. Known as 'search engines', these are special sites which link to a computer that maintains its own directory of web sites. (For a list of the most popular search engines see page 248.) These search facilities are divided into two groups. The first is a collection of topic lists, divided and sub-divided by category and sub-category. The best-known example is the Yahoo site at *http://www.yahoo.com* The main Yahoo page has a selection of category headings, which appear as links. At the time of writing these are:

- arts and humanities
- business and economy
- computers and Internet
- education
- entertainment
- government
- health
- news and media
- recreation and sports
- reference
- regional
- science

- social science
- society and culture.

Beneath each heading is a short list of three or four of the most popular sub-headings. For example, under science are:

- computer science
- biology
- astronomy
- engineering.

These offer quick links to the most used sub-areas. Otherwise, if you click on 'science' itself, you would be faced with a list of 50 sub-headings. Picking one of these – nanotechnology, for example – and clicking on it produces a list of nine web sites about nanotechnology. Some sub-headings are then further divided. At the end of the search through these sub-divisions you are presented with a page of links to the main sites about the subject.

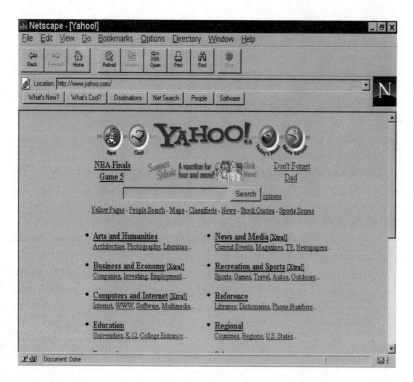

The second kind of search engine uses 'keywords' to find information on the Web. The most popular example is the AltaVista site at *http://www.altavista.digital.com*

A keyword is simply a word that the engine looks for in all the sites in its index. If a match is found, the site will be listed, together with its address and the first sentence or the first few words. Keywords can be combined in various ways. In fact, combinations are usually essential to get useful results. For example, searching for a common word such as 'money' will produce a list of thousands of sites, which is far too many to be useful. So it is vital to make the search criteria more specific. You might choose to look for 'currency exchange rates' or 'stock prices', for example.

You may need to practise to get the best results from a keyword search engine. All of them include help pages which explain how to search for keywords more effectively and how different words can be best combined. It is well worth taking the time to read these pages and do some experimenting to master

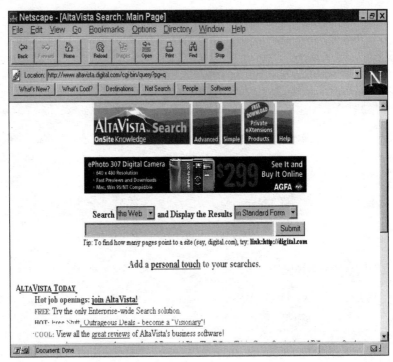

the system. When looking for specific information, choosing the right keyword combinations and using the various advanced search options can sometimes save you hours.

At the time of writing a new search system is being tested on the AltaVista site; it shows the links between ideas in the form of a graph. In theory this should be easier to use than the other two systems, but in practice the connections between words are rather arbitrary, making the system less useful than it might be.

Agents

Agent software, which is starting to be sold over the counter, enables you to create your own personal web search without using any of the existing search engines. You tell it what kind of information you want to look for, then leave it to roam the Internet on your behalf. At this point you can disconnect from the Internet and do something else. As the agent finds information it creates a list of URLs, complete with short descriptions. The next time you connect it copies this list to your computer.

One of the most popular agent systems is called Autonomy, which has been designed to be very easy to use. As soon as you start up the software it appears on your screen as a friendly dog that needs to be 'trained'; you do this by typing your requirements on a blackboard. The words or ideas you are looking for can be typed in plain English, although Autonomy's understanding of what you want is still relatively crude. As you continue to use Autonomy, the dog appears to 'learn' or 'understand' what you want more quickly. Although it is not perfect, the system can be understood by anyone, and is a good example of the attempts being made to make the Internet less technical.

'Push media'

When you surf the Web, you usually make deliberate choices about what kind of information you want and where to look for it. 'Push media' work differently: they send information to you. In this respect they are more like traditional published material, in which you have much less of a say as to how information is presented to you. The advantage is that they are easier to use than other Internet sites, because information appears in your browser without any effort on your part. To use push media you simply 'tune' your browser into a site, and new information will then appear regularly as long as you stay at that site.

Related to push media is Webcasting, which is similar to radio and television. A stream of information – which can be anything from stock-market quotes to sports scores and radio and TV programmes – is sent directly to your computer. Webcasting is still in its infancy, however, and relies on much faster links than are currently available to the general public.

Current examples of push media have many drawbacks. To get the best from them you need:

- **a permanent Internet connection** In the UK this is not a viable option as most people cannot afford one
- **an extremely fast computer system** Even the very latest, fastest models slow to a crawl when working with push media
- **special software** This software, and access to many push media services, is free. However, the price you pay for this is constant bombardment with advertising (usually related to your own particular interests).

Many existing users are scathing about push media and think that it will undermine the Web's traditional ethics of openness and free co-operation. Traditional publishers, however, see push media as a way to bring their products to a new market and increase advertising revenue. At the time of writing it is too early to tell whether Webcasting and push media services will become popular and what kind of effect they may have on the Internet as a whole.

The Web's limitations

Although the Web can be extremely useful, it is not perfect. The most obvious problem is that it can work very slowly; it is not unusual for pages to take a few minutes to appear. The speed depends on two things: the number of people trying to look at a site at the same time; and the speed of the connection between the web site and your computer. At the time of writing an updated version of HTML – the system that holds the Web together – is being considered which will make this connection more efficient. However, lack of speed is likely to remain a problem for the foreseeable future. Anyone who uses the Web can expect a slow service some of the time and should budget for the bills caused by this.

Search engines are useful but not infallible. Sites such as Yahoo have to be maintained by hand to a certain extent, and if a site disappears or a new one appears, it can take a while – perhaps a month or two – for the new information to appear in the listing.

Similarly, keyword searches can date quickly. They rely on special programs called 'spiders' which crawl over the Web looking for changes. But as there are millions of pages to look through, collecting the information is a never-ending process. It is also possible to hide pages from these spiders – either deliberately or by accident – so the index is rarely complete. You need to think laterally when looking for particular information on the Web. For example, when looking for one word, you might also need to look for other words that might lead to it. Non-text information such as images and sounds is not indexed at all. At the time of writing there is no way of searching for a photograph that includes something specific, such as a tiger or a thunderstorm, unless the photographs happen to have relevant text associated with them.

However, it is likely that these problems will have been eradicated by the beginning of the twenty-first century, and the Web will become much more useful than it is currently.

FTP

The Web has subsumed the features of a number of older Internet information distribution systems and can now be used to obtain information from them without the need for the old-fashioned software and working methods they require. A facility known as FTP (File Transfer Protocol) makes it possible to access and copy information from various computers called FTP 'servers' anywhere on the Internet. FTP is a simple copying system. It does not attempt to display the information or do anything useful with it.

FTP servers are most often used as libraries of free or trial software; many companies offer these systems to allow visitors to get hold of new and updated versions of their products directly over the Internet. This is better for the companies as they no longer have to copy the information on to a floppy disk and send it through the post, and better for their customers, who can have the software delivered directly to their computer and start using it immediately. Other kinds of information are also available; books, bibliographies, FAQs for newsgroups (see page 12), photograph archives, and sounds can be copied to your computer using FTP.

FTP works in one of two ways:

- **Anonymous FTP** is open to everyone. All FTP computers – known as FTP servers – require a password and an identifying name before they will allow visitors to copy the information they hold. In the case of anonymous FTP, the identifying name is 'anonymous' and the password can be anything. It is common practice to use your email address as the password, so that the computer's administrators know who has been using the facility.
- **Secure FTP** can be used only if you have a suitable name and password. You will need to obtain these from the administrators. If you do not have a suitable name and password, you will not be able to have the information.

Web browsers can be used for both kinds of FTP and have the ability to make the process much more straightforward than FTP software does. To use FTP from a browser you can either click on a link that says something like 'Download here', or type in an FTP-specific URL – these start with *ftp://* instead of the more common *http://* To use FTP successfully you need to know how the filing system in your computer works so that you can create a suitable folder or directory to hold the new information. Otherwise, you will not know where the information you have copied has been filed.

FTP is related to other, older services such as Gopher, Archie and Veronica, which are discussed in more detail in Chapter 7.

CASE HISTORY – Janet

Janet Anderson subscribed to an IAP in the autumn of 1996 but decided soon afterwards that she needed email software that was better than that provided by the IAP. She decided to look for it on the Web and found something suitable very quickly.

'I found out about this site called Tucows from a magazine. It's a huge list of all kinds of free software, decorated with a picture of two cows. The software is rated so you can see how good it is. It's also divided up into categories to help you find your way around.

'The site has copies – called mirrors – all over the world, so the first step was to find a local one with the same information. You are given a long list showing where the copies are, so it was easy to find the ones in the UK. I had no idea whether any were better than the others so I picked one at random. Apparently some sites respond more quickly than others, but I can't say I noticed any difference.

'The list of categories came as a bit of a shock. I didn't have any idea what most of them were – what's a "DNS server" or a "finger client" – but one of the buttons had "email" written on it in big letters so I clicked on that one.

'The rest of the process was surprisingly easy. There's a long list of the different kinds of software with a brief description of each and its "cows" rating. Eudora Lite had a good mark, so I thought I'd try it. To get hold of the software all I had to do was click on a link and tell my computer where to file it. It took just a few minutes to copy. There were no bills to pay, and I didn't need to give a credit-card number to anyone.

'Eudora – there's a "Pro" version as well as a "Lite" version, but you have to pay for the other one – is much better than the original software I was using. It files mail from different people in mail boxes and maintains my address book.

'Installing the software was easy, setting it up wasn't, so I had to ask for help from my IAP. Luckily they're used to people like me asking them awkward questions and they sent me a help sheet, which answered most of the questions.

'It's strange – I seem to have become some kind of computer expert now. I never would have thought I could do something like this, but it's been much easier than I imagined.'

CHAPTER 5

GETTING SUPPORT AND SHARING INTERESTS ON-LINE

USENET COMMENTS ON ITSELF

Subject: Re: Orrie answers the woodchuck question!
From: Nathan Sullivan <alfonso@cegt201.bradley.edu>
Newsgroups: rec.humor.oracle.d

kirsten@spike.wellesley.edu (Kirsten Chevalier) writes:

> Indeed. It often seems as if the majority of Usenet
>traffic is composed of various rephrasings of the
>command "go stick your head in a pig." Understanding
>this fact would be crucial to any high-level
>understanding of Usenet; whether such an understanding
>would be possible or even desirable is a question
>I'll leave open for discussion.

And if anyone were to ever gain such an understanding,
Usenet will instantly disappear and be replaced by
something even more bizarre and inexplicable.

Some say this has already happened.

Most say it isn't possible.

BECAUSE OF its interactive and open nature, the Internet enables people with similar interests or problems to find, talk to and help each other. Mailing lists (described in Chapter 3) can be used to do this, but a system called Usenet is also available. Where mailing lists use email technology to pass messages between people, Usenet has a special system of its own, which is an important component of the Net. Various on-line services provide their own equivalents of Usenet, which work in much the same way but are for the exclusive use of their subscribers. The information and comments that appear in them are not available to users of the Internet as a whole.

Newsgroups are used in two ways: as a source of entertainment; and for finding answers to specific questions. For entertainment purposes, newsgroups provide access to groups of people with the same interests. As a source of help, they offer the chance to obtain information from people who are experts in their field.

To get the best from the newsgroup system, it is essential to understand the culture of Usenet. Newsgroups have their own traditions, some of which are common to the whole system, while others are specific to individual groups. Newcomers who understand and respect these traditions will find Usenet much more entertaining and informative than those who do not. It is possible to annoy people in newsgroups if you do not behave in the expected way; in return they may well act in an unpleasant manner towards you.

CASE HISTORY – Alan

Alan Marks has an interest in unusual phenomena and was delighted to find plenty of information relating to his hobby on the Internet. But his enthusiasm soon turned to disillusion when he discovered the low quality of much of the debate in newsgroups.

'I have a strange hobby – I'm interested in UFOs, aliens, crop circles and other odd things. The Internet can be great for finding material about these sorts of subjects, especially on the Web and in the numerous newsgroups – the local religions seem to be* Star Trek *and the* X Files.

'When I started using Usenet I saw a long list of groups which looked really interesting, and I got very excited. But when I started reading the messages, reality sank in.

'It was like stepping into a war zone. I was completely unprepared for the personal attacks in some groups. It seems that a number of people spend* their time making sneering put-downs about anyone who disagrees with them. And then the replies are made in kind, and so it continues. I've since found out that sometimes the same arguments and the same insults have been carrying on for years, which is extremely strange but true.

'It wasn't just to do with my interests either – these personal attacks are not unusual and seem to be a common feature of lots of groups. I don't know why, but some people on Usenet are very aggressive. Everyone's postings get equal space, so if someone packs an emotional punch that posting will appear "louder" than the more reasonable ones.

'This seems to have a hypnotic effect on other people; they can't help getting hooked into the name-calling that follows. There are even Net celebrities – people with unlikely names like Archimedes Plutonium – who are cranks who get a lot of attention in the more serious science groups, where they're fair game for experts with time to kill.

'If I was starting now, I'd make sure that I got news software that can filter out the troublemakers and keep the endless arguments off my screen. I have that now, and it's made a big difference. I can watch the filter to see how many messages it kills, and sometimes that number has been a third of all the messages in a group. Is it censorship? Not really – on Usenet you have to look after yourself, and if you don't like someone or something you don't have to read those postings. If someone isn't happy with filtering out the disagreeable postings, Usenet isn't for them.

'And the point is, once you start filtering, life on Usenet becomes much more enjoyable. I've made some new friends in newsgroups, both locally and in other countries. One of them set up a mailing list recently which has been really great.

'Also, you hear about events before anyone else. The Internet had information about Hale-Bopp months before it was mentioned on TV. As soon as a rumour of any kind starts, a newsgroup devoted to it is formed, and someone usually puts up a web page about it too. But you do need to be selective about what you read and how seriously you take it. And life's a lot more peaceful if you stay out of the arguments.'

Usenet in practice

To use the newsgroup system with your Internet connection, you need two things:

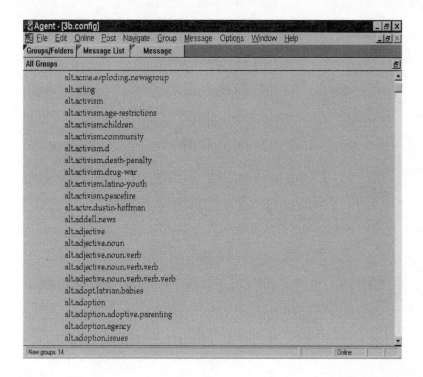

- access to a **'news server'**, which is a big computer that deals only with newsgroup messages. All the main IAPs and on-line services have their own news servers, and you will be given access to one when you sign up for their services
- **suitable newsreading software** The most popular web browsers – currently Netscape Navigator and Microsoft's Internet Explorer – include basic newsreading features, but these are very poor compared with proper newsreading software, which can be bought in stores or copied from the Internet.

Subscribing and posting

Subscribing to a newsgroup is as easy as tuning a radio or TV into a particular channel. You do not need to send an email message requesting to join the group. (In fact, attempting to do so is unwise as it marks you out as being a beginner, and therefore very low down the pecking order that exists in some groups.) Usually

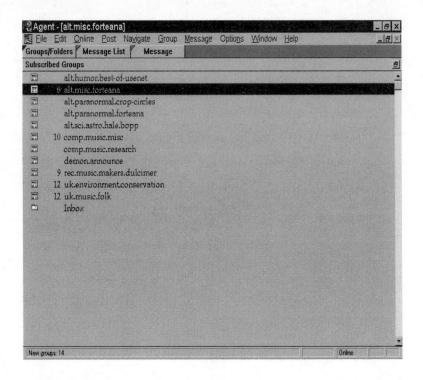

you simply select one or more groups from a long list, and select a 'subscribe' option (or something similar) from a menu. The messages for the groups you have subscribed to will appear automatically next time you connect to the Internet.

Posting a message to a newsgroup is very similar to writing an email, except that the 'address' of the message is the name of one or more newsgroups instead of one or more individuals. All software includes options that let you start off a new discussion in a group or add a comment to an existing one. For the latter, the existing message is quoted and edited in the same way as for email, and many of the same conventions apply (see pages 41–2).

The most significant difference is that the conversation includes more than two people, so it is very important to edit the messages in such a way as to make it clear which comment you are responding to and who said what. Most software has a 'quote phrase', which you set up when you use the software for the first time. This phrase then appears at the top of every message you write when replying to someone else's comment, and automatically includes the name and email address of the person you are responding to. A typical example is set out below.

```
On Mon, 06 Jan 97 14:42:36 GMT, badger@bolthole.lemon.co.uk
(Nick Badger) decided to entertain us with the following:
>In article <QyC$FgAC+hbzFw8M@gthomp.melon.co.uk>
>Gillian Thompson <gthompson@gthomp.melon.co.uk> writes:
>>In article <E9oKts.6yn@csa.bris.co.uk>, "Jai Helden"
>><pz0079@irix.bris.co.uk> writes
>>>I am afraid I can /never/ tell what others are
>>>thinking, which when I was younger led to a few
>>>embarrassments.
>>
>>A good rule of thumb is that others are thinking
>>exactly what you'd like them to be thinking.
>>Remember the world really only exists in your mind,
>>so make the most of it. HTH
>
>Unfortunately that doesn't help cases such as a certain
>person I used to know, who was insecure almost to the
>point of paranoia. If there was a possible negative
>connotation, she'd take it. If not, she'd invent one ...
>
Wow Nick - did we meet in a previous life?

Liz http://www.ginandtonic.melon.co.uk/Liz/
```

The first six lines at the top are the quote phrases, which introduce the people participating in this particular exchange of messages. Quote phrases do not have a standard format. Some people use humorous introductions, while others use much simpler ones such as: 'In article <so and so> <such and such> writes:'. Perversely, quote phrases appear in reverse order, with the most recent listed at the top.

QyC$FgAC+hbzFw8M@gthomp.melon.co.uk is the reference code produced by the various news servers to keep track of the administrative details of the message. This information is strictly for the benefit of the computers involved in passing this message through the Usenet system. It does not contain any information of interest to the people involved in the conversation. Although there is an '@' sign this is not an email address.

Under the last quote phrase is the first message in the exchange: Jai Helden explaining that he cannot tell what others are thinking. Then comes Gillian Thompson's tongue-in-cheek response, then Nick Badger's response to her response. Finally the newest message is Liz's response to Nick. The original message and the replies are shown in chronological order. Liz's response is not quoted because she is the author of the final reply – her 'sig' (see page 101), which includes the URL for her web site, appears at the end.

Although this may look complicated, it is much easier to use the system than to describe it. To keep track of who is saying what, you simply need to count the quote characters ('>') and match them to the person with the same number in the quote phrase. The smaller the number is, the more recent the message. When you post a reply of your own all the text has another quote mark added at the front. You can then edit out the very earliest messages if you think they are no longer relevant. Below is a reply from Steve Casey with the first couple of contributions removed.

```
>On Mon, 06 Jan 1997 17:39:16 GMT
>liz@ginandtonic.melon.co.uk (Liz Purdue) added the
following to the fount of human knowledge:
>>On Mon, 06 Jan 97 14:42:36 GMT,
>badger@bolthole.lemon.co.uk (Nick Badger) decided to
>entertain us with the following:

>>Unfortunately that doesn't help cases such as a certain
>>person I used to know, who was insecure almost to the
>>point of paranoia. If there was a possible negative
>>connotation, she'd take it. If not, she'd invent one

>Wow Nick - did we meet in a previous life?

Maybe we all did. Which is why we decided to live so far
apart this time around.
```

HTH,

Steve

Steve Casey
Skydancer Media Ltd — http://www.skydancer.co.uk

Missing messages

One problem with Usenet is that not all groups, and not all messages, are available everywhere. The Usenet network is rather ramshackle and inefficient, so some groups and messages fall through the gaps. One way in which IAPs differ from each other is the varying quality of their Usenet connection. Some offer a relatively small selection of groups — perhaps a few thousand — while others offer 30,000 or more. Only a tiny minority of IAPs based in the USA carry every single message that appears in every single group. For a variety of technical reasons, UK IAPs do not manage to do this. Some deliberately restrict the number of groups their subscribers can see to limit the demands on their resources. IAPs will sometimes make a particular group available if asked, although this may not always be possible for technical reasons.

Some IAPs may not carry certain groups for moral reasons — for example, those controversial groups that are used for various illegal activities including pornography and software piracy. However, other IAPs do provide access to these, using the argument that they are simply carriers of information and cannot therefore be held responsible for the content. This is a legal issue that will remain unresolved for some time yet, although there are signs that the industry and various governments are moving towards a situation where IAPs can carry whatever they like unless they receive complaints from the police or the public.

For these reasons, newsgroup coverage can be patchy. This is not usually a problem as you are very unlikely to miss a group if you do not know it exists. And unless you have an interest in groups with illegal content, the legal restrictions should not bother you. A more common problem is that messages may be delayed, which can make conversations stall temporarily.

IAPs can also remove messages deliberately. They delete old newsgroup messages from their news computer for the same reason that people remove files from their computer at home: to save space. This is known as 'expiring' the messages. Typical expiry times vary from a few days to a fortnight, depending on the resources of the IAP. A full set of messages for every available group can take up enormous amounts of computer filing space (a few gigabytes a day), and the volume is growing exponentially. So IAPs sometimes set up different time limits for different groups; those with a lot of traffic will have their messages deleted more quickly than others to make way for newer ones.

Newsreading software also includes an expiry feature which performs the same task for your own computer. Typically, you can mark certain messages as interesting, and they will stay on your computer until you decide to remove them by hand. All the other messages will be deleted after a set time to save space.

You can also delete messages once they have been posted to Usenet (both your own and other people's) in an attempt to stop people seeing them. However, this requires specialised knowledge and remains the preserve of Usenet experts, who do this deliberately when they find messages they object to, particularly ones that are attempts to abuse the system. A person with the pseudonym of 'Cancelmoose' runs a system which automatically hunts down and removes Usenet's version of junk mail – commercial messages posted simultaneously across hundreds of newsgroups. In one celebrated case, war broke in a newsgroup when an organisation called The Church of Scientology had some of its secret documents posted anonymously. It tried to cancel these messages, but they were posted again immediately afterwards. After a day or two all parties involved were posting thousands of messages (all conflicting) in an attempt to make sure that the information either did, or did not, become public.

Groups and group names

When you link to Usenet for the first time, your newsreading software will copy a list of all the available groups to your computer – to do this you typically need to select an option labelled something like 'Get all groups'.

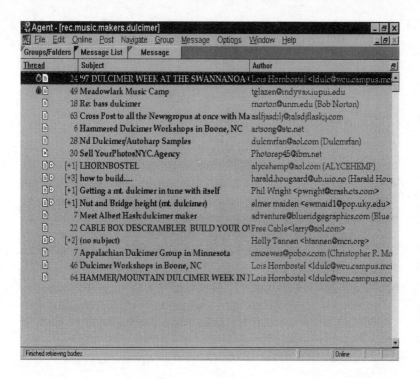

Groups are arranged into categories. These in turn have sub-categories, sub-sub-categories, and so on. Each name appears as a collection of words separated by dots – for example, *uk.business.telework* In this case 'uk' is the main category heading and is used for all groups specific to the United Kingdom; 'business' is a sub-heading that includes all the business-related groups; and 'telework' specifies one particular group from this sub-category – in this case, a group for people who work from home. The name as a whole often, but not always, gives a good indication of what the group is about. When verbally quoting the name of a newsgroup, the dots are not mentioned, so '*uk.business.telework*' is simply 'UK business telework'. Where it is relatively easy to work out the meaning from the context, group names may be abbreviated: '*uk.singles*' becomes '*uk.s*'

Originally, eight main categories existed, but there are now hundreds. Many of the newer categories are specific to certain countries or academic and research establishments, and this limits their usefulness for most readers. When looking for a newsgroup about a specific subject, it is advisable to explore the main categories and perhaps those under the 'uk.' heading before investigating the others.

The traditional category headings are:

rec. – recreation. Hobbies, pastimes, sports, and leisure
biz. – business. Investment and business advice
sci. – science. For scientific discussions and information
comp. – computing. For computers and computer users
soc. – society. For and about various cultures and social and ethnic groups
misc. – miscellaneous. Includes some buy and sell groups
talk. – Idle chatter and repetitive debates
news. – Useful (mostly) information about the Newsgroup Network
alt. – alternative. Anything – literally.

Most of the information on Usenet appears in these groups, and you will find plenty of them to keep you busy. Outside these headings, groups fall into a variety of category types, including the following.

- **Groups set up by IAPs for discussions, help and support for their members** Demon (demon.), Netcom (Netcom.), Pipex (pipex.) and others have their own groups.
- **Groups for various countries** The UK (uk.), Canada (can.), Germany (de.), Poland (pl.), and Mexico (mex.) are typical examples.
- **Groups for various cities** London (lon.), Cambridge (cam.), Ottawa (ott.), New York (nyc.) and so on. Postings to these groups can sometimes get confused when there are cities with the same name in different countries.
- **Groups for various US states** California (ca.), Miami (mi.), and so on.
- **Groups maintained by companies or commercial organisations** These are an anathema to traditional Usenet culture, but are starting to make an appearance. The ClariNet news service (clari.) contains groups which offer a paid-for subscription service for anyone who wants news of the more

traditional kind. Computer software giant Microsoft (microsoft.) has a large number of groups devoted to its products.

- **Groups created by universities and colleges for their own use** uwarwick. groups are for the University of Warwick, utexas. for the University of Texas, and so on.
- **Other local groups** For example, groups for the Triangle area of the USA (triangle.) based around part of North Carolina.

Given these top-level categories, groups are sub-categorised by adding extra descriptive sub-divisions separated by '.' Some examples are listed below:

- **uk.people.consumers** Devoted to consumer topics of all kinds. Mainly for UK readers, but available for anyone anywhere
- **uk.people.teen** Chat for UK teenagers. (Another sub-division of the uk.people sub-category)
- **demon.ip.support.win95** Support for Internet problems for users of the Demon IAP who are using Windows 95
- **alt.family-names-jacoby** Genealogy and general chat for anyone who has this particular surname
- **no.typografi** Discussion of typography in Norwegian.

It should be obvious from looking at the above groups that the categorisation system is rather random. For example, it would make more sense for the London groups to be in the UK category, but in fact they are in a category of their own. Although attempts have been made to impose order on Usenet, the categorisation scheme is very much a free-for-all. This is likely to get worse as more and more people start using Usenet.

It is also difficult to tell what the different groups are about. The information provided above should help you to make an educated guess about many groups, but in practice even experienced Net users often have to experiment. It is not at all obvious what *cns.cbd.cbd-30* is about, for example. Often the only way to find out is to subscribe to the group and read a selection of messages – and even then it is not always clear.

To further add to the confusion, some groups and their names are nothing more than running jokes, while others rely on specialised information that most people cannot be expected to know. An example of the former is *alt.adjective.noun.verb.verb.verb* which – rather bizarrely – consists entirely of postings which start with an adjective, follow it with a noun and add three verbs at the end. At the time of writing, this group was receiving hundreds of messages a week.

An example of the latter is the groups in the *alt.2600* collection of groups, which is the home of various hackers who like to abuse computers and the telephone network. The name comes from the group's history: one particularly famous hacker discovered that a toy whistle, given away in a packet of cereal, produced a sound at 2600Hz when he tried blowing through it into a telephone receiver. 2600Hz happened to be the pitch of the signalling tones used by the telephone exchanges of the time to allow free calls. He then passed on this information to other hackers who started getting free calls in the same way, and the number passed into hacker folklore. This kind of obscurity is typical of some parts of Usenet.

Finding interesting groups

Fortunately, there are more direct ways to find useful groups than reading through the full list of names. Most newsreading software includes a search facility which can pick out groups that contain a particular word, or keyword. It is useful to do some lateral thinking when trying this. For example, when looking for 'hi-fi' you should also check for 'audio' and other synonyms.

Many web search engines also include the ability to search through archived newsgroup postings. These are invaluable when you are looking for conversations about a certain subject. Deja News (*http://www.dejanews.com*) is the best-known service. In addition, some of the web search facilities such as Yahoo (*http://www.yahoo.com*) and AltaVista (*http://www.altavista.digital.com*) include an option for looking through newsgroup archives.

All the search engines work the same way, offering simple searches for occurrences of a certain word or postings by a certain person. More sophisticated options can make a search more specific by including or excluding certain newsgroups, or by looking for postings sent between two particular dates.

Finally, if you want to see what a group is about you can read its FAQ (Frequently Asked Questions document), if it has one

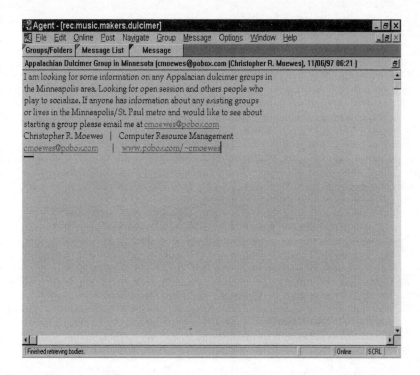

(see page 12). FAQs can be invaluable for finding information or getting practical help about a subject. They are also available on the Web (see page 250 for the relevant details).

CASE HISTORY – David

David Payne decided to get an Internet connection installed at home. His first project was to find out the whereabouts of an old friend with whom he hadn't been in touch for over seven years. He suspected that he would also have an Internet connection.

'Paul is the kind of person who likes to play with computers, so I thought that there was a good chance he would also be on-line. Fortunately, he also has an unusual surname, so I thought it would be easy to find him.

'It actually took only a few minutes. I used Deja News to search for his surname, and it came back with a long list of his newsgroup postings. He'd actually changed his email address halfway through the list, but it

was obvious which was the most recent because Deja News shows the date and time of each posting as well as the subject, the newsgroup and the author.

'He was a little surprised to hear from me, but we met up recently and it was great to see him again.'

Getting the best from groups

To get the most from newsgroups, it is vital to be familiar with Usenet's own peculiar culture, and, in particular, the culture in any group that you may be interested in. All of them are different, and some are much more polite and mature than others, so it is always advisable to watch a group for a while to see how it functions.

Listed below are some useful dos and don'ts:

- **Do** read a group's messages before joining in. If you are looking for help, support or information, you will be able to see immediately if this is the right group for you. You can also gauge the atmosphere of a group, identify dominant personalities who may be either a problem or particularly qualified to help, and find out what kind of issues and subjects make the other members of the group react in a hostile way.

- **Do** read the FAQ (Frequently Asked Questions) list if there is one. It will be posted regularly: at least monthly, and more probably weekly. If there does not seem to be one, it can be worth posting a quick question to the group, saying, for example, 'Is there an FAQ anywhere?'.

- **Do** read the charter, if one is posted. It is a formal statement of what the group is about and a summary of the kind of postings that are and are not acceptable. Charters are sometimes ignored or sidelined once a group has started to thrive, but if one is available it helps to be familiar with it.

- **Do** keep calm under pressure and avoid taking things personally. Even if someone is being intensely annoying, it is best not to get drawn into arguments. If you familiarise yourself with the group before posting you will know who to be wary of. It is possible to make a mistake and ask for information in a way that annoys people. If you have done this, do not try to defend your position, as this will usually make matters worse. It is better simply to ignore the abuse and leave the group. If the mistake was genuine and you want to remain a part of the group, a brief apology can sometimes help. But, otherwise, getting involved in any violent verbal exchange – known as a 'flame war' (see page 105) – is usually a waste of time.

• **Do** edit other people's posts when replying. Reproducing a 500-line message in its entirety with a single short comment at the end is a guaranteed way to annoy people. As with email, it is common practice to leave in only the paragraphs or comments to which you are referring.

• **Do** keep it clear who is responsible for which comment when editing. It should remain obvious who said what, even if some of their comments have been pruned.

• **Do** use software that lets you read and write newsgroup postings off-line (see page 41). Trying to read newsgroup messages on-line is a guaranteed way to run up a huge telephone bill. Plenty of the better software works off-line. If you plan to do more than dabble with Usenet it is well worth either buying a good newsreader (the Internet jargon for newsreading software) or copying one from the Net.

• **Do not** post the same message to more than one newsgroup unless it is absolutely essential. This is known as 'cross posting' and is not popular. Cross posting can start a conversation that spreads between groups, rather than remaining within the boundaries of individual ones. This can make it hard to follow the conversation that results, and also tends to increase the chances of a violent argument breaking out. If you receive a message that has already been posted to numerous groups, you can trim the header list (see pages 234–8) so your reply is sent to only one or two. Typically, software shows a list of the groups that a message appears in, and to trim the headers you simply delete all but one or two groups from this list.

• **Do not** post impassioned comments unless you want a backlash. It is a curious feature of Usenet that people respond more to the tone of a post than its contents. Even if your point of view is valid and you can marshal an encyclopaedia of facts to support it, impassioned rhetoric will infuriate some people.

- **Do not** reply immediately when someone has annoyed you. It is always better to write vitriolic ripostes but wait until the next day to send them. This gives you a chance to calm down, and then decide whether or not to send a more moderate response instead.

- **Do not** be tempted to edit someone else's posts creatively by changing words, adding new ones, or leaving some out. This is acceptable only in a handful of non-serious groups when it is done as a joke and is obvious. Otherwise, it is almost guaranteed to attract a flurry of rude messages.

- **Do not** sell anything in a newsgroup unless you are sure that it is acceptable to do so. Listing a pointer to a web site that tells everyone about you, and perhaps the products or services you offer, will not annoy anyone, whereas posting a three-page advertisement in a group which does not welcome them certainly will. Private sales seem to be more acceptable, but again only certain groups allow them.

- **Do not** post the wrong kind of information. If a group is for text-only messages, posting your holiday snaps to it will not endear you to the group. Similarly, if a group is dedicated to 'for sale' advertisements, having a discussion about something profound will irritate some people.

Good newsreading software can also make a big difference to the ease and efficiency with which you can read and post Usenet messages. Look out for the following features:

- **Killfiles** These are filters that 'kill' (remove) certain messages according to rules that you specify. You can kill postings from particular authors, about certain subjects, or any other type of messages according to set specifications.

- **Off-line newsreading** If you use a browser for reading messages in newsgroups you will have to read them on-line, with your telephone connection running and the phone bill increasing. Off-line reading facilities copy the most recent set of messages to your computer in one go, enabling you to break the connection and then read and reply to them at your leisure.

- **Email facilities** It is usually better to use a proper email package for email, but situations will arise in which you will want to write a follow-up to a newsgroup posting with a private message. Having email facilities included in the newsreading software makes this much easier.
- **News management facilities** Most newsgroup software includes an 'expire' option that deletes old messages after a certain period of time – without this your computer's entire filing space will fill up. It is also useful to have a 'keep' option, which marks messages that are of particular interest so you can keep them permanently without needing to copy and file them by hand. This feature also enables you to organise interesting messages, for example, filing them in folders under different subject headings.
- **Web links** URLs (web addresses) can appear in newsgroup postings. A useful feature of the best software is the ability to start a web browser and pass the URL to it automatically when you click on it, so the relevant web page appears automatically.
- **Threads** Messages are arranged into 'threads' – a long list of all the messages that refer to the same subject. Good newsreading software can show these threads, making it easier to follow one particular conversation all the way through. Some software even shows threads diagrammatically and indicates who has responded to whose comments.
- **Customisation** This facility allows you to change the colour, style and size of text to suit your screen and personal preferences, and also to change the way that unread and read messages appear. (For example, unread messages could be purple and read messages could be blue.)

Trolls, troublemakers, spam, scams and killfiles

Trolls are Usenet's equivalent of an April Fool joke, except that they can happen at any time of year. A troll is a posting that is deliberately provocative or outrageous and is intended to make anyone who responds to it look stupid.

They are not always easy to spot, however. Some postings that look like trolls are actually quite serious, while others that can appear serious are really trolls. A good rule of thumb is to ignore anything that looks too outrageous to be believable.

Troublemakers are a common problem on Usenet. These people repeatedly get into arguments or continue the same arguments for years on end. They are usually quite easy to spot, especially in the more popular groups, as there will be a crowd of angry buzzing messages around their postings.

The best way to deal with troublemakers is to ignore them. They thrive on attention, usually of the negative kind, and getting into an argument with them is a waste of time and quite stressful. It is hard for beginners to appreciate just how nerve-wracking an electronic argument can be. More experienced users, who have learned this the hard way, refuse to be drawn in, no matter how outrageous or offensive the troublemaker becomes.

Spam is Usenet's equivalent of junk mail and is a perennial nuisance on Usenet. It is postings which are made to thousands of groups at the same time advertising goods and services. There is a constant battle between the people who send it – known as 'spammers' – and everyone else. Spammers are usually marketing and sales people who cannot resist the opportunity to send messages to a captive audience of millions for very little outlay. The best way to deal with spam is to use a good killfile (see below).

Scams are postings that claim to offer you instant wealth. They can usually be recognised by subject lines such as '$$$$$FAST CASH NOW!!!$$$$$'. These are electronic versions of the pyramid schemes that have been illegal for a few years, and have been given a new lease of life by the huge number of potential victims available on the Internet. The idea is that you recruit a number of other victims, each of whom send you some cash. They, in turn, recruit others, keep some of their cash and send you the rest, and so on. The problem is that at the bottom of the chain you get nothing and can lose a lot of money. Participating in these schemes is outside the law. David Rhodes, who is often quoted in the preamble attached to these scams, is now serving a sentence for fraud in a US jail.

Killfiles are the solution for most Usenet problems. For anyone who uses Usenet regularly, a killfile option is not a luxury, it is essential. A properly set-up killfile can remove almost all of the most annoying and irrelevant postings that users are likely to come across, and make the experience of Usenet much more pleasurable and useful.

Special groups

Most newsgroups are used exclusively for text messages, but other types of information can also be posted on Usenet. The technology used to do this is not particularly sophisticated, but millions of non-text messages are still sent every day. These messages are segregated into special groups because they cannot be read in the usual way.

These groups pose a serious problem for the Internet because they take up valuable computer time and space that could be better used for other activities. Non-text information is very bulky, and as the volume increases, the whole Internet slows down. This may yet prove to have disastrous consequences. Some experts have warned that the whole Internet may collapse and have to be rebuilt from scratch. Whether or not this happens remains to be seen. For now, non-text groups are something of a liability on the Internet – even if they are extremely popular.

Non-text information is sent to Usenet using a system very similar to that used to add attachments to email. All non-text messages are known as 'binaries', although – rather confusingly – the name is also used to describe groups with certain kinds of content, specifically pictures, video clips, and sound clips.

If you try to read one of these messages as text, you will see a very long string of gibberish. To make sense of this, you need to 'decode' it (see Chapter 7). As with email, the better software does this for you automatically. It can also launch a 'viewer', which will display the information in the most suitable way, for example, as a picture on the screen for images, in a small video window for video, and so on.

The main difference between binaries and attachments is that binary files are almost always sent in multiple parts. A typical binary appears like this: *<description> Some picture.type 1/5*. The first part, <description>, is a very short descriptive phrase, for example 'Balinese temple dancer'. 'Some picture' is the name of the image as it appears in your computer – perhaps

'BALIDANCER'. 'Type' is the type of information: for images and photographs it will usually be 'gif' or 'jpg'. These are popular image formats that can be viewed on most computers. The '1/5' means that the message has been sent in five parts and this is the first message of five. Somewhere else in the group you will find '2/5', '3/5', and so on.

Usenet's unreliability can cause serious problems for binaries: not only do parts often arrive out of sequence, but sometimes one or more go missing. Out-of-sequence binaries are not usually a problem – the better newsreading software can automatically rearrange them, and at worst it is possible to cut and paste the sections together by hand before decoding them. But if a section is missing, the binary is ruined. When this happens it is acceptable in some groups to post a message that says 'Please re-post parts 1 and 2', for example. In others it is not. This depends on the culture of the group.

Sometimes a 'part 0' is posted. This is a short text message that introduces the binary and explains what it contains, both technically so that readers can decide which viewer software to use, and descriptively.

Copying binaries from Usenet to your computer can be very time consuming. A typical photograph may take a few minutes to appear, and a short video clip a couple of hours or more. This makes the binary groups expensive and of limited interest, except for those who are passionately interested in the content. However, binaries will become more popular as the connection speeds increase.

The easiest way to work with binaries is to use good newsreading software. Without it, they can be too cumbersome to be worthwhile. With it, the whole process becomes very streamlined. For sources of software, see Appendix 6, which includes more details about how binaries work and how to make sense of them

Binaries groups

Groups that have the word 'binaries' appear in two ways: either as a group (or collection of groups) that stands alone; or as a group associated with another group used for text messages. The 'catch-all' binaries group is *alt.binaries*. Typically, someone will post a message to a text group saying something relevant to the discussion and explaining that they have copied a corresponding picture, for example, to *alt.binaries*. Readers can then view the picture if they are interested in it, or ignore it if they are not.

As a rule, text and binaries are kept as strictly segregated as possible, and it is another unwritten Usenet 'law' that messages of one kind are not welcome in a group created for the other. This helps make the information clearer for everyone, although inevitably some people ignore the distinction, much to everyone else's annoyance.

Warez

The 'warez' ('wares') groups are the other family of binaries groups. They are best avoided because they are part of an illegal sub-culture on the Net that offers 'free' software. This has been pirated and is then posted for everyone in the group to use. *This software is not legal.* If you are caught with it on your computer you may be liable for prosecution.

If you try posting warez software, it is very easy for the software company in question to get your name and address from your post by obtaining the details from your IAP. Even disguising your message (see page 148) will not stop the company from finding your details. IAPs keep records of who posts what, when, and from where, and can be asked to reveal them to the software company or the police.

Another reason why you should avoid warez software is because it is often infected with viruses. You should always use a virus checker on any software you copy from the Internet, no matter where it comes from.

In addition, warez people are generally very aggressive and abusive, which again makes visiting these groups unpleasant. They use a language of their own called EliTe (the capitalisation is deliberate) which is a warped form of English that is hard for most people to understand.

'Newsgroups' on on-line services

CompuServe and AOL offer their own Usenet-like systems, although these work slightly differently from Usenet newsgroups. (Note that if you use an on-line service you can use these proprietary systems as well as Usenet itself.)

Instead of appearing as a collection of groups in a long list, these 'forums', 'discussion areas' or 'message boards' are usually linked to other related information. For example, a feature about alternative health will typically include a message board where people can swap their experiences and offer help and advice.

As with Usenet, the quality of information may vary from group to group, and the number of discussions that appear can be patchy. However, they are far less prone to name-calling than Usenet groups, and people seem much less keen to take centre stage and present their opinions forcefully. On the other hand, discussions can lack some of the vibrancy of their equivalents on Usenet. Each group has a relatively small number of regular contributors; people seem to visit a group only once or twice before moving on. Temporary visitors to Usenet newsgroups, however, tend to read a group without contributing anything.

Another important difference is that the low volume of messages means that some boards have ones that are a year or two old. As they do not have a formal expiry system, messages remain until they are deleted by the system's administrators – not a regular occurrence – or until the system suffers a technical failure and loses some of its archives. At best, this can make a board a fascinating historical archive, but at worst you have hundreds of messages to look through before you find the most recent and most interesting ones; and many of the original contributors are no longer with the service. (Note that the information in these areas is not archived by any of the Usenet archiving services.)

The great strength of on-line services is that they can offer technical support from various companies. Many computer companies have message areas on these services which relate specifically to their products, and these are read by their support staff. They give you a direct line to someone who knows the product and can answer questions about it. If you do not understand the answer, you can ask another question. Because the interchange is public, companies are aware that getting the answer wrong or appearing to be unhelpful in some other way is bad public relations. The exchange is much more direct than it would be on Usenet, which has a 'non-commercial' ethic that has made it impossible for companies to set up the same kind of service on it.

Because on-line service providers and Usenet offer such different services, they are complementary rather than competitive. The ideal situation would be to have access to both. Usenet is best for 'informal' support and debate. Groups have a much wider range of contributors, and the existence of FAQs (see page 12) is helpful. The on-line services are better for the 'formal' support mentioned above. When a Usenet-like group of regulars appears on an on-line service, it is usually much more tightly knit and dedicated than those found on Usenet. It is also easier to find related information because the groups are closely associated with libraries of software, live chat and other resources.

CHAPTER 6

INTERNET SECRETS: PEOPLE AND CULTURE

THE INTERNET has a language all of its own. Because it is not possible to convey tone of voice or facial expression, various novel ways of communicating emotion and personality have evolved.

The Internet also has a culture of its own. People who use the Net seem to have more unconventional interests and values and express themselves differently. Any newcomers to the Net may find all of this bewildering, so what follows is a guide to those aspects of Internet life that are most daunting to inexperienced users.

Learning the language

Although English is the most widely used language on the Internet, it has been extended to include a variety of expressions and novel forms of punctuation which are not used anywhere else. The language also has certain conventions. These are used in much the same way that 'Dear Sir/Yours faithfully', for example, is used in letters.

Smileys and emoticons

Without the nuance of tone of voice, or the visual impact of body language, on-line conversations can easily give the wrong impression. To compensate for this, many Internet regulars add extra characters to their email messages and live chat to show what they are feeling.

These characters, known as smileys (and occasionally as emoticons – but apparently only in Internet books and never on the Internet itself) are made by combining punctuation marks to draw a picture. Of the hundreds of possible smileys, only a handful are used regularly:

:-) **Happy smiley** Used when someone is laughing, is happy, or has made a joke

:-(**Sad smiley** Used when someone is unhappy

;-) **Winking smiley** Used for sarcastic, ironic or flirtatious comments

;-(**Crying smiley** Used when someone is very unhappy

:) **Shorthand happy smiley**

:(**Shorthand unhappy smiley**

;-> **Biting smiley** Used for a very sarcastic comment.

Some can be emphasised by repeating them. So :)))))))))))) is a very happy smiley indeed. People either love smileys or hate them. In some of the UK newsgroups smileys are considered to be very un-English and rather gauche. (The reasoning is that people have managed to write to each other without smileys for centuries and do not see why they should start adding them now.) In other newsgroups, and in many emails, smileys are both popular and welcome.

Another way of expressing emotion is to spell out actions and comments between angle brackets, thus: <grin>, <sigh>, and so on. More popular examples are often shortened to single letters: <grin> to <g>. Actions are much more versatile than smileys and can be used to express anything: <kick>, <fires gun>, <opens window>, and so on. Some people use a more formal version; the letters 'fx' are added after the first angle bracket. This is short for 'effects' but again indicates an action: <fx: writes Internet book>.

Another similar convention is to put 'emotions' in pairs:

```
<bored>

That's really very interesting indeed.

</bored>
```

This is based on HTML, the system used to create web pages (see Appendix 4). The words in angle brackets work like a sophisticated form of punctuation, which sets the tone or emotion for the words they bracket. They apply to whatever text is written between them and are often used ironically. The first word 'turns on' the emotion and the last word (after the slash) shows where the emotion stops.

Adding emphasis

ON THE INTERNET, WRITING IN CAPITALS IS CONSIDERED SHOUTING. Although this is a rather arbitrary convention, using upper case letters all the way through an email or newsgroup message can make the text hard to read and is considered rude. But capitalising a single word or phrase is a good way to add emphasis.

In print, emphasis can be added by putting words or phrases in italic or bold text. This is not possible on the Internet. To create the same effect words are placed between characters to give them extra weight, thus: /italics/ and *bold*. As with real italics, these effects are best used sparingly.

Abbreviations

Internet users tend to abbreviate common phrases to acronyms. These can be very confusing for newcomers because often there is no easy way to guess what the abbreviations mean. Popular examples include:

LOL   Laughing out loud
ROTFL   Rolling on the floor laughing ('That was very
            funny.')
HAND   Have a nice day
HTH   Hope this helps (Not always meant literally)
IYSWIM   If you see what I mean
IMO   In my opinion
IMHO   In my humble opinion
IMNSHO   In my not so humble opinion
ITYMTP   I think you missed the point

AFAIK	As far as I know
TTFN	Ta ta for now
ISTR	I seem to remember
IIRC	If I remember correctly
YMMV	Your mileage may vary (i.e. your experience may be different)
FYI	For your information
RTFM	Read the ******* manual
FOAD	Please leave quickly and quietly (or words to that effect)
DIMU	Did I mess up? (or misunderstand?)
BTW	By the way
MOTOS	Member of the opposite sex
MOTSS	Member of the same sex
MOTAS	Member of the alternate sex
SO	Significant other
OTOH	On the other hand
BTW	By the way
TLA	Three letter acronym
POV	Point of view

In some quarters the more extrovert abbreviations, such as ROTFL, are considered gauche, but the less colourful ones, such as IMO, are used regularly by everyone.

Sigs

A 'sig' – short for signature – is a short piece of text that is added automatically to each of your email or newsgroup postings by your software. Almost all software includes this facility, although you do not have to make use of it. You type the text that you want to appear into a designated space, and it will then appear at the end of your messages until you decide to remove or change it.

Sigs are used to include jokes, electronic and 'real life' contact details, URLs of personal web pages, and so on. They tend to appeal to novices who have not yet tired of the constant repetition of a sig. More experienced users tend either not to use them at all or to keep them very simple.

In certain newsgroups, long sigs are guaranteed to attract unwelcome attention. A 'rule' states that no sig should be more than four lines long, and some people – including whole newsgroups – will be very aggressive towards someone who has one that is longer than this. (An entire newsgroup – *alt.fan.warlord* – is devoted to the ruthless verbal abuse of people with long sigs.) The rationale is that long sigs waste Internet resources while they are copied from place to place. But given the huge volume of information that moves across the Internet every day, the truth is that this is often no more than an excuse used by some people wanting to pick a fight.

However, it is still a good idea to show consideration for other Internet users when creating a sig. The four-line rule can usually be relaxed slightly if some of the lines use spacer characters such as '-' and '|' to draw boxes. Very long sigs, especially drawings and sketches made out of letters (known as ASCII art), are definitely frowned upon. You should also avoid preaching, religious sigs of whatever denomination or belief, or anything that looks too much like aggressive self-promotion.

Below is an example of a sig that is unlikely to be popular:

```
                                  \ _ /
                               -= ( _ ) =-
                                  / _ \
    .\/\/\.              ,\/,  ,\/.//,                    ,~
   /o//o\\ , . , .     //o\ /o\\o\\                      |\
    |  |  /###/#\       |    |  |                       /| \
    |  |  |'  '|:|     |`=.='| |.                     /_|__\
^^^^^^^^^^^^^^^^^^^^^^^^^^^^^^^^^^^^^""""""""""~~~~~~~~~~~~~~~

     Tina Moriarty   Receptionist   email~ reception@anycorp.com
     Anycorporation     1234 Any Ave,   ZA 72043   215-1234-567
```

But this one will not cause offence to anyone:

```
Richard Wentk    Freelance Widget Services
richard@acompany.com http://www.acompany.com/rjw
```

Although the former may be more cheerful, it causes problems in two ways. The first is that long sigs become less and less appealing with constant repetition. Once someone has seen a sig like this a few hundred times, the novelty value will have worn off completely.

The second is that it does not work on certain computer screens. On some computers, letters on the screen are all exactly the same width (fixed pitch fonts), while on others the widths vary (variable pitch fonts) to create a more natural effect. A sig that works well on one kind of screen will look incomprehensible on another:

```
                          \ _ /
                        -= (_) =-
                         /   \
   .\/\/.        ,\/,   ,\/.//,                    ,~
   /o//o\\ ,.,.,  //o\  /o\\o\\                     |\
   | | /###/#\   |   | |                /|\
   | | |' ':|  |`=.='| |                /_|__\
  ^^^^^^^^^^^^^^^^^^^^^^^^^^^^^^^^^^^^""""""""""~~~~~~~~~~~~~~

   Tina Moriarty   Receptionist   email:reception@anycorp.com
   Anycorporation   1234 Any Ave,    ZA 72043   215-1234-567
```

A good way to make a sig more interesting is to include a link to your personal web site. You can put as much information as you like on these pages, and people can choose whether or not they want to read it. Another option is to use 'sig switching' shareware (the ideas behind shareware are described on page 245) which selects a different quote or comment from a long list for every message you post.

Sig regulars

Although sigs vary, certain ideas are used frequently. The first idea is the 'standard disclaimer'. For legal reasons, company employees who post from a company account are often asked to include a line that says 'This posting is my personal opinion and not in any way that of the company'. This has led to a spate of jokes and puns in sigs about who owns opinions, who pays for them, whether or not they can be hired for a trial period, and so on. The shortest example of a joke is: *#include <disclaimer.h>* which is programmer-speak for 'Include the standard disclaimer that everyone uses here'. (It is a feature of Internet culture that terms and ideas that come from computer programming are very popular, both in sigs and in Internet humour in general.)

Another sig standard is the 'geek code'. This is a shorthand way of summing up the personality, interests, and even the current romantic status of the author of a message. A typical example looks like this:

```
V3.12 GM/CS d s:++ a- C++ U+ p L !E W++ N++ o+ K W— O?
M— V— PS? PE? Y PGP- t— !5 X- R- !tv b+++ DI+ D- G e++++ h-
r z++
```

Each letter indicates something about the author, and the number of pluses or minuses shows how strongly this information applies. The '!' indicates that this particular interest is avoided, and the 'v 3.12' at the start shows that this information is shown using version 3.12 of the geek code.

In the example, 'a–' means the writer is aged between 25 and 29, the 'N++' means 'I read so many newsgroups that the next batch of news comes in before I finish reading the last batch, and I have to read for about 2 hours straight before I'm caught up on the morning's news. Then there's the afternoon...,' and 't–' means the writer is not a *Star Trek* enthusiast. The geek code is maintained by Robert Hayden, and details of the latest version, including a description of what all the letters mean, are available at *http://krypton.mankato.msus.edu/~hayden/geek.html* The code has spawned a number of variations, and it is likely that more and more of these will appear as the Internet increases in popularity.

Rot13

Rot13 is an old Internet tradition used to disguise messages of a dubious or potentially offensive nature. It is a very simple code – each letter in a message is shifted 13 letters to the right, so that 'A' becomes 'N', 'B' becomes 'O', and so on. To read the original message the letters are shifted back. Letters that fall off the end of the alphabet are rotated back via 'A'; hence its name – Rotate 13.

Most newsgroup software includes a Rot13 feature. Its use is generally announced in most messages in plain English before the block of disguised text. If you see a message that looks like a random collection of letters arranged in words and sentences, it is likely that it has been encoded with Rot13.

Flames

Flames are verbal abuse. For some reason, on certain parts of Usenet flaming is considered to be an acceptable, even worthy activity. The most serious flames escalate from newsgroups to private email. Flames do not follow any set rules, and most are not very sophisticated. In fact, the vast majority simply say 'I think you're really stupid', in various more or less colourful ways. A flame war is simply a major outbreak of flaming (the word can also be used as a verb in this way) between two or more Internet users.

Names and addresses

Some email addresses have much more credibility than others on the Internet. They are judged by the 'domain name' – the part of the address that appears after the '@' sign and identifies which business, institution, IAP or on-line service someone is using. Some domains are widely thought to be the homes of troublemakers. Others are not popular because their users rightly or wrongly have been stereotyped as being 'clueless'. (On the Internet, being called 'clueless' is the worst insult that can be levelled at someone. It implies an embarrassingly naive gullibility, a lack of tact and understanding of Internet culture, and ignorance about the technology.) Some people go so far as to killfile all messages that come from these domains.

The main implication is that beginners should choose their IAP or on-line service carefully. However, the prejudice against the less popular services can be surmounted, and if you contribute to discussions in an intelligent way you will eventually be welcomed as 'one of the crowd'.

Local variations

One curiosity of the Internet is that it cannot cope with certain letters or characters. Unfortunately, one of them is the UK pound sign '£'. This character appears differently on various computer systems and can cause a number of other problems. To get round this, an acronym for 'UK pounds' – 'ukp' – is generally used instead. This can be read correctly on any computer.

Another source of confusion is the difference between UK and US date formats. In the UK dates are always shown as day/month/year. In the USA they appear as month/day/year. It is also helpful to remember that many UK words have completely different meanings in the USA – and *vice versa*. Again, these differences can be a source of confusion or embarrassment, depending on the circumstances.

Net culture

The distinction between 'undesirable' and other addresses has its roots in the history of the Internet. Politically, there are two groups on-line and these exist in a state of perpetual tension. The first group comprises the old-timers, the academics and the administrators of the Internet's computers. The other consists of the ordinary users – everyone else. This second group includes a surprising spread of social groups and people with varying interests, including a significant number of users at or near retirement age (who have the time to explore the Net), and a much larger number of women. Originally, this group consisted mainly of students and – mostly male – computer professionals, but this has now changed dramatically.

Initially, the Internet was not designed for the general public. Because of this its original users sometimes show resentment towards the newcomers, who they see as interlopers, especially if they do not understand the system or show no enthusiasm about computer technology. From this point of view, the Net can be unashamedly elitist – an exclusive gathering of technocrats who would prefer the system to remain as it was in the early 1990s before the general public started using it.

These original users left their mark on the culture of the Internet in two ways. The first is Usenet's intolerance of commerce. The Net was built as a not-for-profit facility, which was subsidised with public money. Because of this, no one is supposed to use the Net for private gain, and doing so is seen as an immoral abuse of the system. This is one reason why 'spam' (see page 92) is considered such an outrage. It is not simply an irritation but a deliberate misuse of public resources. The second is to do with the limited resources that were originally available. 'Bandwidth' – the Internet's ability to carry information – was scarce, and activities that wasted it were frowned upon.

To some extent both of these ideals are being marginalised as the Net 'goes public'. Large amounts of bandwidth are now wasted every day on completely trivial activities. The Web is not particularly efficient, and to make matters worse many web publishers are now experimenting with sound and video, which can use hundreds of times as much bandwidth as text does. At the same time, the most popular newsgroups are also being used to exchange binaries of a distinctly dubious nature (see page 95), and again these take up inordinate amounts of bandwidth and so waste resources. Flat-rate pricing for users encourages this abuse. The situation is even worse in the USA, where local calls cost a nominal amount and anyone can create a permanent Internet connection for themselves by installing a separate telephone line and leaving it constantly connected to his or her computer.

To summarise, the Net is changing and shifting from an environment in which users impress each other with their intelligence, knowledge and computer skills, to one that is more open and to which anyone can contribute. The uses to which the Net is put are also changing – less time is spent on research, and more time is spent on mundane activities such as chatting and shopping.

But even with the changes, the qualities and values that have influenced Net culture remain the same. These are discussed below:

- **Constant innovation** In 1994 the most popular web browser was Mosaic. By 1995 it was Netscape Navigator. By 1998 it will probably be Microsoft's Internet Explorer. The Net never stops changing: not only do people come and go, but the technology changes at a ridiculously fast rate. One year's innovation becomes next year's standard and is forgotten the year after.
- **Pranks and practical jokes** The original users of the Internet were much more intelligent than average, and some of them wanted everyone else to know this. Consequently, the

Internet has a tradition of pranks and practical jokes which are designed to make the unwary and inexperienced look stupid. A typical example is newsgroup 'wars', in which one group decides to invade and subvert another. These campaigns can be quite subtle. The invaders start by posting peculiar, but not quite unbelievable, messages to the target group. Then they try to engage their victims in a flame war, either by insulting them or appearing to be so ridiculous that they draw insults themselves. Finally, they instill paranoia by slandering their victims and trying to get them to mistrust each other. Once the group has dissolved in flames and recriminations they announce themselves and say words to the effect of: 'Well, don't take it so seriously – we were only joking'. These jokes have become a fact of life on the Internet. Some – although fortunately not many – web sites have similar 'gotchas'. This kind of humour is rather studenty, but very widespread on the Net.

- **Frank and vigorous debate** At best Internet debates can be fruitful and interesting: for example, *uk.politics* has changed the voting intentions of quite a few people during its short life. But at worst they can degenerate into name-calling and abuse. There is an Internet 'rule' – only half tongue-in-cheek – which suggests that as soon as one person accuses the other of being a Nazi, the debate ends. More experienced users know how to avoid getting into an argument that gets this heated but often only because they have learned what to avoid the hard way. Debate is always informal and people show their private faces much more than they might in the letters pages of a newspaper or in a live radio phone-in. Sometimes the language in debates is frank and explicit. While this may shock some people, these debates provide perhaps a more accurate picture of how most people really are than the rather formal and stylised pictures that appear in the traditional mass media.

- **Tolerance for unconventional ideas** Some of the information available on Usenet and the Web is remarkable by anyone's standards. It is possible to find automatic Shakespearean insult generators, shops that advertise time machines (guarantee not included), big red buttons that do nothing at all, galleries of grotesque art, lists of the contents of people's desks, and even stranger things. Anyone who does not have an open mind or an appreciation for surreal humour may find Net culture difficult to come to terms with. It is possible to avoid these quirkier facets of life on-line by using only email, and ignoring the Web and newsgroups. However, most people would consider this to be something of a waste.

- **Rough justice** Anyone who infringes the unwritten rules of the Internet, such as using Usenet for commercial purposes – especially knowingly and deliberately – can expect retaliation. Net technology can be used in offensive and aggressive ways (such as those discussed in Chapter 8), and these can cause a lot of inconvenience to anyone who finds themselves on the receiving end. Because no central authority exists, there is no one to give a final verdict on what is and is not acceptable. IAPs and on-line services have the last-resort option of 'pulling someone's account' – denying them a service, with prejudice. But individuals and groups also take the law into their own hands at times. Fortunately, random attacks are rare, happening mainly to celebrities, and mistakes and flame wars on Usenet do not usually lead to more than a heated exchange.

Survival tips

A number of other on-line survival tactics can prevent unpleasant experiences. All of these are very straightforward but can help avoid some of more common and petty annoyances of on-line life.

Staying out of trouble

All IAPs and on-line services have a document called an Acceptable Use Policy (AUP) or Conditions of Service (COS), which lists in detail what is and is not acceptable on the service. The content of these documents is not particularly controversial – they consist mostly of common-sense requests not to waste Internet resources or harass other users. Typical points in an AUP are:

- do not attempt to send spam or junk mail, especially for profit
- do not attempt to hack into the IAP's computer systems
- do not attempt to forge email or otherwise misrepresent yourself
- do not attempt to annoy other users in any way.

IAPs differ in the severity with which they treat transgressions. Some will – remarkably – turn a blind eye, even if they have had complaints from other users. Others will terminate their agreement with a user as soon as trouble is reported. It should go without saying that it is best to respect the guidelines in these documents.

Dealing with junk mail on Usenet

Junk mail is unwanted and unsolicited email that advertises a product or service. It can be a serious problem for anyone who posts regularly to Usenet or subscribes to on-line services. It is sent by companies who use the Internet's search facilities to find the email addresses of their intended victims. Once the companies have a list, they simply mail the same message to everyone on it. This can be a good way for them to generate new business. Even if only a tiny proportion of people reply they will still get more leads for less effort than with almost any other advertising technique. Unfortunately for most of the Internet population junk mail is simply a nuisance.

It is possible to avoid it. On Usenet, many people now post using a false address, for example, by adding an extra word such as 'nojunkmail', together with a message in their sig that explains that this word should be removed. This is very quick and easy – the false address is set in the newsreading software the usual way. For example, instead of *sara@sara.demon.co.uk* the address would be *sara@nojunkmail.sara.demon.co.uk* It does not matter which extra words or letters are added. The object of the exercise is to deliberately create a bad address, so that mail sent to it is not delivered to your mailbox. However, it can be helpful to use a word that makes it clear that the address has been modified in some way so that legitimate readers will be reminded to remove it before they attempt to send you email.

With this technique, the unwanted mail will usually be sent straight back to the sender. If enough people did this, junk mailers would be deluged with a flood of returned mail. Unfortunately, some are clever enough to use false addresses of their own. Instead of coming back to plague them, the returned mail disappears into a black hole on the Internet, having wasted the resources of various computers along the way.

An alternative solution is to use a 'mail kill' facility. This is the email equivalent of a killfile (see page 92), but is available only with mail services that use the POP3 system, explained in Chapter 7. Mail kill gives you the chance to see who has sent you mail before you copy it to your computer. Unwanted mail can be deleted before you waste your time and money copying it and reading it.

Mail kill is not as effective an option as not getting the mail in the first place, which is why it is suggested that anyone who uses Usenet frequently should opt for using a false address. The problem with this approach is that some people find it annoying, because they have to change the address by hand when they want to reply to you.

Another way of dealing with junk mail is to include a piece of legalese in your sig which says something like: 'Unsolicited mail is not welcome. All such mail will be charged a proof-reading fee of £500. The sending of such email constitutes agreement with the terms of this contract'. Some people even go so far as to cite a section of the US legal code to justify their claim. The main problem with this approach is that it does nothing at all to stop the mail. Junk mailers do not bother looking through sigs – they simply collect email addresses automatically, and the software they use ignores the rest of each posting. The other problem is that the legal background to such a claim has yet to be tested in court. If someone takes a junk mailer to court and wins because of non-payment, the whole junk mailing system will collapse very quickly. Unfortunately, this has not happened yet.

One final way of dealing with junk mail or spam is to 'mail bomb' the offender. This means sending them one or more huge and inconvenient messages. Although this may be tempting, it can also be counterproductive. You may incite the person at the other end to return the favour, and even if they do not, you will still be making work for a system administrator, who will have to clear up the mess.

Junk mail on on-line services

Users of on-line services do not have the option of changing their address. In any case, when preparing for a mailing, junk mailers compile on-line users' mail addresses in a slightly different way. Instead of searching through postings in the archives, they create their lists by checking to see who is on-line at any one time, and – where available – by checking user profiles (described on page 123) for keywords. This can mean that the more you use the service, the more likely you are to get junk mail.

On-line services take junk mail seriously and make some attempt to block it at source. This means that their subscribers never see the mail – much of it is deleted *en masse* by the administrators of the service, who use software that checks for multiple postings. Unfortunately, some mail still gets through. However, the software offered by these services enables you to check mail before it is copied to your computer. It is relatively easy to delete junk mail before it wastes any of your time.

Complaining about junk mail and spam

If junk mail and spam are sufficiently annoying, you can send an email complaint to the IAP that seems to be the source of the trouble. Some IAPs are genuinely unaware that certain customers are abusing their service and are only too happy to be told so that they can terminate the offender's access to the Internet with extreme prejudice. But other junk mailers have direct Internet connections that do not go through an IAP. Any email complaints will go straight to them in person, and they will, of course, ignore them.

To complain, you need to find out which IAP, if any, the offender is using. Sometimes this is obvious – you will be able to tell from his or her return address. Sometimes it is less obvious, especially if an attempt has been made to disguise the name of the IAP used. All countries have a few dozen IAPs which get most of the Internet business between them, and once you start to recognise these you will have a good idea of where to send the complaint.

The complaint itself should be addressed to an administrator at the IAP. The most widely used addresses are *postmaster@(iap's domain name)* and *abuse@(iap's domain name)* To complain, make a copy of the offending message, including all the headers, and add a short note that explains why you think the message is out of line – whether it is spam, junk mail, and so on. A stronger message is not usually required. Although this appears to be a slightly hit-and-miss method, it can work very well. You will often get a message back explaining that the offender has had their access to the Internet revoked. (For more detailed information about headers, and how to find someone's email address from them if they try to disguise it, see Appendix 5.)

CHAPTER **7**

INTERNET SECRETS: A TECHNOLOGICAL SURVIVAL GUIDE

TECHNOLOGY is unavoidable on the Internet. Although it is possible to get by with only a minimal interest in how the Internet works and what it can do, it is helpful to know about the ways in which technology can be used to make life on-line more interesting and productive. At the very least it is useful to know something about the technology in order to 'beat the system', if only to get the least frustration from its quirks and deficiencies.

The Internet is evolving continuously, and some of the facilities discussed below are no longer at the cutting edge. Others are used only by more experienced Internet users. However, all are included here for reference purposes and for the sake of completeness.

Counting the cost – how to make the best of your connection

An Internet connection is rather like a water pipe. The better the connection is and the wider the pipe, the more information that can flow through it. However, all pipes have a limit and once this is reached a backlog forms, and information trying to get through the pipe has to wait. On the Internet, the amount of 'pipe space' that information takes up is known as the bandwidth. Text needs a small bandwidth, still images and sounds need slightly more, and live video needs the most – enough to be impractical for a typical home connection.

Bandwidth is a limited resource. The most central parts of the Internet – which are known as the 'backbone' and connect countries to each other – use extremely fast connections and have plenty of spare bandwidth. However, traffic becomes congested at the slightly slower connections between the backbone and each IAP, and more so again over the much slower links between IAPs and their customers. On-line services tend to have much faster links to the Internet, and faster links within their own systems. However, they also have far more users to contend with simultaneously, and all suffer from obvious speed problems at peak times.

Wasting bandwidth on the Internet is a 'crime', and – as mentioned in the Chapter 6 – flagrant misuse can attract unwelcome attention from other users. The source of the problem is that traffic on the Internet has been increasing exponentially since the mid-1990s. Before the Internet became available to the general public, research scientists were able to transfer large amounts of information across it relatively quickly. This is no longer possible, even though the technology has improved and there is more bandwidth. It can now take days to copy information that used to take a few hours.

The Internet has its own 'rush hours', and if you want to minimise your telephone charges it is useful to know how to avoid them. Most traffic on the Internet comes from the USA, and once the people living on the East Coast start to wake up – at about lunch-time in the UK – it takes noticeably longer to view certain US web sites. By the time those living on the West Coast are awake as well, three hours later, the whole network has slowed down significantly. The situation is made even worse once everyone in the USA leaves work and goes home to check their email, play on IRC and read their favourite newsgroups. By about midnight in the UK it is almost impossible to access some web sites at all. This USA evening rush hour corresponds to peak traffic in the UK, which happens between about 11pm – after the pubs shut – and midnight.

During these peak periods, Internet access can be four or five times slower than during less busy times. Although this applies to web sites in particular, the same can be said, albeit to a lesser extent, about email and newsgroups. Some IAPs have developed a system whereby newsgroup messages are queued during the peak times, and then processed later in the night, when far fewer people are using the service. Similar delays may also apply to email sent during these busy periods, although IAPs tend to make email a priority in an attempt to make sure it gets through quickly.

The Internet is also very busy at weekends. Although corporate traffic is less heavy, there is much more personal information being sent in the form of email and 'after hours' newsgroup contributions. The peak tends to last slightly further into the night than during the week – people stay on-line longer because they do not need to get up early the next morning.

The best way to avoid the rush is to use the Internet during the early hours of the morning, typically between 3 and 5am, although this is clearly unacceptable for the majority of people. To avoid this problem, many home computer systems, if left switched on, can be set up to send and receive waiting email and newsgroup messages during this period. Windows 95, for example, has a 'scheduler' program which can be set up to start email and newsgroup software at a certain time.

The next best option is to do whatever you can to limit the amount of time you use the Internet during the peak periods. For example, email and newsgroup messages will arrive in your computer much more quickly first thing in the morning than last thing in the evening. Even though the telephone charges are higher in the morning, you may find yourself needing to spend less time on-line to get the same information, so that it becomes cheaper overall. Of course, the length of time depends very much on the volume of information involved. It can be useful to time a typical call at both times of day to see which works out cheapest.

Beware of bank holiday telephone rates; depending on which telephone service you use, the costs may be charged at the weekday rate rather than the cheaper weekend rate.

Speeding up email

Although you cannot do anything to make email reach its destination any faster – apart from switching to a different IAP, perhaps one recommended by a friend, if mail seems to be taking far too long – you can improve the speed at which email is transferred to and from your IAP. The speed limit is set by the speed of your connection, and this depends on the hardware used by your computer and your IAP (see Appendix 2). Even with this limit, there are still a number of things you can do to make the most of the speed available.

The first and most important step is to make sure that your email software works off-line (see page 41); this will make a large difference to your monthly bill, and will also provide you with a more relaxed environment in which to read and write messages.

Text messages are very fast to post, and unless you send hundreds at each sitting, the amount of text you send will not make a big difference to your bill. This is not true of attachments. The secret here is to 'compress' attachments before sending them. A common solution is to use software such as PKZIP to squeeze the information down to the smallest possible size. Doing this can reduce some information to an eighth of its original size.

Before you compress an image you should save it in the least bulky format possible. This is done using an image editor which converts it from one image format another. (Image formats are different ways in which the same picture can be stored in a computer.) Some formats take up much less space than others. For more details of these formats and the best one to choose when sending pictures across the Internet, consult the help documentation supplied with your image editor – and do not forget that good image editors are available on the Internet.

Speeding up newsgroups

Although killfiles (see pages 92–3) are indispensable, they can also slow down the speed at which information from Usenet is copied to your computer. A killfile needs to check each and every article against its 'kill' criteria, and this can take a noticeable and sometimes even an objectionable amount of time. Make a point of checking your killfile settings frequently to see if any can be removed: some spammers change their email addresses regularly to avoid killfiles, and old killfile settings created to get rid of them will no longer apply. Some killfile software has an 'expire' option for each setting, which will automatically has the search for a certain person or subject after a set time. It is worth getting into the habit of using this feature whenever you know that the setting will be temporary.

Another problem with newsgroups is that your list of groups can proliferate. Every month or two, look through the list to see if the groups in it really are indispensable. You may find that you are no longer interested in some of them. If you find yourself spending an hour a day reading and replying to news, you may want to consider whether all the newsgroups are really worthy of your attention.

Lastly, it is tempting to read every single message that appears in case you miss something important by not doing so. However, if you miss a week's worth of messages, you will find that in most groups you can pick up where you left off. If something really is essential you can read about it in the various archive services. These last two points also apply to mailing lists (see page 49).

Speeding up the Web

The key ways to speed up the rate at which web pages appear are: to choose your times carefully, as described above; and to use a variety of tricks and software extras to manage web information.

Images take much longer to appear than text, so one very useful technique is to select 'text only' versions of web pages wherever these are available. Unfortunately not all sites offer these, but for those that do it is well worth ignoring images and graphics – especially of the decorative kind – when you are trying to keep your costs down.

All browsers include a 'new window' option which you can call on while waiting for a slow site. This opens another window that can be used to look at a completely different site at the same time. In fact, you can have three or more windows open simultaneously. However, this may start to slow your computer down unless you have plenty of memory installed. Many pages contain more than one link, and by following two or more links in parallel you can save yourself minutes, or even hours.

Another useful feature of web browser software is the 'cache' facility. This keeps copies of web pages in your computer's own filing space. When you backtrack, pages are read from this local copy instantly. This saves you from having to wait for them to appear over the Internet again. However, the size of the cache is finite, and the oldest information is always removed to make way for the newest arrivals from the Web; this happens automatically.

To get the best from the cache you should set it to the maximum possible size. This can be demanding of filing space and memory, so make sure you have plenty free. Another advantage of the cache system becomes clear once you start creating your own web pages (see Appendix 4). The cache contains the words, images and page layouts used to create every site you have visited recently. Copyright permitting, you can use all of these in your own designs.

'Off-line' browsers are an extension of the cache idea. As well as caching information, these browsers index it automatically and create internal links so that you can view pages as if you were still on-line. You will need a lot of free filing space to get the best from an off-line browser, as web pages can take up a lot of room. Examples of this software are available for free on the Internet, although you can also buy commercial versions.

Speeding up access to on-line services

There is very little you can do to speed up access to these services. You are locked into a proprietary system which gives you minimal opportunity to change anything. Connection speeds vary significantly from service to service, so by trying out different ones it may be possible to find a cheaper service whose connection is faster. This is one reason why free trials of the on-line services (as discussed in Chapter 2) can be so useful.

'Secret services'

Apart from the most popular Internet services (email, the Web, newsgroups and IRC), there are a number of others which, although less widely available, are nevertheless useful. They all require special software, which is often available for free, or perhaps as shareware (see page 245), from any of the many software archives on the Internet.

Finger

Finger is a more direct version of the email autoresponders discussed in Chapter 3. Instead of sending a request for information by email, finger lets you ask a computer for information directly. For example, if you are using a large computer system, such as one at a university, and know someone's email address you can 'finger' that address; in return you will receive some information about him or her. This typically includes the time and date the person last used the computer, and whether or not he or she has any email waiting. Finger may also retrieve a special collection of information called a 'plan', if one is available. In spite of the name this has nothing to do with planning. It is like a sig but does not have any length restrictions. Internet users create plans to tell other users about themselves or to include humorous quotes and other information.

Some IAPs use the finger facility to provide details about the status of their services. Users can finger a specific address to receive an up-to-date maintenance and status report. Another common use is to provide a list of people who are using a large computer system.

Finger is only sporadically useful. Although you can perform finger requests from any computer, many computers on the Net are not set up to offer finger information when asked for it. Often this is done deliberately for security reasons; a curt 'access denied' message will be given.

Telnet

Telnet is used to connect your keyboard and screen to another computer – in effect, you can use another computer from a distance. When you type something on your keyboard, the information is passed to the other computer, which then responds as if you were typing into it directly. Similarly, information from the other computer appears on your screen as if you were connected to it directly.

Telnet is used to play computer games in which many players can take part at the same time, and is also sometimes required for IRC. As with finger, the service has two components: software on the destination computer that accepts remote connections from other computers and gives them access to its facilities; and software on your computer that allows you to connect to them remotely. Although it is possible to install the first kind of software on a home computer, it is more often found on large computers which are designed to have many users, such as the computer systems owned by universities and large companies. The second component can also be installed on any computer.

Ping

Ping is an 'are you there?' message which is sent over the Internet to check the speed and reliability of a connection. Ping sends five messages, which are known as packets, and measures how long they take to return. If the round trip takes a long time, or if any packets go missing, you know that the connection to a particular computer is too slow to be useable. Ping also enables you to see if a distant computer is working, and to check on the speed at which information will flow between your computer and the other one.

Traceroute

Traceroute is an extended version of ping which lists all the steps the Internet takes to make a connection between your computer and another. These appear as a list of computer names, together with 'ping' timing information for each one. You can use traceroute to make an educated guess about the geographical location of an unfamiliar email address. It can also show up problems. To give an extreme example, if you check a computer in the USA and the route shown goes via South Africa, then the Internet is obviously in difficulty, and traffic will be very slow.

Whois

This is a more sophisticated version of finger. Instead of fingering an individual's information, you can check the state of a sub-network. Whois can list all the administrative contacts at an IAP, which can be useful when you are planning to complain about junk mail or spamming.

DNS lookup

DNS lookup converts Internet addresses made up of words into the numbers which the Internet itself uses. All computers on the Internet – including those that are not for public access – have a four-digit address (separated by dots) made up of numbers between 0 and 255. The word equivalent exists to make life easier for humans. As a tool it is really of interest only to system administrators, and has only been included here for completeness.

Time

This sets your computer's local time to your IAP's clock. Many IAPs use clock signals transmitted by one of two atomic clocks: one in Rugby in the Midlands, or one in Germany. Your computer's internal clock will then always be accurate to the nearest second.

On-line 'secret services'

Similar 'secret services' are also available on the on-line services. For example, AOL offers 'Profiles', which are a much-improved version of the finger/plan idea, and 'Buddy lists' which let you create a list of favourite people and show you when they are on-line. There is also a 'locate' facility which shows you the name of the chat room someone is using, so that you can join them there immediately. All of these features are built into the AOL software.

Profiles are like index cards that users fill in, listing their name, location, date of birth, interests, and so on. Some people have turned their profiles into an art form by ignoring the suggested categories and filling the space with poetry or other unusual or surprising information. It is not unheard of for people to lie in their profiles, creating a completely different persona from the one they have in real life.

Buddy lists are a very useful adjunct for anyone who likes to chat or send instant messages to people on-line. You can add and remove people from your list at any time, create sub-lists for different situations or times of day (for example, at work during office hours) and also block other people's buddy lists so that you do not appear in them. The locate option simply shows a chat room name and is included as a sub-option within the buddy list feature.

More about email

The Internet has two types of email system: SMTP (Simple Mail Transfer Protocol) is an old-fashioned and rather crude system which is still used by some IAPs; POP3 (Post Office Protocol 3) is a more modern system which offers a number of advantages over SMTP.

Using SMTP is very simple. When you check for mail, your IAP's mail computer copies it to your computer immediately. SMTP works by checking if you are the owner of the mail. It will then copy the messages that match up with your username/address. There are no facilities for managing mail more comprehensively, although some IAPs include a feature which lets you check if mail is waiting.

POP3 is more complex and has two major advantages:

- You can **read and reply to email that arrives in your mail box using any computer with an Internet connection** – so if you are on holiday abroad and find a cybercafé you can check to see if there are any messages waiting for you. Instead of checking who you are electronically, POP3 asks for a password, and as long as you know the password and the Internet name of your IAP's mail computer (which they will be happy to tell you before you leave) you have the 'key' to your mailbox.

- If you have suitable software you can **delete messages that you do not want to read before they are copied to your computer** – this is useful for dealing with junk mail or other kinds of unwanted email attention, such as mail-bomb attacks.

New mail systems are being developed that will expand on these facilities and make it even easier to manage a mailbox, but these are unlikely to become standardised until after the beginning of the twenty-first century. Plans are even being drawn up for communications systems that use satellite technology to follow you wherever you go by tracking your portable computer or mobile phone.

More about MIME

MIME is best avoided for text messages. One example of a MIME problem is the way that it handles letters that are specific to certain countries. Keyboards are arranged differently throughout the world, and various countries use variations on English roman lettering by adding accents and other extras such as cedillas. Although it is possible to send these variations in a MIME message, attempting to do so may cause more problems than it solves.

Other 'odd' characters, such as the '£' pound sign, also cause problems. MIME treats them in a strange way: it replaces them with a code that starts with an '=' sign and is followed by a two-digit identifier. This can ruin sigs that use these special characters and is also an annoyance on mailing lists, where messages arrive broken up by countless '=' signs which appear at the end of each line because they are inserted in place of the invisible 'carriage return' characters at the ends of lines.

If you need to include a special character in a MIME message, use a work-around (such as 'ukp' instead of the '£' sign) or write it out in words if you possibly can. Most software will warn you against using special characters if you try to do so when sending the message. If a warning appears while you are typing an email, rewrite it, avoiding the troublesome characters.

DIY binaries and attachments

You will not usually need to decode binaries by hand. However, for those situations in which your software does not have the facilities to do the job automatically, it is useful to know what steps to follow. Binaries are sent using one of three systems, each creating a different kind of message. If you know what to look for you can identify very easily which system has been used, and will then know how to decode them.

Uuencoding

The most popular format is 'Uuencoding' (uue), or sometimes 'Uucoding'. The two 'U's are short for 'Unix to Unix'. This is one of the oldest systems in use, but also one of the most reliable. It is widely used for sending binaries on Usenet – in fact someone who tries to use a different system may well be flamed (see page 105). Uuencoded binaries look like the one below.

```
section 1 of uuencode 4.21 of file RW2.JPG by R.E.M.

begin 644 RW2.JPG
M_]C_X``02D9)1@`0$`8`!``$`0$`2`!(``#_X``P2D9)1@`0`$`0$`P0$`P$`
M`0$`0$`Q0$`Q$`1Q$`Q$`Q`(("`@(("@@(#`@("@@(#`@(("@@(#`@(("@+`
MP```"@@(`"@@("@@(#`@(""@@("@@("@@(#`@("@@+`"@@("@@+`"@@("@`@+_
M``````````````````````````````````````````"`````````````````
MP``````````````````````````````````````````````````````````
M``````````````````````````````````````````````````````````
M```````````````````````````````````````````````````````````
38W.#AH:&AH:(B(F)B8J*`````````````````````
M5UA96EA896%F8V1l:2E:bXGaWtyc1d4e3t7f3J+eZ5nmqCgoaKjpKWmp6ipqq
M1K;Klcm5yd3t/g4eLj5OXm5+jp6vLz9PX29/j5+v/aAAwDAQACEQMRAD8A
76U]C9VN'BX^3EYN?HZ>><KQ\O/T]?;3;W
etc.
```

A typical example may be anywhere between a few hundred and a few thousand lines long. The lines at the top define the section/part number of a multi-part file, then the version of the software, and then the name of the file that has been encoded (RW2.JPG). The 'Begin' statement tells the decoding software where to start.

To restore the original information you need to copy the different sections together into a single file, then put the result through uudecoding software. Copying sections together by hand can be a chore, but it is sometimes the only way to retrieve the information. This can be done using any standard word processor, although remember to make sure the results are saved as 'plain text', or 'text only' with no page-layout information (i.e. bold, italics, indentations etc.). Anything other than plain text will confuse the decoding software.

BinHex

'BinHex' is popular with users of the Apple Macintosh. It is not as robust as Uucoding because it does not have any built-in checks for garbled transmission, and this makes it more prone to errors. If you send a photograph using BinHex, it may end up looking disjointed in places. In addition, BinHex may not work properly if you use the wrong version of the BinHex software – the version you should use is listed at the start of the information. Below is an example of a the first part of a BinHex file.

```
(This file must be converted with BinHex 4.0)

:#$!`-$)ZDR"R!%T348Fi3NP0"3!!!+lr!!!L4B-MrpMri!!35NC*4J!"!J%!5!"
)!!$rl3'i8'K[G'pcD'p`)$-Z-!!i3NP0!qN!!!!!!(J!!`!!!%J!5!!!!!!#fJ)
Srq(ri3,j!N8$4`8S!r`!!J!!!%J!5!!!!!!#f!)S!!%!!!"N!!!!3!$!`-!!!!
"*`m!!3!"!!!!!!!!!!!!!!!!D!J!'3'3!!!!!!!!!!!!!!!!!!!!!!!!!!!!!!!
!!!!!!!!!!!!!1%**632Y!!!!!!3!%J!!!!"!!%!5!!!!!%!!6K#!58d$m`!!!!!
!#!!!!!!!!!!!!1%**65F3!!!!!!!+!!%!!!!!!!!!!MK#!58d$p3!!!!!!5!![CQB
!!3"XCQB!"J!!!!!!3![CQB!!3#KQCS!"J!!!!!!3!b!!!!!3"D!!!!"J!!!!!
!!3!e!!!!!3!Y!!!!"J!!!!!!!6K#!58d$q!!!!!!!F!!!rrrrrrrrrrrrrrrrrr
rrrrrrrrr`2S!!!!!2rrrrrrrrrrrrrrrrrrrrrrrrrrm$k!!!!!$rrrrrrrr
etc
```

The line at the top identifies this as a BinHex file and tells you which version of the software (here 4.0) you need to use to be able to decode the file successfully.

Base64

Base64 is not a favourite with the Usenet community. As a general rule, do not use Base64 unless you know that the person, or people, to whom you are sending the information are going to be able to decode it. If you are using MIME, this decision is made for you automatically because MIME tends to use Base64 as a matter of course. For other uses, especially posting to Usenet, Uucoding is much more popular and is also more likely to work successfully. Below is part of a Base64 transmission; the identifying line at the top is present in any Base64 file.

```
Content-Transfer-Encoding: base64
```

```
/9j/4AAQSkZJRgABAQEASABIAAD/7QGhQWRvYmVfUGhvdG9zaG9wMi41OgBIA
```

```
AAASAAAOEJJTQPpAAAAAAB4AAwAAABIAEgAAAAAAyoCQP/x//cDOQJJKgIFeA
PeAQAAAAEsASwAAAAADS8JYAABAAAAZAAAAQEAAQAAAAAAScPAAEAAAAAAAA
AAAAAAAAAAAAAAAAAAAAAAAAP/C/9oNbQmGAAgBAAAAAAAAAAAAAAAAAAAA
OEJJTQPtAAAAAAAQAEgAAAABAAEASAAAAAEAAThCSU0D8wAAAAAABwAAAAAAA
AAAOEJJTQP1AAAAAABIAC9mZgABAGxmZgAGAAAAAAAAAC9mZgABAKGZmgAGAA
AAAAAAADIAAAABAFoAAAAGAAAAAAAADUAAAABAC0AAAAGAAAAAAAAOEJJTQP
4AAAAABwAAD//////////////////////////A+gAAAAA
```
etc.

Although all of these methods may be hidden away by newsgroup and email software, it is possible to find and use software that works with them directly. Such programs are usually awkward to use and old-fashioned; for example on a PC only a DOS, not Windows, version of the relevant software may exist. However, anyone who uses the Internet a great deal and needs to be able to use binaries reliably will find that having this software to hand can save a lot of time and trouble and can rescue information that might otherwise be irretrievable. (For more information on binaries see Chapter 5.)

Getting more from the Web

Although the Internet can deal with any kind of information that can be stored in a computer, individual computers and the software they use may not be quite so versatile. This can usually be remedied with the appropriate software. For example, all the popular web browsers can handle most common kinds of information found on a web site: specifically text and certain kinds of images. But although other information, such as sound clips, can be copied to your computer, a browser may not be able to do anything useful with it.

To solve this problem, web browsers can be extended with software 'plug-ins'. These are small programs – usually free, and almost always available for copying from the Internet – which 'plug in' to the browser and enable it to work with more specialised kinds of information. Hundreds of plug-ins are available, although many use proprietary systems which work only on certain computers or with certain other software. The most popular plug-ins are discussed below.

Real Audio

Often shortened to RA, Real Audio is a 'live' audio broadcast system for the Internet; it is very much like radio, except that the sound is passed over the Internet directly to your computer. The speed of the link between your computer and the Internet determines the sound quality; a slow connection will produce the quality you might expect from a cheap transistor radio. A typical connection will give the same quality in stereo or much better quality in mono. Faster links give progressively better results. If the link is very slow, or if a lot of Internet traffic is using the link at the same time, the sound comes through in gaps and spurts.

Real Audio 'compresses' sound information when it is sent so that it makes as little demand as possible on the Internet's facilities. Your computer then has to reverse this process before you can listen to the sound, and this demands a great deal of computer power. In addition to facilities for sound playback inside your computer, and of course speakers or headphones, you will also need a fairly fast machine to listen to RA successfully. Any computer built before about 1996 will be too slow to reverse the compression without leaving noticeable gaps.

Real Audio has a sibling plug-in called Real Video. While RA is very widely used, live video on the Internet is still in its infancy, and it is too early to know which of the many competing systems will become the most popular. In any case, a standard telephone connection is too slow to show video adequately at present. For the moment there is no point in having a video plug-in unless you have a fast, permanent link to the Internet.

Shockwave and Immedia

Shockwave (made by Macromedia) and Immedia (made by Quark) are both software packages that attempt to expand the facilities that web pages offer. These plug-ins enable you to look at ornately designed pages, with complex animations, sounds and other special effects. (Shockwave and Immedia are also used to create these pages.)

VRML

VRML – Virtual Reality Markup Language – may prove to be the core technology used to create web pages in the future. Instead of a flat image with simple text and graphics on it, which is created using HTML (the current system), VRML creates a three-dimensional environment, in which objects can be animated, and enlarged so that they can be examined in detail. At the moment, a VRML plug-in on a personal computer needs too much computer power to be anything more than a curiosity, but as computer speed and power increase this may change. For now, very few pages offer VRML information, although the system offers an interesting taste of what the future may hold.

Other types of plug-in

- Microsoft's Video for Windows and Apple's Quicktime plug-ins play video clips in one or more of the common personal computer formats.
- MIDI plug-ins can play MIDI files (the computer world's equivalent of the barrel organ).

These two types are not as standardised as RA, Shockwave and Immedia, and VRML, and when you look for suitable plug-ins on-line there will almost certainly be more than one that you can use.

Adding plug-ins to your browser

Plug-ins are usually free, although you may be asked to fill in a registration form which asks you for your email address, and perhaps other personal details. (Information about where to find plug-ins is included in Appendix 6.)

To add a plug-in to your browser follow these steps:

- **Copy the software to your computer** This is usually straightforward. If your browser needs a plug-in to show the information on a certain page, you will usually be asked if you want to 'get the plug-in'; you will then be taken to the page with the plug-ins listed on it automatically. Generally, the only difficult part of the process is deciding which version of the plug-in to use. Sometimes different versions are available for different computer systems and different locations. (Some plug-ins are language-specific.)

- **Start up the software** This will usually start an installation process, which works in exactly the same way as any other software installation. When the installation is completed your browser will be ready to use the new plug-in, which is then available whenever you use your browser in the future.
- **Restart your web browser** The plug-in will then be ready to use.

Using File Transfer Protocol (FTP)

To use FTP you can either rely on your web browser or you can use proper FTP software. Although the former option is much more straightforward, it is not guaranteed to work properly in every situation – browsers sometimes make mistakes which prevent an FTP connection from working properly. True FTP software is intended for more experienced users of FTP, who are not frightened of dealing with a slightly more technical version of the system and who need the extra flexibility that proper software offers.

Using FTP with a browser

It is possible to use FTP with a browser without even being aware of it. This is because FTP is often disguised as 'downloading' – copying information from the Internet to your computer. Whenever a web site has the words 'Download now!' with a link, the link will usually lead to an FTP facility. To copy the information, you simply click on the appropriate link, and then tell your computer where to put the information on your hard disk. (It is sensible to create a separate folder, or directory, on your hard disk to put these downloads in, so that you always know where they are. Otherwise, they can get lost after the download.) The FTP process then starts automatically. The popular Netscape Navigator browser shows that the download is working properly by displaying a cryptic message that says

'Saving location', together with a bar graph which shows how much of the information has been copied.

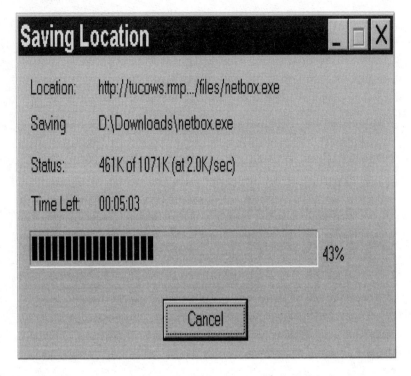

Downloads can take varying amounts of time, from a minute or two to a number of hours, depending on the quantity of information being copied and the speed of the connection between your computer and the Internet. Most browsers show a progress indicator which estimates how much time is left before the process is complete. It also shows the speed at which the information is being transferred. You can use this information to decide whether or not to continue with the transfer – if the process is taking too long you might decide to try at a different time, when the Net is less busy.

The larger and more popular FTP sites have 'mirrors' – copies of the same site on computers in different locations. In theory it is always quicker to access the pages on the computer that is geographically nearest to you. For example, if there is a mirror site in Europe as well as in the USA, it should be quicker to get the information from the computer in Europe (if you live in the UK). In practice, however, this is not always the case. Internet connections to Europe from the UK can be noticeably slower than those to the USA. Sometimes connections within the UK itself can also be slower than those to the USA.

Where mirror sites are available, they are always listed clearly. To get the best possible connection it is often worth experimenting to see which mirror offers the fastest transfer speed. To do this start a download, wait a minute or two for the speed to stabilise, and then check to see whether it is faster or slower than the download from another computer. This is not so important with small chunks of information that can be copied relatively quickly, but with much larger amounts, which can take hours or more to copy, it can save you a lot of time.

The speed of the link is shown as a number of 'K' on the progress indicator and is short for 'thousands of characters per second'. Any speed less than 0.5K is abysmally slow. Rates between 0.5K and 1.0K are barely acceptable – but in some cases are the best possible at the time, in which case it might be worth making another attempt later. Rates between 1.0K and 2.0K are average, and any speed that is faster is good.

Sometimes so many people are trying to use a particular FTP site at the same time that access is denied completely; instead a message appears asking you to try later. Unless you need the information immediately, you should try again during the early hours of the following morning, when the Internet is likely to be less busy.

Once the software has been copied to your computer, you can use it as you would any other. Software obtained from an FTP site is exactly the same as that on a floppy disk, except that you will not generally get a printed manual to refer to. However, if a web site offers a 'shrink wrap' version of the software, it means you are buying a box full of disks and a manual that will be sent to you using the letter post. You can usually download the software anyway – although of course the box will arrive much later.

Using FTP software

If you want to use FTP software, you will need to know slightly more about how computers work and how to find information on them; in particular, you should know how to use directories and how to move up and down through a list of directories both on your own computer and the one at the FTP site.

It is also helpful if you know something about the different kinds of computer systems that are used on the Internet, such as UNIX, VMS, and so on. FTP works very slightly differently on each system, although most software includes an 'auto' option which works out what kind of system you are trying to link up to, and works accordingly.

If none of this sounds daunting, the rest should be straightforward. To start an FTP session you need to type in the location of the remote computer. This appears as a typical Internet address, with words separated by dots. These addresses are listed on web sites and in magazines. You may also need a username on the remote computer and a password. These will be necessary if access to the information you are trying to copy is restricted to certain people for security reasons. (To get a username and password you will need to email the administrator of the FTP computer you are trying to use. He or she has the right to decline your request. For information about 'anonymous' FTP, which uses a password and username but offers information with no restrictions, see Chapter 4.)

You can then attempt to make a connection between your computer and the remote one. The progress of the connection is usually shown in a tiny message window, although information appears here too quickly to read. The different stages the process goes through are indicated here as cryptic numbers and messages. Fortunately, you do not need to understand these to use the system successfully.

Once the connection has been made, most FTP software is designed to show two 'windows': the one on the left lists the contents of a directory in your computer, and the one on the right shows a directory on the remote computer. You can navigate through both these directories in the usual way. To copy a file from one location to the other you highlight the one you want then either click on the 'copy' button or drag the name of the file between the windows.

One final point to watch for is the difference between 'binary' transfers of information, and 'ASCII' transfers. The latter is used for text, the former for images, photographs, artwork, sound and video. All FTP software includes an option to set one of these transfer types. It is important to choose the right one, otherwise the transfer will produce gibberish. When it has finished, click on a button marked 'log out' or 'exit'; your connection to the remote computer will then be broken.

Although FTP is generally used to copy information from a remote computer to your machine, it can also work the other way. This is important if you decide to publish your own web pages (see Appendix 4). The final stage of the publishing process consists of copying your pages to a web server so that they are visible on the Web. FTP software is often used to do this, although if you are using high-quality web publishing software, the process will be hidden away in much the same way that a browser hides away FTP.

Archie and other Internet antiquities

A number of older systems exist to help find information that can then be copied using FTP. However, these are rapidly being made obsolete by the World Wide Web, which offers the same features but is more attractive and easier to use.

Archie

Archie is a keyword–based search facility for FTP sites. About 40 Archie computers throughout the world regularly check through 1,500 FTP sites to see which files are available. When you access the Archie system it works its way through this file list and shows the ones it thinks you may be interested in. The relatively small scope of the search makes it much more focused than a web search, which has millions of computers to look through. However, the Archie system is not as comprehensive, and of course it will not find files on any FTP computer that is not connected to it.

To use Archie you can either use special Archie software – a web search using a search engine should return a list of possible candidates – or you can telnet to an Archie site, such as the one at Imperial College in London at *archie.doc.ic.ac.uk*

Once connected, you simply supply a keyword and Archie will reply with a list of files and the FTP servers they are located on. You can then use FTP to copy these to your own machine. Some Archie software includes proper FTP facilities, which make the process even more straightforward. Archie searches can be slow, so expect to be on-line for a few minutes for each search.

You can spend your time more efficiently by performing an email Archie search. This has the advantage that you can start a search and then disconnect from the Internet. To do this you send your request to *archie@name-of-server-here* Leave the subject line blank. In the main text of the message you need to specify one of the Archie search methods:

• **set search sub** This search asks Archie to find any file with the keyword in the name, ignoring differences between upper and lower case. It will then return all files in which the keyword appears, even if it is not a whole word. For example a search for 'water' will return 'watermelon', 'Waterloo', 'water quality', 'waterfall' and so on.

- **set search subcase** This search will have the same preferences as 'set search sub' except that capital letters have to be matched exactly.
- **set search exact** If you search for 'water' using this method, only files with the whole word 'water' will be found.
- **set search regex**. This method uses a variety of special characters to narrow the search. For example '^' in front of water will return all files where 'water' is at the front of the name, but not in the middle or at the end.

You then type 'find' followed by a keyword to search for, and the word 'quit' at the end of the message. A complete search email might look like this:

```
To: archie@archie.internic.net
Subject: <blank>
Message body:
set search sub
find money
quit
```

After a while – usually more than ten minutes but less than a day – you will get an automatic response from the Archie computer with a list of matching files. Of course, this is not quite as interactive as doing the whole search on-line, but unless you are in a hurry it can be just as effective.

Gopher

Gopher is a precursor of the World Wide Web. It is a text-only system that classifies information into headings, sub-headings and so on, in much the same way that a search engine like Yahoo does (see pages 66–7). Gopher information is kept on special computers – called Gopher servers – which tend to be maintained by governments and universities. Because of this, Gopher information is generally of a more serious nature, such as academic research and government reports, and carries no advertising. Because Gopher is a text-only system, it can be much quicker to use than the Web.

There are three ways of accessing Gopher information:

- **with a web browser**: addresses start with 'gopher://' instead of 'http://'
- **through telnet** (see page 121) – *gopher.tc.umn.edu* is a good address to start from
- **with special Gopher software**, which is free and available from many archives on the Internet.

Once the information has been found, it can be copied using FTP.

Veronica is a keyword search system for the Gopher network. Most Gopher servers include this option, which works with web browsers as well as with the special Gopher software. When you type in a keyword Veronica responds with a list of Gopher 'addresses' which include that particular word.

WAIS (Wide Area Information Services) is an extended, more useful, version of Veronica that searches the text of a document instead of just the description. To keep a search simple it is also possible to look through information categories rather than for keywords. The WAIS network is limited to a handful of academic computer systems, making it of marginal use to anyone without an interest in academic subjects.

CHAPTER **8**

ELECTRONIC BANDITS AND SUPERHIGHWAYMEN

FAR FROM being a superhighway, the Internet is much more like a seventeenth-century mud track. Apart from being slow and inconvenient to use, it can also be dangerous. The perils are both financial and intellectual, and in extreme cases even moral, and Net users should know how to take suitable precautions.

Internet security is a complicated issue. It has two facets: keeping private information away from prying eyes; and avoiding on-line scams and other unwanted attention, such as mail-bomb attacks. The Internet was never designed to be a secure system and few safeguards against malice and trickery have been built in. However, there are a variety of steps anyone can take to improve security, and these are discussed in this chapter.

Hackers and crackers

Like any other human activity, the Internet has its own bandits, criminals and con-artists. 'Hackers' and 'crackers' are the words used to describe Internet users – usually teenage and male – who attempt to abuse the system. (The word 'hacker' was originally used to describe any unusually gifted computer programmer, but the public has now come to regard it as meaning the same as 'cracker' – an Internet criminal. 'True' hackers are understandably offended by this, but the terminology remains widely used.) Typical hacker exploits include:

- breaking into secure computer systems and stealing information

- reading email that is supposed to be private
- collecting credit-card information sent via email
- taking over a web site and vandalising its original information
- attacking an Internet computer so that it becomes overloaded and stops working properly.

A particular class of hacker, known as a phone phreaker, specialises in hacking the computers that operate the public telephone network. Hackers often become phreakers to feed their Internet habit without having to pay the bills. In fact, this class of hacker is less of a nuisance on the Internet itself than others. Apart from illegal access to free calls – at an estimated cost in the UK of £400 million between 1990 and 1996 – phreakers are also fond of listening in on private conversations and playing pranks. A favourite trick is to change a neighbour's settings at the local exchange so that it treats their phone system as a pay phone; it will then not let them use it unless they insert some change.

Keeping hackers out

The only way to create a completely secure computer system is to disconnect it from any networks and severely vet the people who use and supervise it. Some military systems maintain security this way, although even this supposedly fail-safe system is potentially open to bribery and blackmail.

Disconnection is not an option for Internet users, and so a much simpler and more convenient security device is used instead – the password. Unlike more sophisticated systems – such as those that rely on physical keys, such as magnetic cards – passwords do not require extra hardware and are easy to use. But it is important to be aware of their security limitations. A password becomes useless if someone can guess it or work out what it is by trial and error. So it is essential to choose passwords carefully, especially if sensitive information is at risk.

Some IAPs, such as Pipex and Which? Online, supply a computer-generated password, saving you the trouble of creating one. However, most IAPs leave the choice of password to you. The best passwords are easy to remember but impossible to guess, either through psychology or with mechanical aid, such as the war dialler described below. It is not advisable to use names of children, spouses or pets, addresses, phone numbers, maiden names or words related to favourite hobbies. A hacker who is familiar with a person will try all of these first, as well as other words that they know their victim is likely to have chosen.

Picking a word at random is safer, but even this approach has its drawbacks. In the USA in particular, where local calls are either free or cost a negligible fixed amount, it is easy to create a piece of software called a 'war dialler' – an automated password-cracking program. A war dialler will work its way through an entire dictionary of potential passwords in a matter of hours, trying each word in it (which will typically be the list of words in a word processor's spell checker) until the password is found. Home users are unlikely to be targeted like this without good reason, but business users who have a permanent connection to the Internet should choose a password that offers a higher level of security.

Random letter and number combinations are reasonably secure, providing they have not been devised with the help of the standard password-creation software which is widely available on the Internet. Dedicated hackers will have copies of this software and will again combine it with a war dialler if they are determined to get in. The search process is more time-consuming than a straight dictionary-based attack, but hackers can be very patient people. Some are happy to spend weeks or even months trying to hack a computer if they think the information it contains is worth it.

Perhaps the best passwords are those made from a random combination of words from a dictionary and numbers – for example, a password such as 12ARTICHOKE59COTTON would be very hard to crack, even with a war dialler. For maximum effectiveness the number of digits should vary randomly. Of course, the longer a password is, the harder it is to crack. Combined passwords also have the advantage of being easier to remember than completely random strings of numbers and digits.

Password solicitations

Having gone to considerable trouble to choose a secure password, you should, of course, make sure that no one knows what it is. This advice is obvious, but one form of hacker attack – the password solicitation – causes regular grief for the unwary. To solicit a password, a hacker simply asks for it, perhaps by pretending to be someone from the police or from higher up an organisation's hierarchy. Some of the most successful hackers have been able to attack supposedly secure computers by calling someone inside the building and asking for a password.

For business users, the way to avoid this is to make sure that everyone who knows the password also knows who is and is not to be trusted with it. In addition, they must understand that it should be revealed only under very clearly defined circumstances. In a busy office, passwords should never be written down, except in secure areas which are open only to authorised staff. It may be tempting to keep a sticky note of the password under the desk – or worse still, on the monitor – but this is not recommended if security is important.

Password solicitations are a particular problem for users of on-line services. One favourite hacker technique is to access a chat room and send messages to newcomers which suggest that something has gone wrong, and that the user needs to re-confirm his or her password and credit-card details. This kind of message always ends with the threat that if the user does not do this, he or she will not be able to use the service any more. Anyone who falls for this trick can expect to receive a crippling credit-card bill at the end of the month because the hacker will use the password at every possible opportunity. Below is a typical example, copied from an AOL chat room:

```
AOLService: Sector 4G9C of our data base has lost all I/O
functions. When your account logged on to our system, we were
temporarily able to verify it as a registered user.
Approximately 94 seconds ago, your verification was made void
by loss of data in the Sector 4G9C. Now, due to AOL
verification protocol, it is mandatory for us to re-verify
you. Please click 'Respond' and re-state your password.
Failure to comply will result in immediate account deletion.
```

This kind of attack can be extremely effective. With the right tone and convincing use of made-up jargon, this message could easily catch out inexperienced users. AOL (the on-line service provider) makes a point of reminding its users wherever possible that AOL staff will never ask for password or credit-card information on-line, but novice users often forget this. Once a hacker has one person's password he or she can then collect more, and it becomes almost impossible to evict that person from the system. If you receive a solicitation, copy the message and send it to the service's administrators; it makes their job much easier and also helps prevent attacks on other people.

Password solicitations are also sometimes sent as email messages. These work in exactly the same way. The victim receives an official-looking message that suggests they have to supply their password and credit-card details by return. These should be treated in exactly the same way.

Email security

Internet email is not secure. If someone with the required skills deliberately sets out to try to read your email messages, their contents are less secure than those of a standard letter. Fortunately, the tools and the knowledge needed to do this are very advanced, and it is certainly not something a casual Internet user sitting at home with a PC can do easily.

In a number of instances in the USA, 'private' email messages have been intercepted and used as evidence in a court case. It has also been suggested that some hackers have created systems that scan passing email for credit-card details, which they then file away for future use. (Kevin Mitnick, a notorious hacker now serving a jail sentence, had a collection of thousands of credit-card numbers when he was arrested – although there was no evidence that he had ever tried to use them fraudulently. As with many hackers, he was doing it to prove he could, rather than out of malice or criminal intent.) But it is not just hackers who have an interest in email. A web site has details of an alleged US Government email-scanning system called Echelon, which can read a sizeable proportion of the world's email traffic and can be set up to look for certain target words – presumably those related to national security concerns.

It is possible to improve email security by using a secret code. (For more about this see PGP on page 146.) At the time of writing, banks and shops have yet to agree on a way that this can be done commercially. Until they do, Internet shopping will remain moribund.

Email viruses

Email viruses are an Internet myth that regularly catches out the inexperienced. It is impossible to damage a computer or the information on it by downloading and reading a message made of plain text. Information contained in an attachment can only be dangerous in one of two ways: if it is a piece of software infected with a computer virus; if it is a 'macro virus' designed to cause problems with a certain kind of wordprocessor. (For more details, see page 155.) Images and other kinds of information, such as video and sound, sent as attachments are completely safe.

Mail bombs

Apart from trying to read email messages, hackers and other Internet 'undesirables' can abuse the email system in other ways. A 'mail bomb' is a collection of huge and/or very numerous messages, which are sent to your email address and clog up your connection. A mail-bomb attack can be disastrous. You will not usually be able to receive any more email messages until your IAP or on-line service provider sorts out the mess by deleting the unwanted messages.

A more insidious form of mail-bomb attack is the mailing-list subscription ploy. If you are the victim of one of these you will suddenly find that you have been subscribed to thousands of mailing lists, and will then receive thousands, perhaps even millions, of messages a day. A person, who calls himself the Unamailer (after the infamous Ted Kaczynski, the US Unabomber), perpetrated mailing-list attacks on a number of famous people late in 1996. Ironically, he did it to protest against the lack of security on the Internet. It took many weeks to deal with the results of his actions and he was never traced.

Because it is so simple to forge email on the Internet, even a novice hacker can launch an attack such as this relatively easily. More experienced hackers can do it in a way that leaves no trace at all, making it almost impossible to track them down. Apart from being careful about who you annoy on-line, you cannot – unfortunately – protect yourself against this. However, as new and improved ways to manage email become available, attacks will become less destructive and easier to deal with.

Email forgery

It is hard, although not impossible, to forge a handwritten letter. But it is very easy to forge an email message well enough to fool an inexperienced Internet user. With a little thought, it should be obvious how this can be done using almost any standard email package.

However, this simple forging technique will not confuse more experienced users. All email arrives with a long list of information at the top called a 'header'. The information in the header is used to route the message to the correct destination and it includes the name of the computer system the email originated from. If this does not match the suggested return address in the header, then there is a chance the email has been forged. It is possible, but certainly not easy, to forge headers. (For more information about headers see Appendix 5.)

If you need to identify the sender of an email message with absolute certainty, your best option is to ask for a 'digital signature'. This is a special code which contains information that identifies someone as the only possible author of a message. Digital signatures are available when using the PGP system described below. Some US states are beginning to look into the legal implications of digital signatures, and it is likely that by the beginning of the twenty first century all email will be authenticated with digital signatures as a matter of course.

Encryption

Encryption uses secret codes, which rely on complex mathematical techniques that make them virtually unbreakable. A scheme called CLIPPER, which is favoured by the US Government and is being touted as a world standard, has a built-in loophole which makes it possible for government agents to read encrypted email using special electronic keys. This raises interesting questions about who should and should not have access to 'private' information.

In theory these keys would be made available only to the government and under the strictest conditions, such as if there is reasonable suspicion of terrorism. A more sophisticated system called DES is widely used but may also not be completely secure. Many Internet users worldwide distrust the US Government's motives for having access to private information and would prefer to use an alternative system which is secure from all prying eyes, authorised or otherwise.

PGP (Pretty Good Privacy)

At the time of writing, PGP provides the most secure encryption available but is at the centre of complex legal and patent wrangles, which makes it difficult to obtain outside the USA. It is not hard to find on the Internet, although you may, depending on its current legal status, have problems obtaining a copy from a software company in the USA. PGP is very secure and can also be used to encrypt information on a computer's hard disk, but it is also rather complex.

Most secret codes are flawed because at some point the person sending the message has to tell the recipient how the code can be cracked. This is usually done with a 'key' – the information that defines how the code works. If there is no way to communicate a key securely, the code is useless no matter how difficult it is to crack. PGP gets around this problem by using two keys: a private key, and a public key. The private key is known only to one person. As long as he or she keeps it secret, the code will be secure. The public key is made available to anyone. The sender needs to find out from the recipient what his or her public key is and then uses it to encrypt the text of the message with the PGP software. The message is then secure and can be sent in an email in the usual way. The recipient runs the message through the PGP software with both the public key and his or her private key. This process deciphers the message and reproduces the original text.

The reason this system works is because the two keys are mathematically related. If just one key is known, the only way to find the other is to perform billions of calculations. With current computer technology this would take many times the lifetime of the known universe.

Fortunately, you do not need to understand the theory to use PGP. Since 1996 new and improved versions of the program have started to become available. These have 'wrappers' which hide away the technicalities and make the software easier to use. You can buy PGP extensions to popular email packages (such as Eudora) but at the time of writing, for the reasons mentioned above, these are not available over the counter in the UK. As an interesting aside it is possible to use PGP to secure other kinds of communications: a version designed to work with WebPhones can secure private voice conversations.

Interest in privacy, security and encryption has led to the rise of a small sub-culture on the Internet – the self-styled 'cypherpunks'. The existence of uncrackable encryption systems has brought about a new situation in which citizens can be sure of communicating with each other without government interference. To date, governments have taken it for granted that their agents can listen in to 'private' telephone conversations, open letters and take whatever steps they consider essential to maintain national security.

Cypherpunks consider this unreasonable and make a point of using whatever technology is available to help ensure privacy. The situation is a complex one. PGP is used for illegal communications as well as innocent ones. Unless governments ban PGP – and such a ban may well be unenforceable in practice – its use will continue to grow. It is impossible to say what the implications of this are. Some countries – notably Russia, France, Iran and Iraq – have already announced bans of 'unsupported encryption systems'. Anyone who tries to use PGP in some of these countries may suffer serious legal, and perhaps even life-threatening, consequences.

It is important to bear in mind that codes that are unbreakable today will not be so tomorrow. At the time of writing PGP is literally unbreakable – with today's technology, the computer power required to break the code would tie up all the world's computers indefinitely. But because computers are continuously becoming more powerful, it is unlikely PGP will still be secure in the 2020s. New computer designs which work very differently from today's machines are already being proposed, and it is likely that they will be exceptionally good at the kinds of calculations needed to break a PGP code. If you have information which needs to be kept secure for a long time, it is best to take other non-electronic precautions to keep it safe, such as using a physically secure storage facility.

Anonymity

When using email and newsgroups it is sometimes useful to be able to post anonymously, so that the recipient does not know who you are or where you are posting from. A number of 'anonymous remailers' offer this service. These are special email computers which separate the text of your message from its 'header' (the Internet's equivalent of an envelope), give it a different one and then send it on to its final destination. Normally, headers contain information about your name, the time and date you sent the message, the computers your message passed through, and sometimes the software you are using. 'Anonymised' headers replace this information with details that say very little about you.

To use an anonymous remailer, you email a special address and in return receive a unique mail identifier. This is your 'anonymous address'. It works just like a normal email address, except that whenever you send email through it, your true address is hidden. A reply sent to your anonymous address will be forwarded to your true address, although again this process keeps your true address hidden. In effect the anonymous address acts rather like a PO Box, except that you can send mail from it anonymously as well as receiving it.

Anonymous email cannot guarantee total security. One of the most famous and widely used anonymous remailers – which used the address *anon@penet.fi* – was closed by its owner when he was served with a controversial court order, brought by the Church of Scientology, requesting full details of its users. (At the time the Church of Scientology was involved in an Internet 'war' with the members of a certain newsgroup, who were postings its secret documents anonymously.) This is a problem that affects all remailers – if your name appears in a raid like this one, your anonymity will be compromised, even if you have been using the remailer for completely innocent reasons.

It is also possible to track email into and out of a remailer, rendering the anonymising process ineffective, but the skills and equipment needed to do this are beyond the capability of most Internet users.

To increase the security of a message you can send it through multiple remailers. This reduces the chances of having your details handed over to a third party because only the last address in the chain of remailers will have your true address. However, doing this does not make your email any harder to trace electronically. If you do use multiple remailers, you can be sure that the only people who will be able to trace you will be dedicated government agencies who have the kind of computer facilities – if not necessarily the expertise – to track someone in this way. Most people do not need this level of security, but those who do can combine anonymous email with PGP to create an almost totally secure communication channel.

Newsgroup security

From the point of view of security, the main problem with newsgroup postings is that they are archived for posterity. This has some surprising implications. Archiving enables total strangers to see a complete record of everything you have posted on Usenet. This can give them more information about you than you may feel comfortable with. One Internet revenge technique is to look through the archive, pull out postings that might be embarrassing and re-post them in a different context. Many people have suddenly found their more colourful peccadilloes unexpectedly brought to light in this way.

In the longer term, it is worth bearing in mind that the stated aim of the archive services is to make all postings available indefinitely. This means that anything you post to Usenet will remain available there perhaps for hundreds of years. This can have implications for your relationships and family life. Some people have already taken to vetting prospective romantic partners by searching for and reading their postings on the Web. Thinking further ahead, your argumentative Usenet postings will still be there for your children to read when they reach their teens; could this affect your relationship with them? Similarly, you will be able to read their postings once they start making them.

The same applies to a lesser extent to mailing lists. It is not unheard of for someone to pick a posting from a mailing list and put it up on a web site without asking for the original writer's permission. As a result, a number of your comments may be posted publicly without you knowing. Given a selection of these, and your Usenet postings as well, a complete stranger can form an impressively accurate picture of your hobbies, interests and private life. If you have a common surname this will be harder. Because of this you should never post anything that could attract unwelcome attention or which says more about you than you would like other people to know.

To maintain your privacy on newsgroups, you can use an anonymous email address, as discussed above. This should work well but has the disadvantage of appearing odd in the social setting of some groups, in which it would be the equivalent of trying to hold a conversation while wearing a brown paper bag over your head. In others, however, especially those that deal with more dubious information, it is actually expected.

Fortunately, a less demanding form of anonymity is also available. It is possible to bypass the archiving process by including a line that says: 'X-No-Archive: yes' at the start of each posting. This tells the various archiving services to ignore your message and guarantees that it will not be saved for posterity. Note that your posting will appear with your contact details intact, although once it expires, your message will disappear for good. Doing this may also help you avoid junk mail, but is perhaps better thought of as a way of avoiding the attentions of nosey strangers – possibly including your descendants and relatives.

Security on the Web

There are three security considerations on the Web – the security of web transactions, the security of web systems, and various questions about privacy raised by current web technology.

Web transactions

Web transactions, like email, are not very secure. In some situations – such as buying software on-line – you will be asked more questions than you really need to answer. If you are unhappy about giving away your address and phone number you will often find you can leave these parts of the form blank. If the creator of the web page complains when you try to do this, you can supply false information. It is not normally used for anything more sophisticated than sending out information about new products, which you will probably receive via email anyway.

Some web sites are secure (their address starts with 'https://' instead of the usual 'http://'). The system that they use to make them secure is called SSL – Secure Sockets Layer – and encrypts information before sending it to the site. When you look at one of these web sites, your browser will display an icon or some other form of information that tells you it is secure. For example, Netscape Navigator shows a solid key in the bottom left-hand corner when a transaction is secure and a broken one when it is not.

The SSL system is not failsafe. It can be hacked fairly easily, although, again, this requires computer power and skills which most people do not have. It is safe enough to be thought reasonably secure for on-line credit-card transactions. In practice you are less likely to have your credit-card number copied this way than you are to have your card stolen.

At the time of writing, more secure systems are being developed that can be used commercially with complete confidence. These will solve the transaction problem and make using the Web for transactions as secure (perhaps more secure) than giving your number to a mail-order company over the phone.

The latest web technologies such as Java and Active X are not completely secure. To protect yourself from security problems, you should always use the latest version of any browser, as long as it is known to be secure. For more details see your browser's home page; this will always contain information about the very latest security issues.

Web site security

Web sites themselves are not always secure, but this affects you only if you are planning to develop a site of your own, and especially one for business purposes (see Appendix 4). Some organisations – including the CIA and the US Air Force – have had their sites vandalised by hackers, who take the existing pages and replace them with pages of their own design which typically have more eye-catching and controversial content than the originals.

For simple home pages, this is not something you should worry about. Your web pages will be kept on a computer run by your IAP or on-line service provider, and if your site is vandalised – which is very unlikely as hackers usually concentrate on high-profile sites – the attack becomes their problem. Apart from keeping a backup of all the information on the site, there is little you can do.

However, professional web developers who rent space on a commercial web server should always check the security arrangements of their chosen host before signing a contract. A professionally run web site will be able to offer the security features listed below:

- **At least one security expert** He or she should keep track of all the latest security updates posted on the Internet and have modified the existing software used on the server to remove all the common and well-known security risks. This is an on-going process. Much of the software used by the larger computer systems on the Internet has gaping security holes, which are familiar to hackers. These holes need to be closed by a computer security expert. A computer system that does not do this and continues to use the software in the form it was originally supplied, will be vulnerable to attack.
- **A properly installed 'firewall'** This is a piece of software that attempts to isolate secure parts of a computer network from the parts that are accessible from the rest of the Internet. It takes a reasonable level of expertise to install a firewall properly, and a bad installation can be worse than useless. The existence of a firewall is not enough; there should be evidence that it has been installed in a thoughtful and professional way and that all the potential security loopholes have been accounted for. For example, even the best firewall is rendered useless if someone on the network it protects

installs a modem and uses a standard dial-up connection to the Internet.

- **A site policy that follows a document called RFC 1244** This lists sound security practices, and it should be evident that these practices are being adhered to. (If the staff managing a site are unfamiliar with this document it is very unlikely that they know anything at all about practical Internet security.)
- **Regular security checks** These should include checks on personnel and physical security arrangements as well as the software and hardware that make up the web server. Anyone dealing with very sensitive information should have an unblemished security record. Professional hackers and criminals sometimes attempt to bribe key employees instead of hacking in from outside; it is much quicker and easier for them to get in this way. Physical security is important for similar reasons, so keycards or other physical systems should be used to keep strangers out of the most secure areas of the building.

Internet security is not a straightforward topic, and for larger computer installations it is advisable to hire a security consultant to perform a full security audit. The issues are much more complicated than choosing suitable passwords and making sure these are known only by specific trusted people. Questions need to be asked about physical access, backup and recovery procedures, and even the management structure of an organisation. Organisations that do not insist on good answers are leaving themselves wide open to attack.

Web privacy

Whenever you look at a web site you leave a record that shows who you are, which page or pages you looked at, which software you used, which web site you came from, and so on. Usually these details are clumped together and analysed statistically to provide information that can be used to improve the site. But they can also be used in other ways; it is possible to find yourself on the receiving end of junk mail by inadvertently leaving your contact details with a site you have visited.

You can make your web browsing more secure by using an 'anonymiser'. This is a web site that renders the personal details that are usually supplied by your browser 'invisible'. You can then continue to browse as before, without leaving your personal information at any web sites. Anonymisers are very easy to use – you simply visit the anonymising site, and then carry on browsing as before.

'Cookies' are a related problem. These are notes that are passed from web sites you have visited to your web browser and can contain information about the choices you made while you were at the site. The cookie system was created to save users from having to type in the same details whenever they revisited a site. But they can also be used in more underhand ways. For example, some sites use cookie information to change advertising to suit your interests. While not everyone finds this offensive or intrusive, it remains a rather devious way to attract your interest. And cookies can also be used to make a note of all the sites you visit during a browsing session – again, you may not want this information made available for public scrutiny.

It is easy to dispose of cookies. They are created and kept in a file called 'cookies.txt' in your computer's filing system. If you edit this file or delete it at the end of each web-browsing session, your web usage will be cookie-free. You can find software to manage cookies for you, and this is available from many sources on the Net. A search for 'web cookies' should provide a list of plenty of places to look.

Viruses

Software that is downloaded from the Internet should be checked for viruses before it is used. The process of downloading software is quite safe. Any potential problems will appear only when the software is used. Security-conscious computer users should get into the habit of testing any downloaded software with a virus checker. These are available for a relatively small outlay and can save hours or even days of despair caused by a virus that has removed all the information on a computer's hard disk.

Documents also now contain viruses. These are less clever but more insidious than traditional viruses. Instead of taking over a vital part of your PC, they rely on the fact that many of the more popular word processors offer a set of automation tools called macros. (Macros are typically used to create big changes in a document that would otherwise need to be done by hand repeatedly. An example would be changing all the numbers in a table from feet to metres.) These viruses can be included within a document when it is saved to disk and will work whenever someone tries to read or edit it.

An 'autorun' macro will do something every time a document is loaded into a word processor to be read or changed. Because macros can do whatever their creator wants them to, it is very easy to create an autorun macro that deletes all the information in your computer. More playful variations on this theme include a virus that inserts a silly word at random into a document. The latest virus-checking software can deal with macro viruses as well as those of the more conventional kind. It cannot be emphasised enough that a good virus checker is essential whenever you try to download and use any potentially dangerous information from the Internet.

Good Times

The 'Good Times' virus is an email message that travels round the Internet, taking in the unwary and inexperienced, and perpetuating itself indefinitely. The Good Times email claims to be about a virus called Good Times that can be sent via email. The virus is supposed to cause fatal damage to a PC by overheating its chips, and anyone who receives information about this dangerous virus is encouraged to pass it on to warn their friends.

In fact, it is impossible to send a virus as part of an email message, unless it is hidden in some attached software or buried in a document as a macro. The Good Times virus is actually the warning message itself. It attacks people, causing them to believe something that is not true and forcing them to continue to spread the message. In short, Good Times is a fairly typical example of an Internet prank and not a dangerous computer virus at all.

Trojan horses

'Trojan horse' software is a more dangerous version of the Good Times virus. This is software that is claimed to do one thing but actually does something very different and destructive. In the Spring of 1997 a piece of software called AOL4FREE appeared on the Internet. This was supposed to be a PC version of a similar program with the same name that had appeared a few years earlier for the Apple Macintosh. The Mac software was an AOL piracy program that gave people free access to the AOL Service. The PC software was really a Trojan horse and deleted all the information on the hard disks of any computer it was installed on.

Virus-checking software cannot spot a Trojan horse, because technically the program is not a true virus. As far as a virus checker is concerned, a Trojan horse looks like an ordinary piece of software and has none of the tell-tale signs that give away a virus. The only way to avoid a Trojan horse like this is to watch out for rumours and public announcements on the Net. Software that is associated with piracy and other illegal activities is much more likely to cause trouble than ordinary software.

Scams and con tricks

A classic Internet con trick was perpetrated on a number of victims during the Autumn of 1996. Some users in search of thrills found themselves at a certain web site which promised them access to illegal pornography. To use this site they were asked to download a 'special viewer' on to their computer.

The viewer was really a piece of software that broke their existing Internet connection and reconnected their modem – by way of an international call – to a special number in Moldavia, which was set up to charge by the minute. The first that most victims knew of the scam was when their enormous phone bill arrived. As with Trojan horses, the more illegal or dubious the activity on the web site, the greater the chance that some kind of trick will be involved.

The Web also suffers from the problem of commercial verification. How can you tell if someone is who they claim to be? This is a particular problem for share broking and investment services. If you visit one of these in a high street, you at least have the security of knowing that there is a real shop front that has real people working behind it. They may of course be dishonest, but if you ask the right questions you at least have a chance of avoiding fraudsters.

This is not so on the Internet, where anyone can create a 'shop front' which gives a totally misleading impression. A good rule of thumb is that if an investment opportunity seems to be too good to be true, it probably is. To keep out of trouble, it helps to remember the following:

- **Never deal with unregulated companies** These may trade 'outside the law', and you will have no chance of getting compensation if they turn out to be fraudulent or dishonest.
- **Do not invest in anything you do not understand** If something looks appealing, but you are not clear about how it works, get independent advice from an expert.
- **Always do your own research into possible investment opportunities** You can use the Internet's search facilities to check for company names and the names of directors to see if they have ever been involved in litigation or come under some other kind of legal scrutiny.

Children on-line

The Internet can cause something of a dilemma for parents. On the one hand, it can be an extremely effective way to inspire enthusiasm for learning and making contact with others, but on the other hand, some of the information on the Internet is most definitely not suitable for children. At the time of writing, the problem of restricting access to unsuitable material has yet to be solved. Although systems are available that attempt to censor what children can see, none is perfect, and all have the unfortunate side-effect of accidentally barring wanted as well as unwanted information.

On the Internet, the most obvious way to tackle the problem is to use 'Net babysitter' software which attempts to check web sites for inappropriate content, including sexually-explicit material, graphic violence, racism and so on. The software can look for certain words in the text at the site or can use one of the Net's own classification systems, which work very much like film ratings.

The problem with keyword searches is that they are rather unintelligent. While it is easy to get rid of most 'four letter words', a ban on the word 'sex', for example, may make it impossible to read completely innocent sites that refer to certain English counties. Meanwhile, Net ratings are still in their early stages. There is no single standard rating system, and only a minority of sites – ironically often the ones with the most explicit content – bother to give themselves ratings. Many sites aimed at children do not do this, and unfortunately some software bars sites that are not rated. As a result, the sites that might most interest children 'disappear'. The latest web browsers are starting to take notice of ratings but until a system is agreed upon and everyone begins to use it, ratings will remain a patchy and unreliable way to restrict access.

The situation is slightly better on the on-line services, which have a more family-oriented approach. Some services – AOL and Prodigy – offer separate account names for each family member, and these can be set up from the 'master account' so that certain features of the service are unavailable. Access to the Internet can also be controlled from the master account.

One problem is that these controls are set up using a password system, and enterprising youngsters can look over their parent's shoulders so they can 'borrow' their password later. For some children, being left in a special children's web site is not enough, and it is usually very easy to escape and follow links that lead to more adult content.

Chat rooms and IRC can present difficulties of their own. You should explain to children that they should never give out identifying information, including names and addresses, school names, passwords, and so on, to anyone without your permission. Nor should they arrange a face-to-face meeting with someone they have met on the Internet without asking you first. Finally, if they come across upsetting messages which are aggressive and verbally abusive or suggestive you should insist that they tell you immediately.

In practice, the best way to avoid inappropriate information is to rely on active forms of parenting. Finding a balance between effective concern and intrusive paranoia can be difficult here, and the whole subject needs to be handled with tact. Useful possibilities include:

- moving the PC to a living room where you can watch what children are using it for
- checking bookmarks and your browser's history file to see if any explicit or inappropriate sites have been marked. (For the latter, search the filing system for files or folders which contain the word 'history')
- checking new information that may have appeared in your computer's filing system – especially image files (names ending in .gif, .jpg, .tif), video files (.mov, .avi) or archives (.zip).

One problem that is particularly severe on the Web is the prevalence of manipulative advertising aimed specifically at children. Some 'kids' sites' are really thinly disguised corporate attempts to brainwash youngsters into an inappropriate enthusiasm for products and merchandising. It is useful to review these sites in the same way that you would check for information of a more explicitly inappropriate nature. Apart from being better for the children, you will also save yourself the effort needed to dissuade a determined youngster from pressuring you into buying something that neither of you really wants or needs. Parents who would like more advice should try the NCH Action for Children web site at *http://www.nchafc.org.uk*

CHAPTER 9

USING THE INTERNET FOR FUN AND PROFIT

ALTHOUGH THE Internet was originally designed for researchers and academics with advanced computer skills and high IQs, it is now becoming as easy to use as the telephone and television. The uses it is put to are changing accordingly, from software development and the exchange of academic information to commercial applications and entertainment. These new uses are still relatively undeveloped, although, even with the limited technology of today, the Net can already be used as an extremely effective business tool, as well as a wonderful source of diversion.

The Internet for business

Although more sophisticated business tools – such as up-to-the-minute stock quotes and portfolio management services – are only just beginning to become available, it can be surprising how much is already possible with the creative use of email, newsgroups and the World Wide Web. Their power is most obvious when all these tools are used to support each other. Because they are all available to the general public, the facilities they offer can be used by any business, no matter how small.

CASE HISTORY – Jacey

Jacey Bedford is a member of the folk group Artisan and used the Internet almost exclusively to arrange the 1996 US tour for the group. Her story is a good example of the way the different parts of the Net can be used together to accomplish a task that would not be possible with any one of them in isolation.

'We've been singing in England since 1984, and in 1994 we made our first professional trip across the Atlantic. Our most recent tour was arranged via email. Using my PC and working from my office at home, I made contact with venue organisers, negotiated fees and dates and even enquired about airline tickets and car hire.

'To start off, I found a web site which lists American folk venues, state by state. This gave me addresses, phone numbers and, where available, email addresses. Once I found a site with good links it was easy to find other sites very quickly, and I used those links to find still more contacts. I also looked around in the rec.music.folk newsgroup and came across a few folk-related North American mailing lists. One of these was for radio DJs who present folk music, so I emailed them offers of free albums for airplay. The response time is very fast, and lots of DJs said they'd like to have albums, so we sent them out immediately. The DJs on the list have listings of the records they play in each show, so we were able to confirm whether they liked the records and if they were playing them a lot.

'Next I sent out emails to appropriate venues listed on the web venue database, introducing myself and the trio and offering to send out promotional packs and CDs. At the same time, I posted messages to the mailing lists and to rec.music.folk, asking if anyone else would be interested in having us. Then I sat back and waited. There were a few promising enquiries and I traded emails with venue organisers to negotiate dates and fees. Once I had a few gigs confirmed, which took about a month, I posted again to the newsgroups and mailing lists to say "These are the venues already committed to our tour, does anyone else want to come on board?"

'At that point, with the area narrowed down to specific states and dates, I got enough fill-ins to complete the tour. We ended up with 13 dates in 15 days and travelled from Vermont to Pennsylvania, Delaware and then New Jersey. Only two nights on the whole tour were arranged by contact other than email.

'To co-ordinate the travelling, I looked up airline schedules on the Web (using search engines to locate airline web pages) and also checked car hire and prices. In some cases you can actually make your reservations or hire a car on-line. It's easy to turn virtual travel to real travel arrangements on the Web. All you need is nerves of steel and a credit card.'

The Net's great strength as a business tool is that it provides easy access to information and other people. It can take the place of a library full of contact numbers and directories and can make it much easier to find customers and new business partners and *vice versa*. Sometimes, this leads to new business opportunities that would not have been possible with more traditional media.

CASE HISTORY – Samantha

Samantha Eddington discovered that business on the Internet can take on a life of its own and the Net offers opportunities for new kinds of work which are entirely unique to it.

'It started when I decided to create my own web site. I was aiming for something that would help women in business – partly a reference guide, partly an e-zine (an electronic magazine published exclusively on the Web), partly a site where women could get together and talk about the issues involved.

'I mentioned the idea to a few friends and business contacts. I hadn't even got the pages published when I started getting attention from people who were interested in buying advertising space. It was all a bit of a surprise – there was just such was a lot of interest and enthusiasm out there. Really, it's obvious why when you think about it. A full page ad in a glossy magazine can cost a few thousand pounds a month, but on the Web, where anyone can publish pages for next to nothing, amateurs can sell advertising for maybe £50 a year and still make a decent profit. The Web offers a captive, affluent audience, so advertisers love it.

'In the end I turned the offers down because I didn't want advertisements to affect the integrity of the site, and it felt completely wrong for the type of site I was wanting to produce. But I know that other people have started to make themselves a tidy little second income from taking advertising on their pages.

'I should be honest and say that the requests for advertising have slowed down now. There's so much on the Web these days that you'll only get serious attention from advertisers if your site is really popular. That's how the big sites like Yahoo and AltaVista make their money. The advertisers know they'll get millions of visitors, and they're prepared to pay for that. The big search engines can also offer ad tracking – the ads they display will change to match the words the visitor is searching for, so the

advertising is more effective. It's had the effect of squeezing out the little start-ups and the beginners, who either don't want to or can't play in that part of the market. But there's still money to be made if a site caters for a small niche market that can carry suitable ads for a low cost.

'But it's not just advertising that's selling. Once I had published my pages, I got a couple of offers of more web design work. And a friend of mine who started by putting up her own web pages just for fun has set up her own web design and consultancy company. She used to be a graphic designer but now spends her days writing HTML. That's a weird market – you can get "one man and his dog" outfits working from back bedrooms competing with multimedia consultancy houses that perhaps have a background in corporate video or CD-ROM design. Quotes for the same piece of design work can quite literally range from £750 to £10,000. And paying more doesn't necessarily get you a better product either. For anyone with design skills, it's been a bit of a gold rush, although, again, I'm expecting a shake-out over the next few years because, as the market consolidates, there will be less work to go around. On the other hand, it's likely that more and more ordinary businesses – the kind that usually advertise in the Yellow Pages *– are going to want their own sites, and it's possible that there will be a whole new market for designers there.*

'Unfortunately, I had to give up on my own site after a few months because maintaining it was taking up too much of my time. I really started it as a hobby, but it was becoming a full-time job keeping it running. But I learned a lot by doing it, and it was a very interesting experience for me.'

Many businesses make the mistake of treating the Web like an electronic version of a display advertisement or brochure. Although this can work well, it is not necessarily the best way to use the technology. The most effective sites offer the following advantages over traditional advertising:

- **Detail** You can get a lot more information on to a web site than you can in a typical paper brochure, and this gives you plenty of scope for doing things that you would not otherwise be able to do, such as offering a free service or free information which will attract visitors to your site. A good example would be an IAP that provides a free introduction to the Internet on its web site. The 'free extra' attracts visitors who would not otherwise want to see the site, and many of these people will then go on to read the advertising material. An outstanding free extra may even receive a 'web award' – these are rating systems developed by various companies and individuals to mark out particularly good sites. The amount of room on the Web makes it easy to publish large amounts of information in your site. An estate agent, for example, could include details of all the homes currently on the market in a format very similar to the paper flyers that agents currently produce. The extra overhead required to add full floor plans to an electronic flyer is minimal, and the web site serves to distract time-wasters who request flyers or even visits to properties they have no serious interest in buying.

- **Interactivity** Traditional publishing works only one-way (from publisher to reader), but on the Internet all activities can be two-way. Games, email, customer surveys, free prize draws, and so on, can all be interactive. Companies with sites on the Internet can support their customers, either with a mailing list (see page 49) or on the web site itself. Customers can ask questions of the company's support staff, and the answers are then made available for public scrutiny. This saves everyone time because common questions can be answered once instead of again and again. Another useful byproduct of this process is that the support creates a captive audience for the company's advertising.

- **On-line orders** A virtual shopfront has lower overheads than a real one and is open 24 hours a day, seven days a week. Although it may be wiser to give credit-card details over the phone (at least for the moment, see Chapter 8), customers can give details on-line of what they want to order and where they want it delivered without requiring any personal attention.

The Net and money

At the time of writing, the Net's relationship with money is uneasy, although this situation is showing signs of improving rapidly. The biggest problem is the lack of guaranteed security.

Once this is solved – as inevitably it will be – the Internet will become as important to business as the high street and the retail park.

On-line share dealing

The Internet can help with share dealing in three ways:
- it can be used to supply information about share prices and the past and present performance of companies
- email can be used to send buy-and-sell orders to a broker
- help, tips and support are available on-line from other investors.

Up-to-the-minute share information is available from a number of subscription services, such as ESI (Electronic Share Information) at *http://www.esi.co.uk* These offer a range of options, from free trading summaries at the end of each day to up-to-the-minute share prices direct from the London Stock Exchange. A variety of news and other services – for example full summaries of a week's trading, supplied in a form that will work with various popular financial software packages – are also available. These can be copied to your computer and analysed in your own time. Much of this information is also available in paper form, but many people seem to find the electronic option more useful and easier to work with.

The business of buying and selling on the Internet is done via brokers, who accept email requests and provide email confirmation of a trade. Many brokers on the Internet charge a flat fee of around £25 instead of a percentage commission, and this makes them good value for large transactions. The general public is not yet allowed to cut out the middle men and trade 'on exchange' directly – to do so one would need a very secure connection, which the Internet is not yet ready to offer.

For help and support with share dealing, on-line services are the best choice. At the time of writing, there seem to be no newsgroups for share dealing. However, on America Online, the Motley Fool pages provide some useful hints and tips for beginners, as well as suggestions for investment opportunities. Unfortunately some of this information is specific to the US market.

The combination of instant access to prices, speedy buy-and-sell facilities and plenty of on-line help and support make the Internet an unusually potent way to play the markets. The international nature of the Internet also makes it easy to build up portfolios in markets beyond the UK – especially the USA, where it is possible to use US brokers to trade shares on the US markets from the comfort of one's home in the UK. However, investors should be aware that because the Internet is still not totally reliable, it is perhaps best thought of as a useful addition to existing trading facilities rather than a replacement.

On-line banking

For many people, the prospect of on-line banking is much more exciting than the possibility of share dealing. Unfortunately, in the UK electronic banking is currently in a state of limbo, awaiting the development of secure transaction technology. A number of banks, including Barclays and the Royal Bank of Scotland, have been experimenting with pilot schemes, which offer customers the chance to pay bills, transfer money between accounts and view electronic versions of their statements. The Barclays scheme uses a popular money-management software package called Quicken, which makes the whole process relatively straightforward. But until the security problem is solved and banks take more steps to promote their services on-line, electronic banking will not take the place of traditional banking. In any case, prospective customers are well advised to wait six months to a year before signing up for on-line banking, just in case there are any residual teething troubles in the banks' earliest attempts to offer this service.

A related issue is the question of electronic cash (e-cash), which can be used to pay for goods and services on the World Wide Web. It does not require a credit-card number but relies, instead, on the transfer of electronic funds directly from the buyer to the seller. As with on-line banking, a number of trial schemes are in progress, but no one system has proved to be outstandingly popular. One of the concerns is that some e-cash systems can trace every transaction, thereby allowing banks and other institutions to build up a complete picture of someone's spending habits. Civil liberty campaigners are concerned about this and are pressing for a more anonymous system that does not keep these records and allows the completely untraceable transactions that traditional cash offers.

On-line shopping

Whereas on-line banking is still waiting for the starter's pistol, on-line shopping has completed a couple of laps, although it still has some way to go. Again, the big problem is security. Even secure web sites (see Chapter 8) are not watertight, and there are legitimate concerns about credit-card fraud by third parties. Companies are being careful because one or two instances of fraud, followed by bad publicity, could seriously damage the credibility of on-line shopping among the public, as well as a company's reputation. And with such a huge and potentially lucrative market at stake, this would be a commercial disaster.

The Net is an ideal medium for selling certain kinds of goods and services (non-perishable luxury items such as books and CDs) but not so good for others (perishable goods such as foodstuffs). On-line CD and bookstores can carry a spectacularly diverse range of titles and also offer search facilities to make it easier to find specific items. One of the most successful bookstores is Amazon (*http://www.amazon.com*), which sells internationally and can supply obscure titles that many bookstores cannot even find. CD Now (*http://www.cdnow.com*) offers a similar service for CDs. In the UK some high-street stores are beginning to take advantage of the Web: Innovations, which sells gadgets (*http://www.innovations.co.uk*); and Argos, which sells domestic goods of all descriptions (*http://www.argos.co.uk*). The widest range of goods is available on web sites in the USA. These sell all kinds of items, from the mundane – mattresses, for example – to the extremely strange and unlikely – plates that protect the owner from 'harmful negative vibrations'. When you order from abroad, carriage and freight costs are usually reasonable, providing you do not want your purchase urgently. Deliveries can take between a few weeks and a few months, depending on the size and weight of the object. Watch out for customs and VAT charges as these can be considerable on some goods. If you can find someone in another country with whom you can arrange swaps you may be able to avoid paying these costs by having the goods classed as gifts.

For the second category of goods, supermarket chain Tesco (*http://www.tesco.co.uk*) has pioneered electronic stores which serve the area around some of its branches. Goods are ordered on-line and, assuming you live within the required area, are then delivered to your door. At the time of writing only three areas (two in London, one in Leeds) are covered, but the scheme seems to have been well received, and Tesco has plans for virtual stores in other areas. Other supermarkets have been less keen to experiment. Sainsbury's at *http://www.j-sainsbury.co.uk* offers only luxury goods such as flowers, wine and chocolates at its site. In general, many sites are still rather disappointing. Either they are simple electronic brochures with no ordering facilities, or they do not offer the full range of products available from the company.

Meeting people

A lot of the fun of the Internet comes from meeting people. Newsgroups, mailing lists, chat rooms and IRC are the best places in which to make new friends. But other, less obvious, opportunities also exist. The Net has a strong tradition of on-line games and offers users the chance to create and participate in imaginary electronic worlds. These can be intensely social, and for some people the chance to meet other like-minded people is so important that they do not mind the fact that contact takes place at a distance, by way of a keyboard and computer screen.

Another good way to meet people is to publish a 'home page' – an autobiographical web site which list interests, experiences, and so on. Home pages are often set up as a result of pure vanity, albeit usually of a rather mild kind, but are nevertheless an extremely popular part of Internet culture. The best home pages are shrines to the interests of their authors and attract copious attention from visitors who share those interests.

Finally, it is also possible to create your own newsgroup. This is a rather more advanced pastime than the others mentioned in this chapter, but it can also be a very good way to meet electronically a group of like-minded people on a regular basis.

On-line games

Computer games tend to be solitary affairs, but the Internet can remove the isolation and add a new dimension to games by enabling people to play with real opponents. Games fall into two categories:

- **Virtual worlds** are imaginatively social. The main object of the 'game' is to make contact with people and play-act different experiences
- **Networked games** are more limited and simply offer the chance to play a computer game – usually of a rather violent type – against human opponents instead of computer-generated ones.

Virtual worlds

These are completely imaginary environments on the Internet. They are used as a backdrop for participants who can pretend to be someone else for as long as they choose to remain there. MUDs (Multi User Dimensions, or sometimes Multi User Dungeons), MUSHs (Multi User Shared Hallucinations) and MOOs (Object Oriented MUDs – the acronym is always shown the wrong way round) are the areas of the Net in which game players can create virtual playgrounds for themselves and for each other. In MUDs (the generic name for all of these environments), people can battle against the forces of evil, chase dragons, build futuristic cities and create imaginary communities. MUDs vary greatly in character and atmosphere: in some it is bad form to attack other inhabitants, while in others it is absolutely essential. Many are set in a Tolkienesque atmosphere familiar to readers of fantasy fiction. Some settings are based on other literary references, TV programmes or films. In some, the landscape and its features are fixed, while in others players can make their own additions to the imaginary world.

The MUD community is a small but vibrant part of the Net, which attracts a few thousand fanatical people each year. Some players live more of their lives on-line than in the real world. Even imaginary MUD-based marriages have been performed between couples who have never met in person. However, MUDs can be useful and educational too: some host writers' workshops or offer other kinds of virtual teaching.

You do not usually need special software to try a MUD. Some are on the Web, but many rely on vivid textual descriptions instead of graphics. The latter types are used via telnet (see page 121). While the lack of graphics can be limiting, it can also free the imagination and make it possible to create environments – such as a 600-m-high spiralling pink whirlpool – that might look less convincing if presented graphically. (At least without a sizeable special effects budget and more time than most MUD designers have to spare.) For UK users, telneting to USA-based MUDs can sometimes be unbearably slow. However, with a wide variety of MUDs to choose from, it should be possible to find one more locally that responds much more quickly.

Everyone should try a MUD at least once just for the experience. Although they may not interest everyone, by creating environments which nurture fiercely bonded communities, MUDs represent a taste of what the Net may have in store for all Internet users in the future. However, they also encourage a lot of time-wasting on-line. Long-term exposure is definitely not recommended for anyone who is accessing the Net from home – at least not without limitless financial resources.

Networked games

Networked games are conventional computer games that can be linked together over the Internet. A typical example is Quake, which features a gory and violent surreal environment populated by monsters and other players. Most networked games are 'shoot-'em-ups' which rely on killing or disabling opponents. Unlike MUDs, which rely to some extent on imagination and on-line social skills, networked games do not offer much in the way of personal interaction. The attraction comes from having one or more real, as opposed to computer-generated, players to contend with. Very popular games, Quake among them, are sometimes made available on special server computers which are maintained by an IAP. If there is enough demand, IAPs may set up these services on request.

Publishing your own web pages

To publish your own pages you need two things: access to space on a web server, and suitable web publishing software. Many IAPs and on-line services have their own web servers, and customers are allowed to use these at no extra cost. This facility is described as 'space on a web server' because customers are given a small part of the storage space on the server's hard drive. Typically, this is about 5 megabytes, which is enough to publish a couple of books like this one, including the text, the cover art and all the illustrations. Alternatively, you can sometimes find free space on a web server elsewhere; a good example is the Geocities Project (*http://www.geocities.com*), which is an attempt to create a collection of on-line communities arranged according to different themes and interests. When publishing pages you need to check whether the type of information you are allowed to present is restricted in any way. Some IAPs and other web server facilities only allow information of a non-commercial nature. If you are publishing for a hobby these restrictions are not usually relevant.

The choice of web publishing software is endless. Pages are created using a simple computer language called HyperText Markup Language (HTML). HTML is really quite straight-forward. It uses standard English letters and characters arranged in special ways to specify how text, links and other information appear on a web page. It is possible to write HTML by typing text into a simple word processor, although this is not recommended as doing it this way is something of a chore. A better approach is to use HTML editing software. For more information about the mechanics of publishing pages see Appendix 4.

CASE HISTORY – Eileen

It may seem as though there is a lot to remember, but by sticking to the absolute basics to start with, almost anyone can create a home page. Eileen Herzberg, a freelance journalist and author living in Cornwall, found that creating her own pages was much easier than she thought it would be.

'It was surprisingly easy to put up my home page. I did have to phone my service provider a few times to ask some questions, although the people there didn't seem to mind. If I'd known it was this easy I'd have done it ages ago. The package I used – HomeSpinner, a shareware package for the Macintosh – was very straightforward, although to be honest I just stuck to the absolute basics. Publishing was very interesting though. One thing I found was that doing something simple like making the page a different colour had an enormous impact but didn't take much effort.

'I did run into a few problems. To start with I thought I had to put '<CR>' marks at the end of each line to break the text up into paragraphs, but then a friend showed me that putting '<P>' at the start of a paragraph and '</P>' at the end of it worked just as well and had the added benefit of making paragraphs the correct width no matter what size the screen was.

'But that's been about the only problem. So far it's been great. I've had a lot of feedback, which has been useful, and it's really fun getting email from complete strangers who read my pages.'

Creating a newsgroup

Although this is not usually something that most Internet users are likely to attempt, it can be surprisingly straightforward to do. The hardest part is dealing with the politics that surround newsgroups. If your newsgroup is to be successful, it needs to be available on as many newsgroup computers (news servers) as possible. This means you have to persuade the news administrators on the various servers that they should carry your group. Some carry all of them as a matter of course, while others are much more selective. To make the creation process easier for everyone, there is a fixed procedure that you have to follow. If you stick to the procedure, most administrators will carry it, if you do not, your group may be deleted ('rmgrouped' in the jargon) and made unavailable on many news computers.

The procedure is simple. Someone interested in a new group has to post a proposal called an RFD (Request for Discussion) in a special group called *news.announce.newgroups* Everyone who visits this group then says whether or not the group, and the group name, are a good idea. If the proposal gets lots of support, the proposer calls for a vote (CFV). If the vote is carried, the new group is created (newgrouped) by a designated news administrator. Following this procedure means that it is unnecessary for you to know about the technical details involved in creating a group – in effect, it is up to you to sort out the politics, and then someone else who is more technically minded creates the group on your behalf. (While the technical process required to create a group is straightforward and can be done from any computer, a group created without going through the discussion process will be considered a 'rogue' group and not treated seriously. As mentioned above, this typically means that it will be rmgrouped on most news servers, rendering it useless.)

This process applies specifically to international groups. However, a similar procedure is followed to set up more local ones. For example, to create a UK-only group (specifically one that starts with 'uk.'), votes and discussions are posted to *uk.net.news.config* instead of *news.announce.newgroups* Otherwise, the process is identical.

Proposals for both local and international groups need to be formal in character and carefully thought through. It is best if the proposed group has a full charter, which lists what can and cannot be posted and also says whether or not someone has editorial control over it.

Discussions about new groups can be quite heated, and anyone who wants to create one should be warned that some of the comments – especially in the *uk.net.news.config* group – can seem rather petty and narrow-minded. Much of the discussion centres around the names of groups and whether they match their intended function. UK news administrators are very keen to make sure that group names make sense and fit into a clear structure, and their motives are not always understood by outsiders who simply want to create a new group to support a hobby or personal interest. For example, the group *uk.lifts* was removed because the name was supposedly ambiguous. In the event, a group called *uk.transport.ride-sharing* was created in its place. However, soon afterwards, one prankster set up an unauthorised group called *uk.vertical.people-transporters* presumably to make the point that some people might prefer a more relaxed approach to the naming of groups.

In the UK it is important to remember that many news servers are based at universities. (In fact, the UK academic network – JANET – is a major part of the Internet in the UK.) This has implications for the kind of groups that are acceptable. One reason why the UK does not have a collection of *uk.sex.* groups in the way that other countries do, is because academic news administrators worry that students will waste time and computing resources on something that is not relevant to their studies. Similarly, any group that is related to a commercial enterprise – even a book or magazine publishing house – is unlikely to be accepted because of the Net's tradition of allowing only non-commercial use.

These political considerations can be a minefield for anyone attempting to create a group, and, unfortunately, there is no easy way to find out what will or will not offend the people who run the UK's news servers, short of actually going through the process and learning the hard way. Full details of how to create a new newsgroup are posted regularly to *news.announce.newusers* and in the UK to *uk.net.news.config* Details are also available on the Web at *http://www.usenet.org.uk*

This process does not apply to the *alt.* collection of groups (see Chapter 5), and they are more or less out of control. A group called *alt.config* is used for a loose discussion of new *alt.* group subjects, but many news administrators either accept all new *alt.* groups without question or ignore them completely. Either way, it is much easier to create an *alt.* group than any other (proposers simply have to follow the steps that are posted there regularly), and the politics are not quite so prevalent.

CHOOSING AN INTERNET ACCESS PROVIDER

THERE ARE now hundreds of IAPs in the UK, ranging from those with tens of thousands of subscribers to those that have only a few hundred. Although they all do more or less the same thing – offer you a basic connection to the Internet over a telephone link – the level of service they provide can vary tremendously.

The information included in the publicity and advertising materials offered by most services is not detailed enough to base a choice on. The best ways to compare IAPs are to read magazine reviews and to ask for personal recommendations. You can also find out a lot about an IAP by asking the kinds of questions suggested in this chapter.

Unfortunately, irrespective of which IAP you choose, you will almost certainly have problems sooner or later. The Internet is still partly an experimental service, and because of this many IAPs seem to think they can offer appropriately experimental levels of customer care. The situation is improving slowly, but the reality is that your connection, together with the various Internet services at the other end of it, are unlikely to work flawlessly all the time. Even if it seems to start well, the service may get worse over time. IAPs tend to suffer from growing pains; for example, a service that was doing well with a thousand or so subscribers may start having serious difficulties when that number doubles, although after perhaps another six months the problems may be solved and its service may become dependable again. Computer systems can surprise the unwary in this way: once they are working near their limits, a ten per cent increase in demand can create a 90 per cent reduction in service. Most IAPs do not have the experience to be able to predict situations like this, and they tend to deal with problems after they have started happening rather than plan ahead to avoid them. In short, there are no absolute guarantees of quality. However, by following the advice below, it should be easy to spot some of the more reliable companies.

When comparing IAPs, it is worth remembering that while some charge a set-up fee followed by monthly payments, others charge only the latter. Since both sums are relatively small – between £5 and £25 – you may want to consider treating each subscription to an IAP as one month's trial. Although you have to pay for these trials, if you start by drawing up a short list of three or four based on personal recommendations and magazine surveys, you can try them out at relatively low cost before deciding which one suits you best. One disadvantage of this approach is that you will have to change your email address each time. But initially, you may find you spend most of your time exploring instead of using the service seriously. Of course, this option is not available for those IAPs that insist on being paid a lump sum for a longer period in advance. Some offer both monthly and lump-sum payment facilities – if in doubt, ask.

A possible disadvantage with this approach is the clashing software problem described on page 37. However, a good IAP will be able to guide you to a solution – and the speed and efficiency with which the support staff do this is a useful indication of an IAP's competence.

What to look for in an IAP

It is possible to assess the level of service offered by an IAP objectively. When choosing between competing providers you should consider the following points.

Speed

The obvious measure of an IAP's speed is the speed of its modems. The simple rule of thumb is that an IAP's modems should be at least as fast, and preferably faster, than the one that you plan to use. Modem speeds are shown as a number – either 28.8k, 33.6k or 57k. The larger the number the faster the connection. The first of these is now obsolete, the second is the current standard, and the third will be the new standard from about the beginning of 1998. (For more information about modems and modem speeds see Appendix 2.)

But there is more to speed than the modem connection. Significant differences exist in the rate at which IAPs can access information from far-off parts of the Internet and deliver it to you. These differences can be very obvious, for example, with some IAPs, it can become impossible to read certain web pages or copy particular software from the Internet because the information takes an unreasonably long time to get to you, especially during busy periods.

Unfortunately, you cannot check for these kinds of problems without first making a connection, and this means signing up for the service. However, some magazines publish objective tests which compare the performance of different IAPs. It is a good idea to refer to these before making a choice.

It can also be worth asking the IAP about its own connections to the Internet. Some smaller IAPs re-sell the services of larger ones through a slow and relatively cheap connection. If you come across an IAP that does this, it makes sense to cut out the middle man and go directly to its supplier to get your connection. A company that has a thousand-plus customers but is connected to the Internet over a single, relatively slow permanent connection will have serious problems keeping information flowing at a reasonable rate.

You should also check how long it takes for newsgroup messages to appear on a news server and for email to arrive at its destination. In this respect, some of the larger IAPs offer a very poor service indeed. Their facilities are permanently overloaded, and email messages can take hours to pass through the IAP's computers to their destinations. This is a serious consideration for anyone who uses the Internet professionally. If you are using email to deliver something to meet a deadline, using an IAP with a slow email service can be more trouble than it is worth. And of course, if someone sends you a message you should be able to read it almost immediately, instead of a few hours later.

As yet, magazines do not include tests of email and newsgroup delivery speeds in their surveys because objective trials are quite hard to set up. So, unfortunately, the only way to test this part of a service is to do it for yourself. You can easily find out how long emails take to arrive at their destinations by arranging to send one to a friend and asking him or her to tell you when it arrives. Email headers (described in Appendix 5.) also contain time and date information about how long the message took to get from your computer to its destination.

Another point to watch for is the time it takes to get a connection to the Internet, especially during busy periods. If too many people call the service at the same time, they will not all be able to get through at once, and some will be left listening to a 'busy' signal.

In the spring of 1997, America Online (AOL) created a disaster for itself in the USA when it changed its pricing scheme from an hourly rate to a flat, monthly fee. The service was deluged by more people attempting to connect to it than it could handle, and it became almost impossible to get a connection at any time of day other than the early hours of the morning. The resulting lawsuits from disgruntled customers cost AOL hundreds of millions of dollars. This is one reason why on-line services are not very keen to use a flat-fee pricing policy.

Ideally, you should always be able to get a connection the first time you try. Having to dial two or three times once in a while is not perfect but is still acceptable. Having to dial ten times is completely unacceptable – although some IAPs have attempted to offer this level of service to their customers. Smaller IAPs can suffer from the same kind of problem on a more modest scale.

The number of times you try to connect is directly related to the number of modems your IAP has installed at its headquarters, and also to the number of customers who are trying to use the service. This is usually called the 'modem to user ratio'. Five users per modem is a very respectable figure, and the average is usually about ten. Thirty is an unacceptably high number; if your IAP's modem to user ratio is as bad as this, you will certainly have problems trying to get through during busy periods.

To some extent this ratio also depends on the reliability of the modems. With thousands of modems, it is a near certainty that at any one time at least one of them will not be working. As more and more people call and start using the working modems, the chance of getting a faulty one increases. These kinds of problems can be even more annoying than busy signals because each failed call costs a small amount of money – usually 5p – whereas getting a busy signal costs you nothing.

Finally, you should also check if there are any known compatibility problems between the modem you use and the ones your IAP uses. Problems arise in the form of 'dropped lines' – connections which stop for no apparent reason – and connections which fail to complete. If you are having these difficulties, either your modem is not set up properly or your IAP is having trouble. In both cases the IAP should be able to sort out the problem.

Support

Support starts with your first phone call to the IAP, even if you are only enquiring about the service. If problems occur, you need to be sure that help is available. Many IAPs still expect an unrealistic level of technical expertise from their customers. You can eliminate these by making a short investigative phone call. Start by making it clear that you are a beginner and by asking some very basic technical questions. If the answers are far beyond your level of understanding, cross the IAP off your list (they will not be any better at helping you when real problems occur with the service). It is also important to check the times when technical support is available. Help that is provided only during office hours will be of no use if you intend to use your connection from home during evenings and weekends.

Some IAPs provide their own newsgroups, which their customers can use to support each other. These are ideal for slightly more experienced users who want support when attempting more advanced tasks such as creating their own web pages. Newsgroups specific to an IAP will be more helpful than more general support newsgroups because other contributors will be familiar with the IAP's individual technical quirks.

Other options include email support – although this assumes that someone on the other end will actually take the time to reply to your questions – and 'autoresponder' support, which is an email service for frequently asked questions (FAQs) that does not require any human intervention (see page 47). Again, the problem with all of these is assessing the level of technical expertise they are aimed at. It is one of the tragedies of the industry that very few support staff have much of an insight into the kind of frustration that beginners face when things go wrong. It is well worth taking the time to track down an IAP whose staff show some appreciation of a non-technical person's point of view.

The other aspect of support is much more straightforward and can be summed up in one word – reliability. A good IAP can anticipate an increase in demand before it arises and will also have a number of backup facilities installed. If something goes wrong, or if new systems have to be installed to improve the service, you will not be left to suffer while the work is being done. Unfortunately, disasters do happen, and it is impossible for an IAP's staff to protect themselves and their customers from every possible problem. Backup systems, which duplicate vital components to improve reliability, do occasionally fail in unexpected ways. However, it is reasonable to expect that your email account will always be available, that email messages will never be lost and that you should be able to use the newsgroup service whenever you want to.

Not all IAPs can offer even this basic level of service. Newsgroups cause perennial problems because of the huge and ever-increasing amounts of information involved, and even the email system can be accident-prone. It is not unheard of for email to be 'bounced' when sent to a valid address because an IAP's systems were suffering from a glitch at the time. This is a particularly annoying fault, because the missing email leaves no trace.

Free software

An IAP should give you 'click-and-go' software that does not require advanced technical skills, but the software offered by many often falls short of this ideal. The best IAPs do their utmost to hide the complexities of their software from you, while the worst ones provide software that makes the installation process seem like a technical nightmare.

Start by checking how much work you will need to do to get the service working. How much information do you need to type in? Is it obvious what should be typed where? Again, if you make it clear you are a complete beginner and the person at the customer services desk insists on using terms such as 'IP number' and 'nodename', then this IAP may not be the right one for you. Reassurances that the installation process is 'really very easy' should also be taken with a large pinch of salt if offered without supporting evidence.

Next, ask which software is available. At the very least you will be offered a web browser, usually Netscape Navigator or Microsoft's Internet Explorer. This is very much the bare minimum needed to connect to the Internet. A more useful offer would include separate off-line email and newsreading software. (Facilities for newsgroups and email are included in web browsers, but these are very crude and clumsy compared with those available in dedicated newsgroup and email software.)

You can test certain software before you commit yourself to signing up with an IAP. Free versions or trial copies of the packages offered by most IAPs are given away on magazines' cover disks. However, these trials are not as useful as they might seem, because you will not be able to use the Internet properly without a connection. But you can at least have a go at installing the software before going on-line, and see how easy – or difficult – it is to get it working.

It is also worth remembering that once you are on-line, you will be able to pick and choose from the huge quantity of software that is available on the Internet. An initial start-up pack from an IAP should really be considered as a first step on to the Internet and not something that ties you to any particular software. Once on-line you will be able to find software that suits your needs more closely.

Questions to ask

Below are the questions that an IAP should be able to answer to your satisfaction. You will probably find that you do not need to ask all of these, as dubious answers to the earlier questions will render the later, more detailed, questions unnecessary.

How long have you been in business?

The answer to this simple question can tell you a lot if you read between the lines. Companies that have been in business for only a few months should be treated with a degree of suspicion; some companies have asked customers for payment for a full year in advance before disappearing overnight. If the time is very short, it might be worth asking what the background of the company's founders is. Of course, the fact that a company has been trading only for a short time does not necessarily mean that it is staffed by crooks, or that it is any more likely to fail than a company that has been around for a much longer period. But this is still useful information to have, especially when seen within the context of the answers to your other questions.

How much are your services?

Most services charge a small set-up fee, followed by monthly payments. These are usually made by credit or debit card, although occasionally you will be asked to fill in a direct debit form. Ask which payment methods are available.

If you are VAT-registered, ask if VAT invoices are available. Some IAPs will only provide these annually, in return for full payment for a year in advance. Even if you are not VAT-registered, ask about annual payment options – you can often get a sizeable discount by paying this way.

Do you provide local call access?

Local call access means that your calls to the IAP's computers are charged at the local call rate – or in a few cases, because of telephone company politics, at a slightly more expensive rate very close to it. IAPs are either national or local. The ones with national coverage usually offer local call access across the whole of the UK, which sometimes – but not always – includes outlying areas such as the Channel Islands and perhaps Northern Ireland. Local call access is available in one of two ways. The first scheme relies on a network of telephone numbers which cover the UK. You can call any number you like, but only those closest to you will be charged at the local rate. Working out which number is nearest and cheapest, and also keeping track of all this information if you travel, can be something of a challenge. The other, and best, option is a single telephone number charged at the fixed rate, which you can call from anywhere in the UK. This is far more convenient, especially if you travel a lot.

Local IAPs use a more limited version of the same scheme, covering only part of the country. They may offer a small set of access numbers, and again you will be able to use these at the local rate only if you fall into the usual local-rate area. Local IAPs are smaller and sometimes offer a better service than the national ones. However, if you move out of the area you will be forced to make a choice between changing to a different IAP or paying for long-distance calls.

Which software do you provide?

As mentioned above, a web browser – Netscape Navigator and Microsoft's Internet Explorer more or less have a monopoly in this part of the market – should be considered the bare minimum. A much more attractive answer to this question would be a package that includes separate newsgroup and email facilities to complement the browser. Qualcomm's Eudora and Forte's Free Agent are free packages that are often supplied and have a good record with users. Demon Internet offers a free-trial version of its Turnpike package to new subscribers. Opinions are mixed about Turnpike: some people seem to be very happy with it and find it easy to use; others find it badly designed and clumsy. The advantage of a free trial is that you can decide for yourself.

What technical support do you provide?

Find out when telephone support is available and also what other kinds of support are on offer. Does the IAP maintain its own support newsgroups for customers? Is there help available on the Web in the form of answers to frequently asked questions? Does it have an autoresponder service? Some IAPs even provide their own (paper) magazines – although at worst these can be nothing more than advertising and public relations on behalf of the service.

How many users do you have?

This is not a technical question, but asking it does let you know about the size of the company that you are dealing with. It also tells you how informed the technical support and sales staff are – it is not unreasonable to assume that they should be able to answer this question, although unfortunately not all IAPs have staff who can do this.

Who provides your connection? How fast is it?

The ideal answer to the first question is that the company does not buy a connection from anyone but uses its own lines to connect to the Internet directly. As regards the second question, even if the answers sound impressive, with tales of plenty of fast connections to the USA and Europe, you should bear in mind that in practice the speed also depends on the number of users. You can even do a quick calculation to find the ratio of the total bandwidth of your IAP's links to the Internet to its number of users. The greater the bandwidth per user, the faster the connection is likely to be. This is only a very rough guide, and other factors, such as the speed and efficiency of the IAP's computer systems, will also influence the speed. But you should have at least some idea of how fast the connection can be in theory and compare this figure with that of other IAPs.

How many mailboxes do you offer?

For family use, it is essential to be able to use more than one mailbox. Some IAPs offer 'unlimited' email addresses. The information after the '@' sign in the address is unique to you – in the jargon you have a 'unique nodename', which contains a word or name that you specify, followed by your IAP's name – for example: *@mychosenword.someiap.co.uk* With this system you can use as many names before the '@' sign as you like, for example:
myname@mychosenword.someiap.co.uk or
anothername@mychosenword.someiap.co.uk or
mycatsname@mychosenword.someiap.co.uk

Other IAPs give you one or more (typically five) fixed addresses. They specify exactly what goes before the '@' as well as after it. This is a less flexible option. In this case it is useful to ask what choice you get, if any, about your addresses. Some IAPs give you no say at all and expect you to use addresses that start *qx245@....* Apart from being impersonal, these are also very hard for others to remember.

Do you know of any modems that cause problems with your network?

Apart from being a useful titbit of information, this will help you to gauge the sophistication and efficiency of the sales staff and could give you some useful insights into the way the company works as a whole. 'I don't know' is a slightly worrying answer at this point, although serious concern is necessary only if the question is not then referred to an expert.

Do you offer web space?

If web space is available, ask about the size. For ordinary users there is no particular advantage to having 10Mb instead of 5Mb. Most people will use only a fraction of that. As a rough guide, 0.5Mb is too little, 1Mb is a bit cramped, 3Mb is a comfortable minimum and 5Mb should be enough for almost any use – unless you plan to include a very large number of detailed photographs or diagrams, in which case you may need even more.

If you have more serious requirements or plan to run the site on a semi-professional basis, you should also ask about any restrictions on how busy your site is allowed to be. (In the jargon these are known as 'bandwidth restrictions'.) If you get a lot of visitors, each of whom wants to see a great deal of information, you may be asked to change to a commercial server, which you will be expected to pay for. Although this seems harsh there is a good reason for it – too much interest in a single site can become a drain on resources, and access to everyone else's sites will slow down dramatically as a result. Fortunately, this will be a problem in only a very few instances. Finally, ask what you have to do to set up the web pages, and what your URL will be. If it is long and clumsy you will get fewer visitors.

Do you offer POP3 email?

If the answer is no, you will be able to read your mail only by calling in to your IAP. You will not be able to read it from abroad or from a cybercafé. This might not be a problem for you, but in general, POP3 email (described in Chapter 7) is a useful option.

What extra facilities are available on your web server?

Other options include CGI scripts and Real Audio facilities, which can be used to add sound and music to your site. (CGI scripts are described in more detail in on pages 223–4.) Although most beginners will not need these, they are worth considering if you plan to take the time to develop a more impressive site.

Do you maintain a news server?

Some companies do not maintain a news server of their own. Instead, they suggest their users use a different organisation's server, and hope for the best. The problem with this approach is that if something goes wrong with the newsgroup service, you will not have anyone to complain to. Some companies offer the worst of both worlds by supplying a newsgroup server but claiming that it is 'unsupported'. This means that they may try to keep it working, but customers should not expect too much from it. It goes without saying that any company that does this should be given a wide berth.

CHOOSING HARDWARE FOR THE INTERNET

TO USE the Internet you need two things. The first is a computer. The second is a link between the computer and the Internet itself.

Choosing a computer

Computers come in two types – 'traditional' personal computers (PCs), which first became available in the early 1980s and have been improving steadily since then, and the much newer 'Network Computers' (NCs) which are due to be launched towards the end of 1997 or early in 1998.

Personal computers

You can use almost any personal computer (PC), although, of course, more powerful ones will give better results. The most important things to check are the availability of Internet software for your computer system and the speed at which it can handle incoming and outgoing information.

Any PC built after about 1993 which works with Windows 3.1, or a later version, or any Apple Macintosh that works with System 7, or a later version, will be able to use most of the latest Internet software. Users of more modern computers which can use Windows 95, 97 or NT on the PC, and System 7.5 onwards on the Mac will be able to use all the latest software, without exception.

If you have a personal computer other than those listed above, your use of the Internet will be limited. This is because your computer will not be able to read any type of information other than text; the full-colour graphics of the World Wide Web will be inaccessible, as will some of the special software needed to use an on-line service. What is and is not possible for any particular computer is changing continuously. For the latest information you should check one of the relevant specialist magazines.

Network Computers

Today's personal computers are far too complicated and expensive for many home users, and even business users have found them to be more expensive than they at first seemed because the cost of maintaining them is much greater than the initial outlay.

Network Computers are an attempt to solve both these problems. They are designed to be cheaper and easier to use than a personal computer. Instead of working with software that has been installed internally, NCs retrieve it from a network (the Internet, an Intranet or a more traditional business network). Because of this, NCs need only enough working space to store the software while it is in use. Some NCs are even simpler than this and are a modern version of the old-fashioned display and keyboard combinations that were used in large centralised computer systems in the 1950s and 1960s. These NCs are very simple indeed – all the work is done on a larger computer system elsewhere, and they are used only to type in information and display the results.

NCs come in a variety of shapes and sizes. Some are budget PCs which – unlike existing PCs – cannot have new memory or other extras added to them. This makes them simpler to design, build and maintain. Others take a completely new approach, which is unrelated to existing PC designs. These use the Java system (explained in Appendix 4) to create a computer that is essentially a web browser in a box.

Home users are unlikely to find NCs useful until the bandwidth problem is solved. The existing telephone system is far too slow to make the 'remote software' concept a practical option, because it takes too long for the software to be copied over a telephone line. Cable and satellite systems do not have this disadvantage, and the combination of these with an NC system has obvious potential. By the early part of the twenty-first century it is quite likely that the NC idea will be successful and will probably combine telephone and TV services with Internet access. In the meantime, there are suggestions that a number of companies, including those that make computer-game consoles, are experimenting with adding Internet and perhaps TV-related facilities to their products using more conventional technology.

If you are considering any of these systems, it would be wise to wait for this new potential market to stabilise and standardise. You should be wary of any new products that are not yet standardised across the whole industry, as they stand a good chance of becoming obsolete very quickly.

For business and corporate users, the low-maintenance approach of the NC concept has obvious attractions. But the usefulness of an NC relies upon the speed and dependability of its supporting network, and some companies are finding that maintenance costs are simply being transferred rather than reduced. There are also questions of security when information is centralised, and 'future proofing' – how well will the network cope with the new load if a company expands? Issues like these require the skills of an experienced network consultant. Although some parts of the computer trade are touting NCs as a solution for all kinds of problems, in practice they bring new ones of their own. These need to be assessed carefully when you are deciding whether or not an NC system is the best possible solution.

Links between computers and the Internet

Although most people use what is known as a modem link, this is in fact the slowest way to connect a computer to the Internet. Faster, more expensive, options are available, although these will be beyond the means of most home users.

Choosing a modem

A modem (modulator-demodulator) is a unit that converts computer information into 'rasps and squeals' that can be sent over a telephone line to another computer. Modems for personal computers are now relatively affordable and available over the counter in computer stores, and in fact some new computers are sold with a modem already built-in. But how can you tell whether a modem is any good? And if you already have a computer, how do you decide which modem to buy?

As with other computer components, the price of modems has come down dramatically since the middle of the 1990s. As a result, there is very little reason to settle for a modem that is not of very high quality. The main points you should check for are discussed below.

BT approval When the Internet first started to become popular in 1994, 'illegal' modems – those that had not been tested and approved by BT – were widely available. Although it was illegal to use them on the UK telephone network, it was perfectly legal to buy and sell them. Some of these modems had minor compatibility problems, such as an inability to recognise a 'busy' signal. But they were also significantly cheaper than certified modems, and some people took the risk and ignored the legalities.

With the explosion of interest in on-line services, modems are much more of a commodity item now, and this shady practice is no longer necessary. Almost all modems are now fully BT-approved and marked with the green triangle symbol (as opposed to the red circle that indicates the absence of approval). It is still wise to check, just to make sure, because there is no reason why you should settle for a non-approved modem when an approved one with the same features at a similar price is available.

Internal/external modems Internal modems are supplied as a circuit card without a case that needs to be fitted inside your computer. External modems sit outside the computer at the end of a special cable.

Unless you are very experienced you should *always choose an external modem*. They are slightly more expensive, but you will almost certainly save yourself hours of frustration when you try to install the modem and get it working. Internal modems are notoriously difficult to set up properly and require a combination of technical knowledge, persistence and –

apparently at least – plain luck before you can get them to work. External modems are much more straightforward to set up.

When buying an external modem, check whether or not a certain type of adapter is included in the package. The connectors on the back of a Windows computer can have either 9 pins or 25. If you have an adapter you will be able to use either of these. It is likely that you will need an adapter, so you may save yourself time if you get one on the spot. These adapters cost a pound or two at most, and it can be worth asking for one to be included for free just to close the sale. If you have a Macintosh, make sure your modem includes an MCC8 cable to fit your Macintosh's serial socket.

Speed is the single most important factor to consider when you are buying a modem as it sets an upper limit on how quickly information can move between your computer and the Internet. This can make a significant difference to your phone bill. Slower modems are adequate for occasional use but leave you no room for expansion if you find your interest in the Internet starts to take off. Faster modems are, of course, more expensive, but prices are dropping steadily. At the moment the very fastest models available cost about £200, while the slowest models start at about £40. A peculiarity of the modem market is that while more expensive models than those mentioned above are available, they do not go any faster and seem to offer few, if any, advantages over their cheaper siblings.

Until recently, a confusing system of code letters (the 'V' standard) was used to describe modem speeds, but in most advertising this has now been replaced with a straight measure of the speed in bits per second (bps) or thousands of bits per second (kbps.) The latter two are a direct indication of the speed at which the modem works: a 28.8kbps modem will move information twice as quickly as a 14.4kbps model, and a 57.6kbps model will move it twice as fast again. You will sometimes see this shortened form of the speed with a 'k' instead of the '.' – thus 33k6 means the same as 33.6kbps.

A 9600bps modem is adequate only for very occasional email, while a 14.4kbps is the absolute minimum needed for Internet use. More serious users need a faster modem: 33.6kbps has leap-

Speed (bps)	Speed (kbps)	Code
2400	2.4	V.22bis
9600	9.6	V.32
14400	14.4	V.32bis
28800	28.8	V.34
33600	33.6	V.34 (A separate code was not agreed for this speed)
57600	57.6	(No code or standard agreed yet)

frogged 28.8kbps as the standard speed, although in practice the maximum speed is impossible to reach on anything other than a crystal-clear telephone line. Many people find that 33.6kbps modems work only at the slightly slower speed of 31.2kbps. This depends on the quality of the modem and the telephone line and the modem's compatibility with the IAP's modem at the other end. When looking for a modem, read comparative reviews very carefully to see if this problem is mentioned.

The 57.6kbps speed suffers from similar problems. Modems can work at this speed only by stretching the limits of the UK telephone system and by relying on special techniques that bypass some of its shortcomings. These techniques work only one-way – from the Internet to your computer – so in practice these modems work at two speeds: 57.6kbps when receiving information, and the more usual 33.6kbps when sending it. Most people receive much more information than they send, so this is a relatively minor drawback. These very high-speed modems are even more susceptible to telephone line noise and interference than their slower predecessors, and in practice you will not usually get them to go any faster than about 44kbps.

At the time of writing, a proper standard for this speed has yet to be agreed. Unfortunately, this means that not all 57.6kbps modems are guaranteed to work at their top speed with each other, because the technology used by the two main manufacturers – US Robotics (x2) and Motorola (dialX) – is not completely compatible. If you have a modem of one type and your IAP or on-line service uses the other type, you will not be able to take advantage of the speed increase. If you attempt a connection, the modems will still work together, but will 'fall back' to the slower speed of 33.6kbps. However, when the system works correctly it obviously speeds up the transfer of information significantly. And compared with the cost of a single ISDN line (see page 195) this 57.6kbps option offers exceptionally good value for money.

'Flash' modems use special chips inside them to hold their operating software. The operating software is fixed in most modems, but in a flash modem it can be changed by copying the latest version from the Internet.

Extras and special deals

Many modems include free trial offer software for the major on-line services. While this should not sway your decision as to which modem to buy – these offers are freely available elsewhere – the free trials are a useful bonus to have.

Some modems are now being sold with Internet access. When you buy the modem, you also pay for a year's access to a service provider. These deals can seem appealing, if only because they save you a certain amount of research and shopping around. But you should never sign up for a deal like this without thoroughly checking the credentials and reputation of the service provider in the usual way (see Appendix 1).

Finally, it is well worth looking into the extra features that a modem may offer. All modems can send and receive fax messages – although remember that you will be able to send only a fax that has been created inside your computer. (If you want to send a map or hand-drawn diagram, you will need an extra piece of hardware called a scanner, which can copy an image from the outside world into your computer, or a digital camera, which can copy in photographs without requiring film or film processing.)

Some modems also include voice-mail facilities, which transform the modem into an answering machine, complete with a pre-recorded message and the ability to store incoming messages as recordings inside your computer. This is a useful feature, although it means that you have to leave your computer turned on all the time. In practice, an external fax/answering machine is usually a more convenient and more reliable, although also a more expensive option.

Portable modems

So that a modem can be used with a portable computer, the circuitry has been shrunk to a size that will fit into the wafer-thin PCMCIA cards used in portable computers. PCMCIA modems work in exactly the same way as their full-sized counterparts but they are significantly more expensive. From the point of view of installation and setting up, they are equivalent to external modems.

One point to check is whether the modem can be set to work ('homologised') with foreign phone systems – an important consideration for anyone who plans to spend a lot of time abroad. Also, check the sockets on the modem for any sign of weakness. If it is likely to get heavy use it is important to be sure that this part of the system will not fail at an inconvenient moment. If you are travelling abroad, remember that almost every country has a different-shaped telephone socket, so you will need suitable plug adapters.

Cellular modems (data cards)

While conventional modems use the existing telephone network, cellular modems use the cellular networks built for users of portable phones. These modems are still fairly expensive to buy and use but they do offer the advantage of truly wireless communication with the Internet. At the time of writing, the maximum speed available is 9600bps, which is slow enough to make call charges something of a worry for all but the richest of users. Some modems are starting to use a 'data compression' system which makes information take up less space before it is sent over the network. This can improve transmission speeds significantly, although it will not work with files that have already been compressed on a computer. In practice, this means that email, web and newsgroup access should be up to four times faster, but anyone intending to download software from the Internet will find it much quicker and cheaper to use a telephone modem.

Remember also that cellular calls are not known for being secure. The older analogue cellular networks can be monitored by anyone with simple and affordable equipment, which can be bought over the counter in many parts of the UK. Digital networks are more secure, but even so it is wise to encrypt all email, especially if it contains sensitive information.

When considering a cellular modem check that your Internet service provider or on-line service provider is sure that it will work with their system. Some companies, such as Demon, have negotiated deals with certain cellular phone companies, so check also if there are any special offers available that combine the two services.

Faster options

The maximum speed the current telephone network is capable of is 57.6kbps, and unless British Telecom or a consortium of cable TV companies invest in a national rewiring scheme to replace old-fashioned copper cables with high-speed fibre-optic links – something that seems extremely unlikely at the moment – Internet users will have to look at other ways to speed up their connections. Some options offer much better value for money than others.

ISDN

ISDN (Integrated Services Digital Network) is a digital-only connection to the existing telephone system. The cumbersome process by which modems convert information into sound (and back again at the receiving end) is bypassed completely. As a result, ISDN systems offer higher transfer speeds and can also create a connection much more quickly – typically within a second or so, as opposed to ten seconds for a conventional modem. Instead of modems, ISDN systems use 'terminal adapters' (TAs). These connect your computer directly to the exchange over the link.

Another advantage of ISDN is that it can use a clever system known as dial-back. With a dial-back connection, your IAP's computer will call your ISDN link whenever information is available but hang up before the call is completed. This costs the IAP nothing but lets your ISDN connection know who the call was from. Your side of the link will then immediately call back automatically to retrieve the information. Dial-back can simulate the permanent connection offered by a leased line (see page 198) at a fraction of the cost. Unfortunately, after experimenting with this option, most UK's IAPs seem to have decided not to offer it to their customers, although this may change in the future.

If you are a professional Internet user, ISDN can save you money (although only if you use the Internet almost continually). It also has the potential for very fast fax transmissions using the latest generation of 'group 4' fax machines (existing models use the older and slower 'group 3' system), video conferencing and high-quality audio connections.

However, the savings are not as clear cut or as certain as they might be. In Japan and Germany, ISDN systems are available for the same price as conventional phone lines. In the UK, BT maintains a complex pricing scheme which gives you the choice of trading off an initial outlay against an annual call allowance in a number of different ways. Installation charges are extortionate, as are line-rental costs. Call charges are the same as those for conventional calls, although if you choose a payment scheme with a call allowance you will, in effect, be getting calls for free – or at least as a compensation for the huge increase in line rental.

Some cable TV companies will fit and run an ISDN line for much less than this, although most seem to charge broadly the same amounts as BT does. If you are considering ISDN it is a good idea to check with your cable TV company to see what kind of deal it can offer you. Some also offer free off-peak telephone calls, which can save you money even if you have a modem. In either case, you may be able to arrange significant savings for yourself by asking a few simple questions.

ISDN hardware is more complex than the typical socket-in-the-wall most people are used to. There are actually two variants: ISDN2, which is suitable for home users, and ISDN30, which is suitable for large businesses.

ISDN2 offers two 64kbps channels (known, for no obvious reason, as type Bs) and a separate signalling channel which runs at 16kbps (known as a type D). The two faster lines can be used at the same time to give a total speed of 128kbps – the signalling line is more or less an 'overhead' line and does not contribute to the speed of the system. It is vital to note that at this higher speed the call charges can start to mount up because the two lines are counted as separate calls running in parallel.

ISDN30 offers 30 'B' channels and 1 fast 'D' channel. It can run at up to 2000kbps. (2mbps). It is usually supplied as a fibre-optic link and is much more expensive than ISDN2. ISDN30 was originally designed for businesses that need multiple telephone lines, and not as an Internet connection, so it is quite hard to run all 30 channels in parallel as a 2000kbps Internet link. Some companies, such as Mercury, will very occasionally fit an ISDN30 system for free in return for a guaranteed number of calls over the course of a year. It is sometimes possible to negotiate deals like this on any ISDN30 line, although some companies will be more receptive to this than others. An important consideration with ISDN is whether or not your IAP supports it. The smaller providers are unlikely to do so, as it requires a sizeable investment.

With so many hardware options, pricing schemes, questions about availability and also its future in the UK, the whole area of ISDN is a very complex one. Anyone considering an ISDN30 system for their business should think seriously about hiring a telecommunications consultant to help ease the process, because linking the switchboard with the business's computer network and from there to the rest of the world is not a job for the technically inexperienced. A reputable consultant should be able to oversee the process and can help to prevent expensive mistakes, for example, leaving a 'trapdoor' open to the exchange which hackers can exploit easily to give themselves free telephone calls.

ISDN hardware

Although the technology used is rather different, ISDN terminal adapters (TAs) are now being sold in much the same way as modems. The costs are comparable, and TAs are also available in internal and external varieties. The external option (as with traditional modems) is a better bet, as setting up and installation are simpler.

TAs are more demanding of computer hardware, and any computer built before about 1995 may have problems coping with the speed of the link, especially when two ISDN lines are running in parallel. When looking for an ISDN TA, check for the following:

- **V.110 or V.120 connections** These are the standard systems used for ISDN and offer the ability to link two channels together to create a 128kbps connection
- an **'analogue port'** Somewhere to plug in a phone. If your ISDN link is used only by your computer you may not need this facility.

Leased lines

If you run a medium-sized business and your staff need regular access to the Internet, an even faster and more expensive option is the leased line. A leased line is a permanent direct connection to the Internet. Mail appears in your mailbox as soon as it arrives, instead of being held at your IAP's mail computer until you dial-in. You can also maintain your own private connection to the Usenet news service. The most important advantages of a leased line are:

- **speed** Your connection is permanently available. To some extent, you can 'queue jump' users of dial-up accounts. Leased lines can also be much faster than dial-up links – tens of times faster in some cases
- **the possibility of creating your own personal web site with your own computers** This is done instead of hiring time and space on someone else's system – typically an IAP's. Using your own computers saves you monthly rental charges and means you can make your web site as big as you would like it to be with no restrictions. It also means that you get exclusive use of your web server and do not have to share bandwidth with other users whose sites may 'steal' it from yours, making your own site slower.

Leased lines are very expensive. Prices start at about £7,000 a year for a 64kbps connection, and increase to as much as you can bear to pay, depending on the speed of the link and on the length of the line (a leased line must go from A to B, definite points). You get a fully professional level of service with engineers who can be paged immediately whenever a fault develops, and often 24-hour access to support calls. At this price a leased line is obviously not something that most private individuals can consider. But medium-sized businesses will find it can save money compared with the cost of equipping hundreds of staff with modems and dial-up accounts. And, of course, all the computer equipment and information can be kept on-site, where it is easier to maintain and manage.

Apart from the physical cost of the line itself, it is important to be aware that a leased line has implications for the security of your system. Because your computer system is now permanently on-line, it is open to millions of Internet users. You have to take precautions to make sure that the system is as secure as it can be. (For more details about this see Chapter 8.) This means that installing a leased line is a major undertaking, and you should consider and cost out all the implications before deciding to install one.

A number of companies have recently started to offer 'pseudo-leased' lines, which use a telephone link via a modem that is left permanently connected. It offers the advantages of a leased line at much lower cost – typically less than £2,000 a year. Although these pseudo-leased lines are slower than ISDN – typical speeds are 33.6kbps – they can be cost-effective for anyone who uses the Internet professionally and would like to be able to set up a private web server for a relatively small outlay. In practice you will need to be doing a lot of business from your web site to make one of these links cost-effective.

Satellite links

High-speed Internet access is also available by satellite. This is not quite as complex as it sounds – in fact, it is no more difficult than installing a satellite TV system. Of course, this is easier in some parts of the UK than others. No one will think twice about yet another satellite dish in central London, while inhabitants of rural areas may find that they have to abide by planning laws, and perhaps run into resistance from neighbours, and this can make the installation of a satellite terminal problematic.

It is very likely that during the early part of the twenty-first century, the Internet will 'go wireless' and leave the telephone system behind completely. Proposals exist for a number of global satellite networks which will offer this service.

In the meantime, satellite access gives higher speeds than ISDN at a price that offers relatively good value. Two systems are available:

- **true two-way satellite links** are about half the cost of the cheapest leased line but give speeds of around 400kbps. This is very fast indeed and offers the kind of access most home users only dream of. Businesses may find this kind of access well worth considering. It provides some of the advantages of a leased line at a fraction of the cost
- Slower, but cheaper, access is also available by way of a **combined system from Hughes–Olivetti**, which works together with a conventional modem. The satellite dish can only receive information, and a modem link is still used to send email and web-page requests. This is not much of a limitation in practice because most people need to receive a lot more information than they send. At just over £1,000 for the hardware, and with a variety of payment schemes that are based on the amount of information that is actually received, these systems are still expensive. But for many users they are likely to offer much better value for money than an ISDN link.

The disadvantages of satellite systems are their relative vulnerability to weather conditions and perhaps slower technical support, compared with that available with a leased line system. Satellites are one-off installations that are supposed to work permanently, and if there is a problem it may be a while before an engineer can get to your site. This makes them less suitable for applications where reliability is very important. But for a company that wants to get large amounts of information from the Internet very quickly, they are worth considering.

If you are thinking seriously about a satellite system, it is important to have a demonstration first. Although 400kbps sounds fast, web pages may not appear any more quickly than they do over a 64kbps link. The bottleneck is at the other end – if a site is getting a lot of attention, it will not be able to supply information at a reasonable rate. This puts a practical limit on the speed at which information can be received and makes very high-speed systems less effective than they might otherwise be.

Cable modems
Some cable television companies are now experimenting with faster modems – in some cases as fast as 10mbps, which is

roughly 300 times faster than a 33.6kbps telephone modem. These use a system called ADSL and 'piggy back' on the existing TV channel system. They are designed to offer much faster access to the Internet than is currently possible.

These systems are not for sale commercially, and it is unlikely that they will become widely available until the twenty-first century. This kind of very high-speed access will transform the way the Internet is used and make it possible to send live video information from place to place as easily as an email can be sent today. If access is available at a reasonable price, these new networks are likely to render the existing telephone system redundant, and the high-speed links that result will help make the Internet a part of everyone's daily life.

The Internet for business users

Some businesses use the Internet with a standard dial-up account. If only a handful of people are working in an office on a network and they use the Internet for occasional email and perhaps for looking at the Web, a dial-up account is perfectly adequate.

However, business users can benefit from a number of other Internet-related services. These include Intranets, customised email addresses, professional web design services, and so on. These are provided by a range of consultancies and other Internet-oriented businesses which cater for the more professional user.

Professional Internet facilities

Internet access can be enhanced with a number of optional extras. These are available from the larger IAPs and also from smaller specialist business-friendly IAPs which advertise in the Internet press. It is possible to use either type of company for all of these facilities or to use one for one service and a different one for another.

Customised Internet addresses

Apart from a certain on-line cachet, personalised email and web addresses free you from dependence on any one IAP. If you or your company change IAPs – or even move to a different country – you can keep exactly the same address.

Two steps are involved in creating a customised email or web address. The first is to lay claim to the address itself. This is known as 'registering a domain name'. The second is to tell the computers on the Internet that this address is yours and that any information that accesses it should be directed to your computers. This is known as 'mail forwarding' for email and 'web forwarding' for the Web. If you have a permanent Internet connection (using a leased line or other system), this second stage will not usually be necessary. However, it is essential for anyone who connects to the Internet via an IAP or on-line service.

Domain names are relatively cheap, and you can claim one with very little effort. This process involves a one-off payment to a registration bureau – examples can be found in the more serious Internet press – and then a regular annual payment to the organisation in the USA that administers all domain names (called the InterNIC).

At the time of writing, a bureau may charge about £70 to deal with the paperwork, although charges seem to be falling. The administration fee payable to the InterNIC is $100, which covers two years – payable in advance – and then $50 per year after that. In return for the payment, you get exclusive rights on the Internet to your domain name.

There are two problems with the current domain name system. The first is that domain names need to be unique, and many of the more popular names are already in use. For example, if your company is called Ipswich Banana Merchandising, you will not be able to use the *ibm.com* domain because it has already been registered by IBM.

This is less of a problem in the UK because you can often use the *.co.uk* extension instead of *.com* to create a unique name. However, the pace of registration is speeding up, and even with the latest set of possible extensions (see Glossary), it makes sense to register a domain name as soon as it becomes obvious that you will need it – and, if funds allow, preferably even sooner.

The second problem is a legal one. Some names are registered trade marks, and in some cases different companies in different countries may have a legitimate claim on the same name. At present, the law is unclear about how these should be handled. After some interesting legal wrangles, the InterNIC made it clear that no one would be allowed to register a name that was not in some way connected with his or her business or personal interests. You can no longer make a claim on *mcdonalds.com* or *mtv.com* in the hope that you will be able to make a profit by selling on the name – something that a few early net entrepreneurs attempted, with mixed results. However, it is less clear what will happen if you register a name in good faith, and are then sued a year or two later by a company that feels it has a prior claim. As with a lot of corporate law, the result seems to depend on which party can afford the better lawyers. Because of this, it is wise to check that your proposed name is not a trademark in the UK, the USA, and preferably anywhere else in the world. Unfortunately, this kind of check will usually be too expensive or time consuming to be practical, but if you are at all unsure about a name, it is worth doing this if you can as it may save you a lot of legal difficulties later.

The InterNIC recently muddied the waters even further by suggesting that in those cases in which a name registered outside the USA conflicts with a USA-registered Trade Name or Service Name, the USA company will get prior claim to it – even if the other claimant registered it first. To confuse matters even further, a self-styled *ad hoc* committee of domain-name users has been pushing for a relaxation of the present tight rules about the forms that a domain name can take. In effect, they are trying to introduce a much wider selection of domain-name types, for example, *.com*, than is currently available. These *ad hoc* domain names are not recognised by all of the Internet, and if you try to register one you will find that in some circumstances it will not work properly. However, the committee does have a point: the existing restrictions seem to be jealously maintained without a reasonable supporting rationale.

Note that most domain registration bureaux do not offer any legal services to help you make sense of these different considerations. Their job is to check that the domain name you want is free, and then fill in the paperwork to make sure that it is reserved in your name. They also set up their computers so that the rest of the Internet knows where to send information intended for your domain. But their responsibilities end at this point. If you want to avoid legal troubles, you will need to get professional advice from a suitably qualified law firm.

It is possible to check for domain names on-line. A number of registration bureaux offer on-line search facilities which can tell you in seconds whether or not a given name is already registered. It is wise to use these when selecting your name. Although some registration companies also offer a free postal or telephone checking service, running through a list of hundreds of names only to find that they are all taken already will probably try their patience. It is a better idea to do the searching yourself and then present them with a name that you know is available. In some cases you can even register on-line immediately and follow up the registration with a cheque or credit-card number to pay for the service. You can find these services advertised in the Internet press.

Legal considerations aside, you should consider a potential domain name's 'user friendliness'. The name will be printed on cards, and you and your employees will also have to give it over the telephone. It makes sense to have a name that is short, apt and easy to remember. Names that are ambiguous, very long or hard to spell should be avoided.

Mail forwarding

This service offers the email equivalent of a Post Office box. A company whose official domain name is, for example, *adomain.com* may really be using the mailbox supplied by an ordinary IAP. As soon as mail forwarding is set up, all mail sent to *adomain.com* will be forwarded to the registered domain. This service is typically offered by domain-name registration bureaux, whose computers will perform the forwarding operation for a small annual fee – typically less than £50 a year.

Email illustrates some of the most obvious advantages of a customised domain name: it is good for public relations and looks much more impressive and business like than an address with an ordinary IAP, and it makes it easy to create an infinite number of personalised mail addresses. Although all forwarded mail is sent to the same address, it includes the original 'To:' information. As an example, consider:

the-boss@adomain.com
the-secretary@adomain.com
the-tea-person@adomain.com

Mail sent to these different individuals will all be forwarded to the same mailbox, but because the 'To:' information in the header is different, it is possible to separate it later and forward it to different people within the same company. Many of the most popular email software packages include features which can direct mail to the right person in this way. If the different mailboxes are protected with passwords, the email will remain private and secure. There are no limits on what goes before the '@' sign. You could create an absurd address such as: *this-is-a-ridiculously-long-address@adomain.com* and this will work as well as any other. This kind of flexibility keeps your options open for the future. Even if you suddenly find yourself with tens of thousands of employees, a single domain name will still fulfil all your needs.

You can also use your domain name to hide your address when sending email. You can do this by changing the 'From:' and 'Reply to:' settings in your software to a suitable address at your domain. Although your mail is still sent by your IAP, it will now appear as if it was sent directly from your domain name, and your correspondents will be able to reply to you at your official address in the usual way.

Web forwarding

Web forwarding is the Web's equivalent of email forwarding. You can leave your site on your IAP's web server, and then create an 'official' address for it which will route visitors to your IAP's web server automatically. As with mail forwarding, this hides your real address away and suggests that you can afford your own permanent Internet link. The difference in cost between a web forwarding and a web hosting service (see below) is often negligible. In most cases the latter is preferable.

Web hosting and mailboxes

These services stop you from being dependent on an IAP. Instead of using your IAP's computers for mail and web space, you use those of the bureau that maintains your domain name. Apart from – possibly – a more reliable service, the biggest advantage is that your web pages will be kept on a professional computer system, which may offer faster connections and extra features, such as a wider range of CGI scripts (see page 223) and better visitor tracking.

Dial-up connections

Some domain registration bureaux also offer dial-up connections to complement their web servers and mailboxes. This breaks the final link between you and your IAP because, with such a service, the new company becomes your IAP and you can cancel your subscription to the old IAP altogether.

Choosing a suitable package

If your business is small or medium-sized, it pays to shop around and weigh up the pros and cons of the offers made by the various companies. Many provide special business-package deals which include mail forwarding, web hosting and a selection of other services for an annual flat fee. These can seem appealing, but you need to ask yourself how these packages compare with the existing services offered by your IAP. If you do not expect enormous amounts of traffic at your web site and do not need any special security facilities, it makes sense to use the free web space offered by your IAP, together with a small extra payment for mail and web forwarding.

This is an area in which many companies are being conned. If you are paying only £5 a month to an IAP for a dial-up link with some free web space, it is not wise to swap to using a different IAP for a similar service costing ten times the amount just because it claims to specialise in 'business solutions'.

The difference in cost can be justified only if the 'business' IAP can offer a suitably professional level of service. In fact, when negotiating a contract for business use, you should be careful to specify an SLA (Service Level Agreement). This should include details such as the modem-to-user ratio, minimum bandwidth from the IAP to your computer and also to the rest of the Internet, and any other features that affect the speed and reliability of your connections. IAPs that are more used to

207

dealing with the public than businesses will not be able to offer an SLA unless you order a leased line from them. Business-oriented IAPs should be more amenable to agreeing acceptable service levels in a contract, even for a straightforward dial-up link.

Once you have agreed a contract, it is worth checking regularly to see if the terms are being adhered to. If you try to visit your own web page and it takes ten minutes for the information to appear then you have the right to ask questions about the quality and commitment of the service you are paying for.

Apart from a good-quality service, business IAPs should also be able to offer more advanced facilities such as ISDN and leased lines (see Appendix 2), in addition to business-oriented payment terms with full VAT receipts. It is useful to check the cost of an ISDN connection to see how it compares with that of other IAPs. Some companies charge a hefty premium for ISDN access, while others charge exactly the same rate as they do for dial-up connections.

One final consideration, especially for anyone buying space on a web server, is security. If the IAP does not seem to have a properly maintained and managed security policy in place you should not sign up with it.

Given the international nature of the Internet, it is well worth bearing in mind that you can buy every part of the service from abroad, except for the basic dial-up link. If you do not own your web server you will find no particular advantage in limiting yourself to buying web hosting and other services from companies in the UK. Equivalent services can be significantly cheaper in the USA, and there will not necessarily be any practical disadvantages to keeping the information abroad. The only significant concern is that you will have to pay more for calls if something goes wrong and you need to complain.

Technical consultancies

Unlike the various business-oriented Internet facilities, which are used on a continuing basis, the services offered by technical consultancies tend to be one-off projects which are required when developing a business presence on the Internet.

LAN connections

A LAN (Local Area Network) connection is a special link to the Internet which is essential if your company already has a computer network of its own. Although individual computers on the LAN can be equipped with modems, it makes much better business and technical sense to fully integrate the company network as a whole with the Internet. A special computer called a 'bridge' or 'router' is used to do this. Companies that offer LAN connections will install routers and set up the associated software to make sure that internal and external email are seamlessly integrated. LAN connections often require the co-operation of your IAP, and you should discuss this with them before going ahead. LAN connections are also prone to the security flaws discussed in Chapter 8 and should be designed with security in mind.

Intranets

Designing and installing an Intranet is a major undertaking and something that only a few larger IT companies will be able to advise you about. The advantages of an Intranet are: improved communication, for example, company-wide announcements can be made over the network; and easier workgroup management. The disadvantage is that more time is spent maintaining an Intranet than a traditional network.

Web design consultancies

Many businesses are interested in being on the Web but do not have the time, the inclination or the skills needed to design their own pages. Since 1995 the web design market has undergone explosive growth as professional graphic designers and artists, beginners with a knowledge of HTML, and any number of others, have tried to make new careers for themselves as professional web designers.

HTML is relatively easy to use, and with a little help from some well-designed software, almost anyone should be able to create their own pages. But there is a big difference between creating an amateur home page and creating a professional site in a business setting. The latter requires a much better knowledge of how the Web works, how to use it for promotion, how to make the site accessible, informative, interesting and easy to use, and also some basic knowledge of graphic design. These are not skills that amateurs are likely to have.

Choosing a web designer or web design company can be nerve-racking because of the large range of possible candidates. This is a new industry, and some companies are start-ups that do not even have proper business premises. Others are spin-offs from existing large design companies that have all the impressive trimmings but do not necessarily have any practical experience of designing pages. Quotations for similar work can vary over a ridiculously wide range, and some designers are undoubtedly cashing in on the Web's popularity – although as more people experiment with HTML for themselves, the Web's mystique is starting to fade. To sort out the wheat from the chaff, it is helpful to find out about the following points:

- **Communication skills** The Web is all about communicating, and if a prospective designer cannot show that he or she understands what you need, you will probably not be happy with the end result. Unfortunately, some of the larger design houses have a reputation for arrogance and will attempt to force a grand vision on their clients whether or not it is appropriate. This is always unacceptable. You are not looking for a design that will impress other designers and win awards, but for a design that will reach the intended audience. Designers should show that they understand this well enough to know how to shape the site accordingly.
- **Previous work** A portfolio – which can be on-line – is essential. But apart from examples of work, you should also ask about the success of the work. Was there an increase in business as a result of the site? Was the site successful? How was this success assessed? Is there anything that should have been done differently?
- **References** Reputable designers should not mind if you want to get in touch with previous clients. If you take up this option, do not just ask about the success of the site but also

about how easy it was to manage and finish the task and whether or not the designer was easy to work with.

- **Reliability** For a really big project, you can protect yourself to some extent by including a penalty clause for non-delivery in any contracts you negotiate, and also by breaking the design work down into clear stages. Another excellent idea is to have a contingency plan, perhaps in the form of one or more backup companies that can step in at short notice. If a designer seems to be struggling, you should cut your losses and swap to someone more reliable as soon as you can.

- **Maintenance and documentation** You should always have access to the notes, the raw HTML files, and any other information that your designer has created while building your site. Where appropriate, a good way to save yourself money in the long term is to ask for a site that you can add information to yourself. Your designer can do this by creating a site that relies on a small number of templates which can be filled out with information by anyone at your company. High-maintenance sites, where every single page is designed from scratch, are very expensive and not usually necessary.

AN INTRODUCTION TO HTML

THE SYSTEM used to create web pages is called HTML. Below is a more detailed introduction to HTML and further information about what happens when you try to view a web page on a remote computer.

How the Web really works

When you select a page from a link or a URL, the first thing the browser has to do is to find the page's position on the Internet. This means finding the location of the computer system that 'hosts' the page, which is why the remote computer is often known as the 'host'.

To do this, it passes the address you have selected to one or more 'domain nameserver' (DNS) computers. These maintain a kind of 'telephone directory' and convert the name – which is written in words for the sole convenience of humans – into a list of numbers, which is the 'true' Internet address. You will sometimes see addresses listed as these numbers, and you can type these in in the usual way. But it is more common to use words in a URL because they are easier to remember and more informative.

If the nameserver cannot find the address in its directory and cannot get the information from any of the other nameservers on the Internet, it sends a message back to the browser explaining that it cannot fulfil the request. The browser passes this message on to you, and you will see a cryptic error message that says something like: 'The remote server does not have a DNS entry'.

Otherwise, the nameserver passes the address to the browser, which then attempts to create a connection. If you look at the bottom left-hand corner of your browser while all this is happening, you will see a message that says something like: 'Connect: looking up host'. This tells you that the browser is still trying to find the address. Once it has found it, this changes to: 'Connect: contacting host'.

When this appears, the browser is attempting to create a connection between your computer and the remote one. This involves making contact and then negotiating a connection so that the remote computer knows that it needs to give your computer some attention. The process sometimes stalls at this point, either because of heavy traffic across the Internet or because the remote computer is too busy to respond. Occasionally, it is because it has been switched off and is not working. If this is the case, the browser keeps trying for a few minutes and then gives up, showing a message that says something like: 'Could not contact host'. It is sometimes worth trying again if this happens, although it is usually a better idea to give up and try later when traffic is not so heavy. Even if you do get a connection after an error like this, the chances are that it will be too slow to be useable.

Once the two computers have agreed to connect to each other, the raw HTML on the web host is copied to your computer, together with any images and other information that is needed to display the page. This happens in spurts. While it is happening, your browser is attempting to display the page – or at least as much of it as it can. You can follow this process by looking at the status line at the bottom left-hand corner. The amount of information needed to show each part of the page is shown as a percentage. The browser and host try to copy all the parts at once, which is why this percentage seems to switch at random – each percentage refers to a particular part. Unfortunately, you cannot check how many parts are involved or see the percentages for all of them at the same time.

Eventually, all the information arrives on your machine and the page is shown with the text and images. If you click on a link, the process starts again with a different page. However, if you then click on the 'back' button, the original page appears immediately. The browser is clever enough to 'cache' a copy of the information inside your computer – this means it keeps a copy for its own use, so it does not have to wait while the information is transferred again.

HTML for beginners

Although at first sight it can seem rather daunting, HTML is really very straightforward. In fact, it is possible to create a simple page very quickly. The language has two parts: 'keywords', which are special words or letters that have a specific function, and 'content', which is the text and other information that you are publishing. Keywords appear within angle brackets '<>' and are always used in matched pairs. The second word in the pair is the same as the first but with a '/' character added in front. Anything between these two keywords will be influenced by them in some way. Note that quite a lot of other information may be separating the first word in the pair from the second. Keywords will not appear when you look at the page with a browser – they are simply there to tell the browser how to display the content but remain 'invisible' otherwise.

It is easiest to understand this with an example. On web pages, text is arranged in paragraphs. The start of a paragraph is marked with the keyword <p>, and the end with </p>. This is repeated for the next paragraph, and so on, for example:

```
<p>Here is a short line of text</p>
<p>Here is some more text, which will appear on a new line.
Without the paragraph markers it would be added to the end of
the previous line, even though you typed it on a new line.</p>
```

Keywords are really just a novel and elaborate form of punctuation. For example, text between the <b> and </b> markers will appear in **bold** type, while <i> and </i> set *italic* type. More complex keywords such as <A> and </A> specify that the text between them is a URL (address) or a link. The actual address appears within the angle brackets following the 'A', and this is followed by a line of text that appears underlined on the screen. This makes it possible to create links that say things like:

And you can see my other page here.

Clicking on 'here' will take you to a different page. Below is a short example of a complete page which demonstrates how this works:

```
<HTML>
<HEAD>
<TITLE>This is a page of HTML</TITLE>
</HEAD>

<P><B>Welcome to my home page!</B></P>
<P>This is a link to my email address:
<A HREF="mailto:somewhere@someaddress.com">My email
address.
</A>
</P>


<P> This is a link to my web site:
<A HREF="http://www.somesite.sometype/">My web site
</A>
</P>
</HTML>
```

It does not matter how the information is laid out, so it is more likely that the page would appear like this:

```
<HTML>
<HEAD>
<TITLE>This is a page of HTML</TITLE>
</HEAD>
<P>Welcome to my home page!</P>
<P> This is a link to my email address: <A
HREF="mailto:somewhere@someaddress.com">My email
address</A></P>
<P>This is a link to my web site: <A
HREF="http://www.somesite.sometype/">My web site</A></P>
</HTML>
```

Although it is no longer clear where the pairs of keywords are, a web browser will still display all the content correctly. In fact, you could squeeze all the information into a single long, completely incomprehensible line, although this would be a bad idea if you ever wanted to make any changes.

Useful shortcuts

Very few people take the time to create whole pages by typing in HTML by hand. It can be done but it is a very time-consuming and inefficient way to do the job. It is much easier to use a 'WYSIWYG' ('what you see is what you get') HTML editor package. This lets you design pages by typing directly on the screen so that you can see your page developing in front of you, and the HTML remains hidden away. These are often supplied with templates – sometimes called 'wizards' – which can help you design pages very quickly.

Another alternative is to use the 'save as' feature available in all browsers to copy the HTML from someone else's web pages to your computer's, so that you can use them as a template and read and edit them at leisure. It would be unwise to publish exactly the same pages with precisely the same content because this would be a breach of copyright. However, people do sometimes use edited versions of a page as a quick way to create a framework for their own content. Very few pages have completely distinctive and unique designs which could be identified by their authors, so there is no reason not to use this shortcut.

Whichever shortcut you use, it is still useful to understand how HTML works so that you can make small changes to the HTML created by a WYSIWYG editor if the need ever arose. One situation in which you would need to know how HTML works is in the use of 'meta tags', which are described below. More advanced facilities are available on some recent word processors, including Microsoft's Word 97 and Corel's Wordperfect. These include built-in web publishing features which can convert a document into a web page at the touch of a button. This is usually done by choosing the 'save as HTML' option in one of the menus. Although it can take much of the hard work out of designing pages, this software lacks some of the more advanced features that true web design software has. They can also have the annoying habit of re-interpreting the layout of a page in unexpected and unwanted ways.

A much quicker and simpler option is to use the web design shortcuts offered by some IAPs and on-line services. These are electronic forms that are provided by the IAP or on-line service on its own web site. To create a page of your own, you simply fill in the form with your name, email address, hobbies, and other details. The rest of the process happens automatically, and suitable pages appear with no further effort on your part. Although these pages are relatively crude in comparison with some of the elegant and artistic designs possible with proper software, they offer a quick and easy way for beginners to start publishing on the Web.

The most sophisticated way to create pages is to use one of the popular web editing and design packages. These allow you to design your pages on-screen and then convert your design to HTML once you are satisfied with the layout. Some of these are very sophisticated and can make use of all of HTML's special features, such as blinking words or sentences or 'frames' which break a single page up into areas that can show separate information. The best software offers templates so you can get started very quickly, but at the same time gives you the option of producing more sophisticated pages as your knowledge grows. The features to look for in web publishing software include:

- **WYSIWYG publishing** With this kind of editor, any changes will take effect immediately. This is much more convenient than other kinds of publishing, in which you either have to guess the results of your changes or use separate software to see how your page is progressing. For example, it is much more convenient to be able to move a picture to a position where it looks right rather than type in numbers that specify where it should go, check how it looks, and if it is wrong, type in different numbers, then check again, and so on.
- **Site management** This phrase describes a simple need – the ability to make sure that all the links across the different pages you have created work properly. Without site-management

features you have to keep track of cross-links by hand. This is straightforward if your site has two or three simple pages, but anything more complex will benefit from automated help.

- **Wizards and other shortcuts** These include: page design templates; shortcuts to help add sophisticated features such as animated graphics; and detailed help when attempting to FTP your page design to a web server.

- **On-line editing** Some software lets you edit pages on the server itself as well as on your computer. This can be very useful if you need to make small changes to a page. It will save you from having to move your site back on to your computer to make a change, then copy it back on to the Web.

- **Image-editing tools** Image editors can be used to crop and re-touch photographs, change the number of colours in an image, and so on. But it is convenient to have image-editing tools that work closely with the web-page software itself. A particularly useful extra is an animated GIF editor, which can be used to add simple flip-book animations to your pages.

Hints and tips for designers

Page design is as much an art as a science, and you can look at many excellent sites on the Web for inspiration. When designing pages, it is important to make sure they can be seen correctly by as many different people as possible. Because there are so many kinds of computers on the Internet with so many different specifications you should keep this in mind when working on your pages, and this means considering the points below:

- **Screen size** Computer screens are like a grid of tiny lights, which are measured down and across. The smallest common size is 640 dots across by 480 dots down. The largest is 1,600 dots across by 1,400 down, although larger sizes are used occasionally. HTML has facilities to check the size of the screen, and it is important to scale the position of the text and images so they appear correctly. There may be situations in which one screen size is preferable to another, in which case it is useful to include a note to this effect somewhere at the top of the page. Ideally, this should be avoided and the page should work well on all the common screen sizes. If possible, try them all out to see what the page looks like and make changes if you need to.

- **Screen colours** Each tiny light on a screen can be one of a number of colours. The number varies between two – black and white – to hundreds of millions. If you are including photographs, convert them to 256 colours wherever possible. This gives reasonable quality when viewed with most browsers and avoids some of the nasty side-effects which can occur when an image with more colours is viewed on a screen that only shows a smaller number. Also, the more colours the image has, the longer it will take to appear in a browser – another incentive to keep the number of colours to the bare minimum.

- **Connection speed** The more information you have on your page, the longer it will take for a browser to display it. Text appears relatively quickly, but large, very detailed images such as photographs can be too slow to be practical. This can be handled in three ways. The first is to produce a text-only version of your whole site and include a link to it from your 'welcome' page. This gives visitors a chance to decide whether or not they want to see pictures. The second option is to use 'thumbnails' – small versions of larger images – on your pages which, in effect, provide a small sketch of each image. Each thumbnail includes a link to a full-sized version of the image, with perhaps its size (for example, 300Kbytes) listed underneath. Again, visitors can decide for themselves whether or not to view the full version. This approach works particularly well with photographs. Finally, it is possible to list descriptions of images instead of using thumbnails. If you do not want to follow any of these suggestions, it is a good idea to keep the number and size of images to a minimum – otherwise, visitors will get bored and leave before they have seen the whole site.

- **Text attributes** You can set the colour of both the text and the background for your page. Some people use unusual colour schemes on their computers, such as white text on a blue background, because they may find their scheme is easier on the eyes for long periods. It is important to make a point of setting your own text and background colours because if you do not you can leave your visitors trying to read white text on a white background.

- **Browser compatibility** Not all browsers are the same. Older versions of the same browser will not be able to show certain kinds of information properly. For example, the ability to divide a page up into 'frames' (different windows with their own distinct contents) only came with version 3 of Netscape Navigator and Microsoft's Internet Explorer. If your page has special features like these it is traditional to include a line that says 'This page is best viewed with <suggested browser name>', which features a link to the latest version of the browser so that visitors can download it before they try looking at your site.

- **Artwork** As you will notice when you start exploring the Web for yourself, images appear in two ways: line by line starting from the top of the image, or all at once with increasing detail. The latter is by far the better option because it gives visitors a chance to change their minds about seeing an image once they can see enough of it to be able to tell what it is. To specify the way an image appears you will need to use suitable image-editing software. The 'increasing detail' option is known as an 'Interlaced GIF' and is a feature of most popular image-editing packages.

- **Animations** These are always welcome as they can make a page look much more interesting and appealing. It is possible to create animations without resorting to using Java (see page 221) and other complicated options. Most animations on the Web are of the 'flick book' variety. They consist of a series of still images shown in sequence and are known as 'Animated GIFs'. As with Interlaced GIFs, this feature is available in many image-editing packages. Do bear in mind, though, that it is wise to keep both the size and the number of images in the sequence to a minimum because they have to be copied to a browser in full before the animation appears.

- **Site layout** When you start designing your own pages, you should first sketch a map which shows the links between the different pages. Web surfers tend to be impatient, and as a rule of thumb, the more links visitors have to follow to get to the pages that interest them, the less likely they are to bother to continue looking at your site. You can expect to lose half of your visitors for each extra link that takes them further from the main welcome page and contents list.

- **Optional extras** You can add all manner of extras, such as audio clips and special effects, to your pages, but these are best left until you have mastered the basics.

- **Things to leave out** You should avoid using 'This page is still under construction' notices because they tend to look rather apologetic. (In any case, most pages are permanently under construction.) As long as all the links that are available work properly, you do not need to advertise the fact that the site is not yet as comprehensive as you would like it to be. Some people include links to places on the Internet that are already very popular, such as the various search engines. However, most web users bookmark these locations right away anyway, so adding these links is not a particularly helpful thing to do. Instead, make sure your links are genuinely interesting and innovative and lead visitors to places they might not take the time to see otherwise

- **Things to put in** Your email address; the date the page was last modified; a link on each page back to the main welcome page – visitors may jump into your pages at any point, and if you do not include this link they may be stuck where they landed; copyright notice, especially if the content is unusual or particularly interesting.

Extending your pages with special effects

A number of advanced techniques are available to add interest to web pages. Very few people need to know enough about these to be able to work with them professionally, but it is useful to know what they do in outline and what the different words mean.

Java and Javascript
Java – a programming language – has caused something of a sensation on the Internet. Most software is created to work with one particular kind of computer system – for example, software

for the Apple Macintosh will not work on a computer that uses Microsoft's Windows system. This has been a major source of difficulty in the computer industry, both for software developers, who are forced to create multiple versions of the same software for different computers, and for users, who have a confusing array of choices to make when buying and using both computers and software.

Java gets around this problem because Java programs – known as 'applets' – work the same way on any computer that has Java installed. Fortunately for users, Java is simply built into all the popular web browsers. This means users can benefit from Java's features without even knowing they are using it – all they see is a web page that does something more clever than usual – and programmers can create software for Java without worrying about the details of a user's machine.

Unless you already have programming experience, adding Java features to your own web pages so that they, too, do clever things is probably beyond your scope. The Java system is not hard to learn but it does use advanced software techniques and ideas, making it beyond the skills of most beginners. However, anyone who would like to know more can experiment with Java 'development software', which is very affordable. Some books about Java even include this software for free. Java programming skills are currently much sought after and this makes Java worth considering for someone in search of a new career.

Java may possibly have an important part to play in the future of the Internet and of computers in general. Sun, the company that invented Java, has created a hardware version of the Java system. The version of Java used in web browsers is rather slow, and this makes it unsuitable for certain tasks, such as those which try to display lots of information that is changing constantly. The hardware version uses specially designed computer chips which work much more quickly. What this means in practice remains to be seen, but it is possible that the result will be a range of small, cheap computers designed for home use to integrate with the Internet and do everything personal computers do today, except with much less bother. Java is not tied to the Internet, it can be used for anything. So far, however, it is most widely used for Internet-related purposes.

Javascript is a version of Java that is built into web browsers. Instead of separate applets, Javascript is included within the HTML that describes a page. There is no particular advantage or disadvantage to doing this, it is simply another way to use the Java system to create enhanced pages.

ActiveX

ActiveX is Microsoft's answer to Java. ActiveX offers very similar features, but to date – in spite of Microsoft's efforts – practical demonstrations of it remain tied rather closely to Microsoft's Windows system. As a result, ActiveX lacks Java's universality. Microsoft is very influential in the personal computer trade and in the past has often been able to impose its wishes on the market. However, the future of ActiveX's relationship with the Internet remains uncertain. Many Internet users do not use Microsoft's Windows, and unless ActiveX can match Java's ability to work on any machine it may remain something of a side interest for the Internet.

CGI

In the same way that Java is a computer language that was originally designed to add extra features to web browsers, the Common Gateway Interface (CGI) was designed to add features to web servers. CGI programs are known as 'scripts' and make it possible for web servers to perform a variety of useful tasks with web-related information. Examples include search facilities for a site, on-line registration forms, counters that show the number of times that a site has been visited, and so on.

The biggest difference between CGI and Java is that Java software is copied to your computer before it does anything, whereas CGI software stays on your IAP's web server. Because CGI is a very powerful tool and has a much higher security clearance than most software, many IAPs are reluctant to allow full public access to CGI facilities on their machines. For example, Demon Internet offers a number of pre-written CGI scripts to its customers, which they can use in their own web page designs. Other scripts are banned. This makes sure that knowledgable customers cannot 'beat the system' and change someone else's pages without permission, take complete control

223

of the web server, or perhaps intercept someone else's mail. For professional users who need CGI facilities, Demon offers a different server, which is available at extra cost.

CGI programming is a job for professionals, even more so than Java. If you have an aptitude for computers, the language is not hard to learn, but using it properly – and avoiding disasters, especially of the kind that can compromise a system's security – requires a high level of skill. For most web publishers it is easiest to use 'off-the-shelf' scripts such as those offered by Demon and other IAPs. These come with instructions, so you can use them without a detailed knowledge of how they work.

Perl

Perl is another computer language, which is designed to extract and process information from large amounts of text. A simple example would be searching for a certain word in the text of an email or showing the differences between two messages. Perl is frequently mentioned in the context of web-page design because it is often used to write CGI scripts. Again, this is a language for computer experts, and beginners will not usually need to know how it works – although knowing what the name means can sometimes be useful.

Front Page Extensions

These are used with Microsoft's Front Page web design software, which includes a number of CGI-like features that work using Microsoft's own proprietary system. As with ActiveX, these extensions work only with other Microsoft products. This means they lack the universality of CGI and Perl, which will work with any web-related computer systems. However, they are easy to install on a web server, and many professional web server companies offer them.

Publishing your pages

Once you have completed your pages and tested them on your personal computer, you need to transfer them to a web server so that they appear on the Internet. This is done using FTP (see Chapter 7). Someone at your IAP will explain to you how this should be done for that particular server and will tell you what the main URL for your pages will be. Remember that you will need to copy all the information associated with your pages, including all the HTML, the images and anything else that may be relevant. The copying process should not take more than an hour or two, even for very big pages.

Once the information is copied you do not need to do any more. When your IAP's web server receives a request for the pages located at your URL, it will send the information you have prepared over the Internet in the usual way, and your pages will appear on someone else's browser. If you make changes, you can copy the new HTML over the old information and use FTP to add to or delete the other information.

When your pages are on-line, the final part of the process is to let the various search engines know where to find them. This makes sure that if someone searches for a word mentioned in your site, it will be listed by the search engine. In theory, they search the entire Web, but in practice they follow only links from other pages. If no one includes links to your pages, they will remain invisible and will not be included in any listings.

You can make sure your pages are listed properly in two ways. The first is to use the on-line forms, which some of the search engines provide, to submit details about your pages manually. On Yahoo, for example, you can specify which categories and sub-categories you would like your pages to appear in. A submission service – Submit It! at *http://www.submit-it.com* – offers a free service which will submit your site to all the major search engines on your behalf.

The other way to determine how your pages are listed is to use 'meta tags'. Normally, when a search engine visits a web site it notes the first few lines of text it finds there. This text appears whenever the site turns up in a search, and is often cut off at random. For example:

```
'Welcome to our home page! This is the home page of' ...
```

Clearly, there are situations in which this can be less than informative. Meta tags solve this problem by telling the search engine two things: the first is the text that you would like to appear when your site is listed; the second is a list of relevant keywords that apply to your site, which will make it appear in a listing whenever anyone searches for them.

For example, adding:

```
<META name "description"
content "We specialise in breeding pink parrots in West
Yorkshire.">
<META name "keywords"
content "pets, breeding, parrot, West Yorkshire">
```

to your site will make sure that when someone looks for information about pets, breeding, pink parrots, or West Yorkshire on a search engine they will see the following:

```
Pink Parrots.
We specialise in breeding pink parrots in West Yorkshire.
http://pink.parrot.co.uk/ — size 3k — 29 Feb 97
```

APPENDIX 5

INFORMATION FOR EXPERTS

THIS APPENDIX is an introduction to some of the more advanced features of the Internet. The information that follows is intended for anyone who feels they have a basic working knowledge and would like to get more from their hardware and software. Some of these techniques are 'trade secrets' used by established Internet users. Others are included here for reference, to explain some of the more intimidating jargon that is used or simply for the sake of completeness.

How the Internet really works

The Internet was originally designed as a computer network that could survive a nuclear strike. Its most distinctive feature is its lack of centralised control. Instead of one big computer that controls everything, the Internet is a rather ramshackle network of all kinds of different computers. It only works at all because everyone who uses it agrees to use the same technology.

Once you start using the Internet, you will notice that information seems to travel across it in fits and starts. In fact, information travels in 'packets' – small chunks of information that act independently of each other. Packets can go across the Internet via any available route. The real world equivalent would be a newspaper delivery service that sends one page via the next street, another via the next town, another through a different country and another to the moon and back, before finally reassembling the newspaper and pushing it through your letterbox. This may seem wasteful but it allows the Internet to deal with problems intelligently. If one computer fails, packets are sent over a route that avoids it. This switching process happens instantly and no information is lost.

The Internet's other great strength is that the system that controls packets – called TCP/IP (Transmission Control Protocol/Internet Protocol) works in exactly the same way on every computer. TCP/IP is powerful enough to do the job of creating packets and reassembling them when they arrive – even if they arrive out of sequence – but simple and undemanding enough to work on small personal computers as well as large scientific and commercial ones.

Personal computers use a small piece of software called a 'TCP/IP stack' to do this job. (This is supplied with some Internet software, but in many cases it is included with your computer when you buy it.) This provides the 'pipe' that makes information flow in both directions between the personal computer and the Internet. If the stack is not working, the Internet connection will be dead. When you buy a connection from an IAP, what you are really paying for is the technology needed to link this 'pipe' to the IAP's own network, which has a permanent direct connection to the Internet. All the software you use relies on the stack being in place and working correctly.

On personal computers that use Microsoft Windows, the TCP/IP stack is often known as 'Winsock' – short for Windows Socket. Sometimes, when Internet software does not work properly, you will see a message that refers to a problem with the Winsock. Setting up Winsock from scratch is not a job for the beginner. Windows 95 has its own version, which – to some extent – sets itself up automatically. Unfortunately, Winsocks for older versions of Windows have to be set up by hand. Some Internet software packages install a Winsock of their own, which again – in theory – sets itself up automatically. This works just as well, providing you do not already have software from an existing IAP installed on your computer. If you do, the two Winsocks may conflict with each other, and the connection will not work. Unravelling this problem is again a job for an expert – yet another reason why it is important to check an IAP's technical support before subscribing.

On-line services do not generally use the Winsock system. Instead, they use either proprietary software of their own which works differently, or a unique Winsock which works only with their software. It is sometimes possible to replace the unique Winsock with a 'proper' Winsock, allowing you to use standard Internet software instead of the software supplied by the on-line service. The browsers offered by some services are not as good as the 'standard' Netscape or Microsoft browsers that the rest of the Internet uses. By installing a suitable Winsock, you will be able to use one of these standard browsers, while at the same time keeping all the facilities of the existing software offered by the on-line service. You may need to do a little research to find out if this is possible, and if so, how to do it in practice. You will usually be able to find help in one of the computer forums specific to the service.

Servers, clients and hosts

On the Internet, computers and their software are often divided into three categories. A **'server'** is a computer system that offers access to a particular service or facility, usually on the Internet. A mail server collects and stores all the mail that arrives addressed to an IAP's customers, and a news server does the same for news. A web server 'serves up' web pages on the Web so that they can be read by anyone. A news server 'serves up' copies of newsgroup postings, and so on.

Although servers are usually big, fast and powerful computers that can handle thousands of requests for information every minute, it is possible to install server software on any computer. One common situation in which this is necessary is when someone is developing a web site on a home PC. Pages can be viewed with a browser while they are being developed, but without a 'personal web server' installed on the home computer none of the links between pages in the site will work. This makes it hard to check that the links are working properly. With a server, all the links within the site will work correctly because it will be able to 'serve up' the relevant pages when asked. This means that you can test the site in private at home before making it public by copying it to an IAP's web server.

'**Clients**' are computer systems that copy information from a server to you and display it in a form that you can use. An email client connects to the mail server, finds your messages out of the thousands of others that are stored there, copies them to your computer and organises and displays them for you so you can read and reply to them. In practice, most Internet software used on home computers is client software, even though it is not always labelled as such.

The client/server idea is an important one and may have a big effect on the way that the Internet develops in future. One proposal is the 'thin client' – a computer system that is not much more than a screen and keyboard, with some memory, a processor chip to do the work and perhaps a hard disk. The thin client concept attempts to move the maintenance usually associated with personal computers – especially the frustration which software installation can sometimes cause – over to a big general-purpose server computer. Instead of installing the same software on many machines, it needs to be done once only. In theory, this thin client computer should then be much easier to use. ('Thin client' is really another name for 'Network Computer', discussed in Appendix 2.)

You will sometimes see the words 'server-side' and 'client-side'. These are industry jargon for 'used by servers' and 'used by clients'. For example, server-side software is simply software that can be used on a server.

'**Hosts**' are more or less the same as servers. A host computer is one that hosts some action or exchange of information. In most contexts the word simply means 'the computer at the other end of the link'.

Making sense of addresses

A common mistake made by beginners is to assume that Internet addresses are written in English and therefore all the normal rules about grammar, capitalisation and punctuation apply.

This is not true. Addresses are always typed in lower case. The only exceptions to this rule are the addresses used internally by certain on-line services, although once these are converted into Internet addresses, they also always appear in lower case.

Addresses should always be typed in exactly as shown, with no extra spaces and with all the punctuation intact. It is easy for beginners to get this wrong and to miss details such as the difference between the backslash '\' and the forward slash '/' characters. If you are trying to use an address and it is not working properly, check your typing before trying anything else. Even experienced users sometimes misspell names – although using the address book feature, available in most email software, can help minimise this.

Although Internet addresses may seem like a random jumble of letters and punctuation, they have a definite logic of their own. Knowing how they work can make it easier to spot errors, to find useful information about someone on-line and even to correct mistakes in addresses that are printed in magazines and other publications.

Email addresses

These have two parts: a 'public' part, which makes sure the information is sent to the right computer system on the Internet; and a 'private' part, which tells the computer system whose desk or computer terminal to send it to. For users of IAPs, the public part is the address of their IAP, and the private part is their own personal mailbox. In all cases, for all addresses on the Internet, these are separated by the '@' sign, pronounced 'at'.

In essence, all email addresses are simply *name-'at'-location*, where the location is the name of a computer system. The location – which is known in the industry as a 'domain name' (see Appendix 3) – has to be unique because otherwise the Internet would be unable to work out which computer to send the mail to. Apart from the name of an organisation, domain names also include information about the type of organisation that uses the domain and the country it is based in. These appear as short codes separated from the main name by dots. A typical domain name is *intelligent.co.uk*. The first word, 'intelligent', is the short form of a company called Intelligent Realtime Information Systems. The full name would be too long, so it has been shortened to make it more convenient. This is standard practice among companies on the Internet – either a single descriptive word is used for this part of the address, or a long name is shortened to its initials. The next part, '.co', is short for company and indicates that this is a commercial address. Finally, '.uk' is the country code and shows that the company is based in the UK. If it was based in Australia, this part of the address would be '.au', if in Belgium '.be', and so on. The full list of country codes is very long and is included in the glossary. The full list of organisation codes is much shorter. Most are used internationally, but some are relevant only to particular countries.

While the rules about what can go after the '@' sign are quite strict, anything at all can go before it. Any restrictions on this part of the address are specific to each domain. For example, someone using AOL has to limit his or her name to ten characters without spaces, anyone using Which? Online will have an address that looks like *firstname.secondname@which.net* and someone who uses CompuServe may have an address that consists of two long numbers: *1234.5678@compuserve.com*

Address conversions

Email sent between users of the same on-line service follows different rules. Because the email remains within the same organisation there is no need for a domain name. There are no '@' signs, and the address follows the service's own conventions. Some people include this internal form of their address on their business cards and letterheads. If you are not a member of the same service and try to send email to this internal address, it will not get through. So it is useful to know how to convert internal addresses into working Internet-style addresses:

- **CompuServe** Old-style CompuServe addresses look like this: *1234,56789*. The number of digits in each section can vary. Note that a comma is used instead of a full-stop. To convert this to an Internet address you replace the comma with a full stop and then add *@compuserve.com* – thus: *1234.56789@compuserve.com*. CompuServe has now changed its address system and allows words instead of numbers. To convert these newer addresses, similar rules apply. As long as you add '@compuserve.com' to the end and make sure that any words in the first part are separated by full stops, your email should get through.

- **AOL** These addresses can be any combination of letters and spaces. Letters can be in upper or lower case. To convert this to an Internet address that works you need to strip out any spaces, change all the letters to lower case, and add *@aol.com* So, for example, *Sorcha V* becomes *sorchav@aol.com*
- **Other services** Similar rules apply for all the other services. Usually, all you need to do is add *@servicename.com* to the end of the address, where 'servicename' is the name of the service. This rule has one or two exceptions. A handful of Internet addresses use a different addressing system called X400. X400 addresses are long and extremely complicated and include lots of '/' and '=' characters. The conversion process is equally complex and can sometimes even confuse experienced professionals. If someone is using an X400 system, the easiest way to work out that person's address is to ask him or her to send you an email, so that you can use the 'reply' option in your email software. If you have tried all these methods and nothing seems to be working, as a last resort you can either email or call the postmaster at the service to see if someone there can help you with the conversion.

Finding an email address
The easiest way to get an email address is to get someone to mail you first, but, of course, this is not always possible. If not, try the following:

- **ask for it** For addresses of people in the UK, it is easier to ask for an address in person or over the telephone than it is to get it any other way. This is not so true of addresses abroad, especially those that are in very different time zones.
- **consult a paper directory** Bookshops now sell Internet directories, and some of these include interesting and useful email addresses. This technique can work well if you want a commercial email address or one belonging to one of the less net-shy celebrities.
- **consult an on-line directory** The InterNIC directory and database at *http://ds.internic.net/ds/dspg01.html* is a 'directory of directories' that lists all the widely used public access on-line directories. These are useful for commercial or

educational email contacts, but may not include information about anyone outside these kinds of organisations.

- **consult an on–line archive** Doing a web search on someone's surname can turn up some surprisingly useful leads, as can searching through the Usenet archives. If someone has posted to Usenet his or her email address will appear there. Obviously, this approach works best for people with unusual surnames, although adding a first name can narrow the search down significantly. On the Web, someone's name may appear if he or she contributes to any of the mailing lists that are archived there.

- **Mail 'postmaster@...'** If you know the name of the organisation where the person has an email account, you can mail the postmaster, who will often send the full address by return.

- **Try 'finger@...'** Most of the large Internet service providers and many universities and other institutions have machines that can be fingered to see who is connected (see page 120). If a name looks likely from the long list you get back, you can finger that name in turn and see if it is who you think it is. Some universities offer search facilities which can be accessed with the finger command. If you finger a name you will receive a 'best match' and perhaps more information on possible leads and other contacts. On IRC, the '/who' and '/whois' commands give people's nicknames and often provide a clue to their email address. Again, finger can be used to get more information about these. Some people, notably famous academics and other celebrities, like to keep their email addresses very private. You will not have much luck getting hold of these.

Making sense of headers

You will often see 'headers' referred to in newsgroup postings. Headers are extra lines of information that arrive with each email and newsgroup message. They are rather like envelopes and contain the Internet's equivalent of address and postmark information. Normally headers are hidden – they are not very interesting and tend to clutter up your screen. But there are times when it is useful to be able to read them and pick out the useful information they contain.

To do this you need to get your software to show header information. Most software has a menu option somewhere that says 'show headers'. If you select this option when looking at a message – either email or news – a number of lines of gibberish should appear above the text of the message. (To get rid of the headers you will usually need to select this option again – otherwise they will appear for every message you look at.) If your software does not have such an option, look for 'headers' in the on-line help facility or the paper manual. If all else fails, try calling the relevant technical support number for an explanation of what you need to do.

Headers are arranged in lines, each of which tells you something about the message. The most common entries for email messages are:

To: This is usually your email address. If the email was sent to more than one person, their addresses will also appear here.

From: This is the email address of the sender.

Sender: Again, the email address of the sender.

Return–path: This is also the email address of the sender. However, sometimes this and the 'From:' line are different. This might be due to a number of reasons: some organisations have a single incoming address but multiple outgoing addresses; occasionally, the person's software is not set up properly; the sender could be trying to anonymise the email (see Chapter 8) or make it look as if it is from someone else by deliberately changing one of these settings in his or her software. To decide which applies, you will need to use your judgement and consider the context.

Subject: The subject of the message.

Date: The date and time. The time is the local time that applies when the message was sent, and includes a local time zone – for example, email sent in the UK will have 'BST' when British Summer Time applies. Sometimes the time is also the Greenwich Mean Time equivalent of local time.

Precedence: A priority measure set by the sender's IAP. This is usually set to 'bulk', which means the message gets no special treatment.

Message-id: This is another header set by the sender's IAP. It is the code number left in the log of the IAP's email server as the message passes through its system.

Received: There is usually a string of these lines. They should be read from the bottom upwards. They list the different computer systems that the email passed through on its way to you. Included in each line is:

- time and date of arrival of the message
- the message-id on that particular computer
- the make, version number and/or operating system of the email control server used by that computer (this is optional).

Newsgroup messages include many of the same lines but also have the following:

Newsgroups: This is a list of the newsgroups the message was posted to.

Organisation: The name of the poster's organisation (often a joke name if the poster is not at work).

References: A long list of news message-ids which refer to related messages in the same thread. Unfortunately, these are different for every news server, which makes them unhelpful.

Path: The newsgroup system's equivalent of the 'Received:' lines. This is a summary of the computers that the message passed through on its way to you. Starting from the computer that sent the message at the end of the line and working backwards, it is possible to trace the route the message took. Each step is separated by a bang '!' character.

NNTP-Posting-Host: The name of the IAP's newsgroup server. When present, this tells you explicitly which IAP was used to send the message.

Both email and newsgroup messages can include any number of lines that start with 'X-'. These include extra information supplied by the sender's software. Examples include:

X-newsreader: Tells you which newsreader software the sender is using.

X-mailer: Tells you which email software they are using.

X-noarchive: Tells the Deja News archive service whether or not to ignore the message.

This may seem like a lot of very dull information to wade through for no good reason – and for most messages it is exactly that. But this information can be useful in two types of situation: dealing with 'spam' and junk mail, and checking for forged email.

As mentioned in Chapter 6, it is possible to complain about spam and junk mail by sending a message to the postmaster – the administrator – of the IAP that the offender posted from. However, some 'spammers' and junk mailers attempt to disguise their tracks by using false addresses.

By checking the headers it is possible to guess which IAP the poster is using. This information will appear in the 'Received:' lines in an email and the 'Path:' line in a newsgroup message. (Some offenders are inept enough to leave this information in the 'From:' line as well.) To find the source, read the lowest 'Received:' line or the rightmost couple of 'Path:' entries. With experience, you will be able to recognise an IAP's name among these. You can then compose a message to the postmaster at that IAP, even though an attempt has been made to hide this information from you.

Note that headers, especially email headers, contain computer names rather than domain names. For example, one of Demon Internet's email computers is called *punt2.demon.net* You probably will not get a response if you send a message to the *postmaster@punt2.demon.net* because this is an 'administrative' computer that works behind the scenes, rather than an official address. But if you leave out the computer name and make an educated guess at the domain name – in this case 'demon.net' – you will be able to work out an address that will get your complaint to the right person.

Forged email can be spotted in a similar way. If the person's return address or 'From:' line does not match the computer or domain name listed in the original 'Received:' line, either the email is forged or the sender has used a mail-forwarding service (see page 205). You should be able to decide which is the case, depending on the context. To find the source of junk mail, you can follow a similar process of elimination to work out the address of the IAP being used.

Making sense of URLs (Uniform Resource Locators)

The word 'Uniform' in 'Uniform Resource Locator' is something of a mystery to many net users. Most people associate URLs with the letters 'http://' and assume that URLs always follow the same format.

In fact, web browsers can read and make sense of other kinds of information. The 'http://' part of an address will be changed accordingly. From a technical point of view, one of the clever things about the Web is that it ties all kinds of addresses into a single uniform format that can be accessed with a single piece of software. This is the source of the 'uniform' description. The most common kinds of addresses are:

http:// 'Hypertext Transfer Protocol', or a web site

https:// 'Hypertext Transfer Protocol, secure' or a web site with security features. Credit-card numbers should be safer here

gopher:// a Gopher site

file:// a file (usually of HTML information) on the user's own computer. (Note that this is always followed by another backslash. This refers to the first part of the address − or path, as its known − of the information on the user's hard disk)

localhost:// information from a local web server − typically on a user's own computer

ftp:// File Transfer Protocol − an FTP site.

Knowing this information enables you get more from your browser. If, for example, you come across a Gopher address you can use the 'gopher://' prefix to view the information with your web browser instead of finding and installing special software.

If you try a URL and it does not seem to work, you can sometimes still find a way to view the information by doing some exploring. A useful trick is to leave out the rightmost parts of the URL one by one until the browser responds. A part is defined as anything after a slash '/'. For example, you would start by trying: *http://www.somename.some-extension/someword/etc1* and then *http://www.somename.some-extension/someword* and finally *http://www.somename.some-extension*, which is as far as the process will go ('http://' will not work as a URL – there have to be at least two words separated by dots after it). This trick works because URLs with lots of parts actually take you straight into the middle of a site. As you backtrack you will sometimes find you get closer and closer to a 'welcome' page which introduces the site. Often this welcome site lists all the options available – perhaps including the information you are looking for. This technique is not infallible and should be used only as a last resort, but it is worth trying if you have problems.

When using an IAP's web server, your address will look like this: *www.(your iap's web address)/(your user name).htm/*

Making sense of killfiles

Killfiles (see page 92) work by downloading newsgroup headers, scanning them to look for certain information and then marking the articles that fail the tests. Some software does this with a 'mark as read' option, which copies the article to your computer, but makes it look as if you have read it already. This is not as effective as the 'skip' or 'delete' option, which saves time and money because the offending article is never copied to your computer in the first place.

Killfile scans can be set up in two ways. The simplest way is to list all the offending authors and subjects. The more complicated approach is to killfile by creating a set of rules which attempt to pick out unwanted postings. Not all software gives you both options.

To use the second approach you need to understand the meanings of certain symbols. The most useful are:

'*' This is a 'catch-all' symbol. For example 'new*' would kill all information that started with 'new'.

'|' This means 'or'. So 'new | old' would kill all information that mentioned the words 'new' or 'old'. By combining these symbols with the relevant words, it is possible to kill a wide range of messages with a single killfile entry. Thus:

```
subject: (((fast | free | get | mak* | legal | quick | easy)
& (cash* | money* | dollar* |$10*| ($ |$50*))) | ($$|$$$*) |
make$* | $$cash* | ca$h* | $mo* | fastcash* | fastmoney* |
(DOLLAR* & week*))
```

will kill most 'get rich quick' scams.

Other useful tricks include killing all messages from authors using a certain IAP – *author: (iap's domain name goes here)* – and anything that asks you to call a free number in the USA – *subject: (1-800*)*.

If your software has the facility, it is also useful to killfile all articles that have been cross posted (see page 89) to more than one newsgroup. You run the risk of missing something interesting this way but you are more likely to save yourself the trouble of reading through a lot of annoying postings. You can also set up some software so that a killfile entry is temporary or specific to a certain newsgroup. Killfiling takes quite a bit of time, so it is useful – as well as cheaper – to keep your criteria as short and as simple as possible. A list of useful killfile criteria posted on Usenet includes the following:

- all posts by people who do not use a real name
- all get-rich-quick scams
- all advertisements
- anything with 'sex', 'nude' or 'teen' in the subject line
- any argumentative subject line, for example, 'You are all idiots'
- any subject that has more than one thread
- anything that has been cross posted
- posts with more than two paragraphs of quotes.

Initially, you may need to set up some of these by hand after encountering an offensive article or thread, but from then on all articles in that thread will no longer appear. Following this advice will make your experience of Usenet much more pleasant than it might otherwise be.

Finding or starting a mailing list

The easiest way to find a list is to search the newsgroup archives and the Web for a word that describes your interest and add the word 'mailing list' to it. New mailing lists are always announced in newsgroups, and a news archive search will reveal the relevant article/s. Similarly, back issues of some lists are published on the Web.

If this approach does not produce anything, the next step is to find a newsgroup related to the subject matter. This will either have an FAQ, which contains the appropriate details, or the newsgroup's members will know of a suitable list. As a last resort, it can be worth trying to search through the Liszt list directory (*http://www.liszt.com*) This is an automatic search system that scans the Internet looking for mailing lists. In its current incarnation it does not seem to be particularly reliable, and many lists which should be included appear to be missing. But it can be a good source of leads, and if all else fails you can always email the maintainer of a list dedicated to a related subject to see if they know of one that is closer to what you have in mind. Some lists occasionally list other relevant lists. Finally, do remember that news of mailing lists is often passed by word of mouth. Friends who share your interests may know of something suitable.

If all else fails, it is possible that no such list exists. At this point you have the option of starting one yourself. This is fairly straightforward. Some IAPs offer the facilities for you to do this and may even help you get started. Starting a list implies that you have volunteered for the job of moderator, and, of course, this is not a role that everyone will feel comfortable with. But if you feel confident that you can keep a group of people in order and 'on-topic' without being too heavy-handed or getting drawn into unnecessary personal conflicts, then creating and maintaining a list can be a very satisfying exercise.

To offer a mailing list service, your IAP needs to have a list server running one of the popular list maintenance systems – either Majordomo or ListServ. If they do not have this facility and are unwilling to install it, you will have to look elsewhere. If they do, you will need to set up your list by following the instructions your IAP sends you. This is only slightly harder than setting up an email account and much more straightforward than creating a web site. The next step is to advertise the list to make sure you get enough interest. You can do this on your web page, if you have one, but by far the best approach is to announce the list in one or more relevant newsgroups. The rest of your job will be maintenance – you will sometimes need to add and remove people from the list by hand if they forget how to leave or join the list or if they step out of line, but otherwise the software does most of the maintenance for you.

Some lists do occasionally lie moribund for days or weeks on end, but most come to life immediately. If after a while you find the list is taking up too much of your time, you will usually be able to find a volunteer who will take on the job of moderating it. Like newsgroups, once a certain number of enthusiastic posters has appeared, a list can become self-sustaining and will carry on indefinitely.

FURTHER INFORMATION

THIS SECTION includes a summary of the various resources available on the Internet. It is not in any way comprehensive – a full survey would fill a whole bookshelf – but it does provide some useful starting points for further exploration.

Unusual Internet facilities

This is a selection of some of the more unusual options and facilities that the Internet offers. Some are experimental and are included because they are a taste of what the Internet may offer in the future.

Video Conferencing

You can find out more about CU–SeeMe and try a free version of the software at *http://www.cu-seeme.com/biw.htm* The company also has a UK distributor who can be emailed at *sullivand @e92plus.co.uk* Tiny video cameras and suitable software are made by Connectix at *http://www.connectix.com*

WebPhones

There are a variety of WebPhone options. WebPhone software is beginning to be standardised to the ITU (International Telephony Union) H.323 standard. Any WebPhone that uses this system should work with any other. Free trial versions of suitable software are available form Intel at *http://www.intel.com* and IBM at *http://www.ics.raleigh.ibm.com/ics/icphone.htm*

Details of other products are regularly announced in the Internet press.

MUDs

Some MUDs are on the Web, but most require telnet access. A comprehensive list of MUD-related resources, including lists of MUDs, details of what MUDs are and how they work, FAQs, links to relevant newsgroups, and so on, is available at *http://godlike.com/muds*

Fax/email gateways

A rather technical description of this service is available at *http://www.tpc.int/* or *http://www.dis.org/fax/faxsend.html* This explains which kinds of attachments are and are not allowed with emailed faxes.

Privacy resources

Privacy resources are used to make up for the Internet's security flaws, to keep private information away from accidental or deliberate public scrutiny.

Anonymous remailers

A list of links and information about remailer-related facilities is at *http://www.cs.berkeley.edu/~raph/remailer-list.html* The site seems fairly technical at first glance, but some of the linked articles are written at a level more suitable for beginners.

Anonymisers

The anonymiser site at *http://www.anonymizer.com* lets you view web pages anonymously.

PGP

PGP has its own newsgroups – *alt.security.pgp* and *comp.security.pgp*

– and these have their own FAQs. A copy of the *alt.security.pgp* FAQ is available at *http://www.rivertown.net:8080/pgpfaq.html* Both cryptography and PGP require a reasonable level of computer literacy, so you may find you need to do some background research before you can start using the system for yourself. There is a non-commercial PGP home page at *http://www.ifi.uio.no/pgp* and a commercial page at *http://www.pgp.com* The latter includes free trials of the older and clumsier version of PGP called PGPmail, as well as news of commercial versions which can work with popular email packages.

Resources for business opportunities (and how to vet them)

The Securities and Investment Board (SIB) site at *http://www.sib.co.uk* includes information on how to distinguish between scams and genuine investment opportunities. FraudNews (*http://www.silverquick.com/fraudnews.htm*), the Fraud Information Centre (*http://www.fraud.org*) and Scambusters (*http://www.scambusters.com*) are good sources of information about the latest scams and con tricks. The newsgroup *uk.finance* is also well worth reading.

Software resources

Software on the Internet appears in three forms: commercial software, which you need to pay for immediately; shareware, which is offered on a 'try before you buy' basis; and beta software, which is offered for free in an unfinished and possibly accident-prone state, and which you use at your own risk. Some software is also available for restricted use – typically, if you use the software commercially you are expected to pay for it but if you use it at home for your own non-commercial use it is free. Most software states clearly which category it falls into. Shareware demands a certain amount of honesty, and if you do find yourself using a piece of shareware regularly you should pay for it. Some shareware authors rely on these 'voluntary' payments to make a living, and the existence of shareware is a resource that benefits everyone.

Browsers

At the time of writing, the browser market is the scene of a pitched battle between two companies – Netscape and Microsoft. Netscape – the browser market leader – offers Navigator Version 3, which is the most widely used browser. (Earlier versions are still available and are offered by some IAPs as part of the software they supply when you sign up. If you have an earlier version you should change to version 3 as soon as possible.) While it is an excellent browser, Navigator's email and newsgroup facilities are rudimentary.

Navigator Gold is a more sophisticated version of Navigator and includes basic HTML editing facilities, which you can use to create your own web pages. However, these are very basic compared with those available from other web page creation software.

Communicator is a package intended for business users who share the same network – an Intranet. Communicator includes an extended version of Navigator, slightly improved email and news facilities and a selection of features that make it easier for people to exchange information with others in a group. Netscape has plans for a completely new product, which will be available in 1998, but no details were available at the time of writing.

The Netscape site at *http://www.netscape.com* has full details of all these products and also offers downloads so you can copy them to your computer. Navigator is not free, although free beta versions are widely available and Netscape offers a free restricted-use licence for certain users, such as those who are using the product in a non-commercial setting.

Microsoft offers Internet Explorer Version 4. Unlike Netscape, which works on most computer systems, Explorer has many features which link it to Microsoft's Windows 95 operating system – as well as related systems such as Windows 97 and Windows NT. Explorer also works well with Microsoft's Office business software suite. As with Navigator, older versions of Explorer are still available. Version 3.01 contains security loopholes which allow hackers to gain access to the information inside your computer. If you have this version you should change to version 4.

Microsoft's site at *http://www.microsoft.com/ie/default.asp* has full details of the latest version of Explorer.

Plug-ins

The latest list of Navigator plug-ins is available at *http://home.netscape.com/inf/comprod/products/navigator/version_2. 0/plugins/index.html* The list is very long and increasing all the time. As a rough guide, it is not usually worth getting a plug-in until you come across a site that demands it. Some plug-ins are very obscure, and you will not need them at all unless you work in a specialised technical field. The most popular ones – Shockwave, Real Audio and VRML – are widely available. At the time of writing it was not possible to find a corresponding list of plug-ins for Internet Explorer. Some plug-ins will work with both browsers, but there are technical differences between Navigator and Explorer which make these plug-ins the exception rather than the rule.

Other software

Many excellent collections of software are available on the Internet. Tucows at *http://www.tucows.com* is a very comprehensive list of sites that offer Internet-specific software of every conceivable kind, arranged by category and rated for quality. Software is available for PC compatibles that use Windows, and for the Apple Macintosh and its clones. Tucows has over 200 mirror sites around the world. When downloading software, use the mirror site that seems to be the fastest, even if it is not necessarily the closest to you geographically.

A similar list of software is offered by download.com at *http://www.download.com* for both PC and Apple Macintosh computers, together with newsgroups and links to a variety of other useful Internet software and information sources presented in a magazine-like format. When choosing newsgroup and email software make sure that it works off-line. A number of IAPs and other services offer on-line email, which is needlessly expensive. Off-line software is much cheaper, and well worth copying from the Internet.

Search systems

Use these search systems to find information about anything and everything on the Web. Search systems appear as 'search engines' which find web sites that mention specific words, and 'web directories', which are lists of sites arranged in categories. Some offer both types of search.

Search engines

The most popular engines are:
AltaVista   *http://www.altavista.digital.com/*
Yahoo   *http://www.yahoo.com*
Lycos   *http://www.lycos.com*
Webcrawler   *http://www.webcrawler.com*

Meta search engines

Instead of searching with one engine, these set up a search using many engines simultaneously, and then collate and present the results for you. They offer a handy way to check lots of engines at once. For a list of these see *http://www.yahoo.com/ computers_and_internet/internet/world_wide_web/searching_ the_web/all_in_one_search_pages/*

Mailing lists

The Liszt list of mailing lists at *http://www.liszt.com* is an attempt to create a complete directory of all the mailing lists on the Internet. This is an experimental service which is not as comprehensive as it aims to be, but it offers a good starting point for anyone looking for a list devoted to a particular topic.

Web site announcement services

Submit It! at *http://www.submit-it.com/* is one of the most popular site announcement services. When your pages are ready to be put on the Web, you can send the URL to this site and it will forward your details to the 20 most popular search engines for free.

Commercial users can pay a small fee to have the URL copied to over a hundred search engines. Submit It! also includes the Link Exchange service, which offers free banner advertising for participating sites. This works in the same way as commercial web banner advertising, but no money is exchanged and the banners display information and act as links to other sites in the scheme.

On-line information sources

Unsurprisingly, much Internet-related information is available on-line. The examples that follow are a very brief indication of the huge number of resources that can be used for free.

RFCs (Request For Comment)

RFCs are the Internet's technical manuals and include full details of how the different parts of the Internet work. Each document is really a proposal, although some proposals have gone on to become Internet standards. The language and the ideas used in most RFCs are really quite impenetrable to outsiders. They are technical documents written by computer experts, for example, RFCs 1034 and 1035 include full technical definitions of the domain name system (see Appendix 3), including the theory and how it works in practice. However, a handful – such as RFC 1855, which is a guide to Netiquette (Internet etiquette) – are intended for a wider readership. Apart from being reference tools, RFCs are also a historical record. The numbers are sequential (lower-numbered RFCs are older than higher-numbered ones), and taken together RFCs provide the definitive documentary record of the Internet's development. The system is still being used: for example, RFC 1876 is a proposal for including latitude, longitude and altitude in domain names – an idea that may come into its own once satellite and mobile systems become more widely used.

The full set of RFCs is available in many places on the Internet, usually via FTP. Copying them to a computer takes a sizeable amount of filing space, so most people read them on-line instead. To find a local site that holds these documents try using a search engine to look for RFC, RFCs or RFC Index.

On-line dictionaries

WhatIs – *http://www.whatis.com* – offers a comprehensive dictionary of Internet and computing terms as well as short articles about writing HTML, how the Internet works, and so on.

FAQ finders

A list of literally thousands of FAQs is available at *http://ps.superb.net/FAQ* You can search for FAQs by keyword or by following a list of headings and sub-headings.

Traditional media

Books and magazines can still be extremely useful when you are trying to master the Internet. The information available covers the full range of Internet facilities, from help for total beginners to reference materials for professionals.

Choosing books

Hundreds, if not thousands, of books have been written about the Internet. They fall into three categories:

- technical reference manuals
- web site and other resource directories
- beginners' guides.

As far as beginners are concerned, almost all reference manuals are pitched at a level somewhere between intimidating and incomprehensible. They are written for people who want to know about the nuts and bolts of the Internet, and the specialised information they offer requires much more sophisticated computer skills than most Internet users are likely to have or need. If you need to know how to write your own CGI scripts or how to get the best from Perl, then you may find them useful. Otherwise, they are best left on the shelf.

Directories and listings are the tour guides of the Internet. Some are sober and straightforward, while others – especially those that concentrate on the more controversial aspects of Internet life – are written in a jaunty and colourful journalistic style that often matches the culture of the Internet itself. These guides can be surprisingly useful but can also date quickly because sites appear and disappear. Although the writing may be entertaining, it is often better to use the Web's own search facilities to find information on a given subject instead of relying on printed information – in fact, the information in most guides is collated by doing just this. On the other hand, these directories can point you in the direction of resources you might not have thought of looking for. And, of course, having a ready-made listing in print is often more convenient than having to do the searching yourself, even if one or two URLs no longer work.

Beginner's guides vary hugely in both usefulness and price, with no guaranteed correlation between the two. The majority of books are written for the US market, and many of these include trial offers for US IAPs. These are, of course, useless for UK readers, who would need to pay transatlantic telephone charges to take advantage of them. When choosing a guide, look out for the following:

- **Free software** Although copying software from the Internet is relatively straightforward, getting it free with a book in the form of a CD-ROM or floppy disk is even simpler. However, the software offered by some books falls into the category of 'shovelware' (it is not particularly outstanding and has been included only to fill up the CD-ROM), while others offer more useful products and packages. An ideal book/CD-ROM combination provides plenty of examples of all the different kinds of software you may need, including web browsers, and email newsreaders, FTP software and plenty of useful extras such as telnet, Traceroute and Finger. Most books supply software on CD-ROMs now instead of floppy disks, so your computer will need to have a CD-ROM drive fitted if you want to try out the software.
- **Free trials and special offers** Free trials for the UK (which are usually offered for on-line services, but occasionally for IAPs or combined services) are always worth having, although you should read the small print to see exactly how much of a

saving a special offer really gives you. All free trials are given in the hope that you will continue to use the service as a matter of habit. Even if you sign up for one of these, it is still worth looking at the advertising in the various Internet magazines to see if another service can offer you a better deal in the longer term.

- **Computer specific advice** Many books are written for users of the Unix operating system because it is so popular on the Internet. Unix computers are completely unlike personal ones, and their software works in an entirely different way. You can spot a book that takes a Unix approach to introducing the Internet by checking if it concentrates on Unix-specific Internet software packages such as Pine and Elm. Unix software tends to require lots of cryptic typed messages, whereas personal computer software is much more visually oriented and easier to use.

Choosing magazines

There are far fewer Internet magazines than general computer ones, and this makes it much easier to find quality information. Most magazines are general-purpose titles that include newsgroups, software reviews and listings of interesting web sites. The best offer useful features to help beginners get started. Only one or two are aimed specifically at beginners.

Connect (Future Publishing)
This is an Internet listings magazine, very much like an Internet version of the *Radio* or *TV Times*. Billed as 'The Essential Guide To Net Entertainment', it concentrates on the less serious side of the Internet and includes a CD-ROM with various entertainment-type software, including trial versions of the latest games. The style is slightly tabloid-like, but it has plenty of information about unusual web sites.

.net (Future Publishing)
.net is *Connect*'s older brother and is aimed at more experienced Internet users. The style is frank and explicit and can be deliberately controversial. The breadth and depth of the content and the colourful style can leave newcomers feeling baffled. Two

versions are available: one with a cover CD-ROM, which offers free trials and software, and a cheaper one without.

Wired (Wired Ventures)

An attempt to produce an Internet lifestyle magazine, this US publication tries to inspire a vision of what the Internet should be about. It has topical and futuristic stories about what may happen on the Net next, self-consciously historical Internet retrospectives and topical features about the most controversial issues of the moment, such as censorship, privacy, electronic cash, and so on. The design is garish, and the articles are aimed squarely at 'geeks', who either make a living from computers and the Internet or would very much like to. It does not have any 'how to' articles, and even the web listings are short and stylised.

Beginners may find the style of this magazine heavy going, but some of the more forward-looking and topical articles can be thought-provoking.

Total Internet (Rapide Publishing)

This is a good all-round magazine aimed at slightly more experienced net users and has an interesting range of news, product reviews and background articles. Most of each issue is devoted to a large web directory listing, which covers a huge range of topics which changes every month. Also included are a list of IAPs – although only their contact details and prices are provided – and cybercafés.

Practical Internet (Paragon Publishing)

This is another all-round magazine which specialises in product reviews, introductory 'how to' features and various topical background articles. The content is slightly pedestrian compared with some of the other magazines, but beginners should be able to derive some benefit from most of the features. Also included is a comparative table of IAPs, which includes prices, geographical coverage and other useful information.

Internet Today (Paragon Publishing)

Internet Today is a fairly standard collection of news, reviews, listings and general background features. It is not strong on 'how to' articles or information for beginners. The content and presentation are less imaginative than *Practical Internet*. A brief list of IAPs is included.

NetUser (Paragon Publishing)
A comparatively bland listings magazine, *NetUser* focuses on a small number of topics each month. It does not have any other features or background information, and the amount of information in it is limited, given the price.

Internet Magazine (Emap Business Communications)
Bulky and glossy, it successfully balances informative features, topical stories, news, reviews and listings. The writing style is sober and informative without being dull. Articles cover a wide range of topics with plenty to interest both beginners and more seasoned Internet users.

Also included in the magazine is a comprehensive list of UK IAPs, with objective consumer tests of the performance of the most widely used ones. Advertising is perhaps more comprehensive and informative than that in the other Internet magazines and includes products and services of interest to both home and business users.

Internet Business (Internet Business Magazine Ltd)
Aimed squarely at business users, this title includes a variety of business-related features written for anyone who uses, or is thinking of using, the Internet in a business setting. The style is serious and professional, and the content includes useful business-related news stories and information that does not appear in any other title. Although it does not have any directories, business-oriented IAPs advertise heavily in it. It is perhaps best thought of as a monthly manager's Internet briefing: strong on business ideas and background but lacking practical 'nuts and bolts' details.

Internet World (VNU Publications)
This is another business-oriented title that includes the usual mix of news, reviews and listings. *Internet World* includes plenty of reviews of both services and software and also useful and unique case studies – these take the place of web listings and provide a detailed and critical look at the strengths and weaknesses of the featured web sites.

On-line services

America Online	(0800) 2791234
CompuServe	(0990) 000200
MSN	(0345) 002000
Which? Online	(0645) 830240
Virgin Net	(0500) 558800
Line One	(0800) 111210

Other web sites mentioned in this book

Eileen Herzberg	*http://www.users.dircon.co.uk/~eileen*
Jacey Bedford and Artisan	*http://www.artifact.demon.co.uk*
Glastonbury Framing	*http://www.isleofavalon.co.uk/gframing/gframing.html*

GLOSSARY

Acceptable Use Policy (AUP) A set of rules outlining what users can and cannot do on the Internet and what the consequences are likely to be if they break these rules.

account A particular user's Internet connection, so called because it usually has to be paid for.

address The electronic equivalent of a postal address – a unique string of words, usually separated by dots, colons, slashes and other punctuation, that is used to send or retrieve information from a certain computer or email account.

America Online (AOL) One of the world's largest on-line service providers.

anonymous remailer A special email forwarding address on the Internet which can be used to make email messages and newsgroup postings anonymous.

ARCHIE ARCHIE exists to make it easier to find files using FTP (*q.v.*). It searches for keywords in text files and in file descriptions.

ASCII (American Standard Code for Information Interchange) The coding standard used in the computer world to make sure that when a user types an 'A' in an email message and sends it to someone else, the recipient sees the letter 'A' and not a completely different letter, and so on.

ASCII art Art made of letters and other symbols.

attachment One or more binaries (*q.v.*) which are attached to an email using Uuencoding (*q.v.*), MIME (*q.v.*), BinHex (*q.v.*) and Base64 (*q.v.*).

backbone An extremely fast connection on the Internet that acts as a trunk route between two major computer centres.

Base64 A system used to translate binaries into text so they can be sent over the Internet.

binaries Any information that is not text – for example, word processor documents with formatting, sounds, images or video clips.

BinHex A system used to convert binaries (*q.v.*) to text so they can be sent over the Internet.

bookmark A feature of most web browsers, which marks a web page so that a user can go straight to it on another occasion.

bot (from robot) A computer that does something 'intelligent', such as holding a conversation on IRC (*q.v.*).

bounce When email cannot be delivered it is returned to the sender with a brief note. It is then said to have bounced.

browse The act of looking through pages on the WWW, sometimes with a goal in mind, sometimes just to see where the links take you.

cache A place on your hard drive where your browser stores copies of the last few web pages you have visited.

CompuServe A very large international on-line service.

Deja News A popular archive of newsgroup postings at *http://www.dejanews.com* combined with an easy-to-use search engine.

DNS (Domain Name Server) See 'name server'.

domain (also called domain name) The part of an Internet address that identifies one particular computer or Internet service.

down A computer that is not available is said to be down. See also 'up'.

Dynamic HTML The latest version of the HTML (*q.v.*) standard.

email (electronic mail) The name given to messages in electronic form that are sent from computer to computer.

expire Used for newsgroup postings – these are deleted after a set period to make room for new postings. An expired posting is no longer available.

e-zine (electronic magazine) A web publication that is updated regularly but usually produced by amateurs for others with similar interests.

FAQ Frequently asked question list. A document that answers the most commonly asked questions on a particular subject. Most newsgroups have one.

file format A description of the kind of software needed to understand what is inside a file, for example, avi – Microsoft Video for Windows video player; mov – Apple Quicktime video player; jpeg – jpeg image file; gif – gif image file.

finger An Internet tool used to get information about a remote computer system or a distant email account, for example, the location of a particular user's terminal or when he or she last logged on to a particular server.

firewall An Internet security system that protects an internal network.

flame A nasty message sent to someone who has been annoying.

flame war An endless round of flames.

forging It is possible to make an email message appear as if it has come from one person when really it has come from another. This is called header forging.

FTP (File Transfer Protocol) The system used on the Internet to copy information from one computer to another.

FTP site A computer that offers an FTP facility on the Internet.

gateway A computer on the Internet that links one part of the network, or one service, to another.

geek The stereotypical Internet user. Geeks are good with computers but are typically socially inept and tend to spend most of their time on-line to the exclusion of other interests.

geek code A collection of letters and other symbols added to some sigs (*q.v.*), which give a shorthand account of the writer's personal and professional circumstances.

Gopher A primitive text-only precursor to the WWW.

groupware Software designed to work on a network, such as the Internet or an Intranet (*q.v.*), which makes it easier for a group of people to work together.

header The section at the top of an email and newsgroup message that contains information about where the message has come from, when it was sent, and so on.

host An Internet computer that has been set up to offer a service to users.

HTML (Hypertext Mark-up Language) The computer language used to create web pages.

http:// The letters added at the beginning of a web address (or URL) that let the browser know it is supposed to be accessing a web server.

hypertext Text with links in it.

Internet access provider (IAP), or Internet service provider. An organisation that supplies a connection to the Internet, usually in return for a fee.

Internet Explorer (IE) Microsoft's answer to Netscape Navigator (*q.v.*) – a very popular web browser. It works very closely with Windows 95.

Intranet Internal computer network used within an organisation.

IRC (Internet Relay Chat) A system which connects thousands of people around the world. Unlike other Internet services, IRC happens 'live'.

Java Programming language which enhances web pages.

junk email The electronic equivalent of junk paper mail.

keyword Keyword searches look for occurrences of one or more words.

killfile An invaluable feature of email and newsreading software which blacklists certain subjects or postings/messages from certain people so they no longer appear. A good way to deal with flames and junk email (*q.v.*).

link A word, phrase or address that appears on a web page, underlined or in a different colour, and links to a different related web page, email address or newsgroup.

log-in (or log-on) Connect to a computer.

mailing list A list of people with common interests.

MIME Multipurpose Internet Mail Extensions – a not-quite-standardised system used to send binaries (*q.v.*) within email messages.

mirror Some FTP sites (*q.v.*) have replicas in different locations. This is done to make it quicker to access the information locally and also to take the load off the main site.

MOO Object Oriented MUD – yet another variation on the MUD idea (*q.v.*).

MUD Multi User Dungeon – an on-line game system in which players can explore a virtual world and interact with each other in various more or less violent ways. Often accessed via telnet (*q.v.*).

MUSH Multi User Shared Hallucination – a more elaborate version of the MUD (*q.v.*) idea, in which players can help to build the environment they are in instead of simply exploring it.

name server Sometimes abbreviated to DNS, a name server is a computer that converts an Internet address into a string of numbers.

Netscape The company responsible for Navigator, one of the most popular web browsers.

newsgroup International discussion areas. There are about 20,000 devoted to almost every topic imaginable.

news server A special computer that keeps an up-to-date copy of the thousands of daily postings made to Usenet (*q.v.*).

off-line Not connected to the Internet. For example, it is possible to write an email off-line, then connect to the Internet to send it. This saves you money.

on-line Connected to the Internet, and – by implication – spending money through phone charges, connection charges or both.

on-line service provider Apart from providing the usual Internet services, an on-line service provider adds extra facilities such as software libraries and live chat.

packet The basic unit of information on the Internet.

PGP Pretty Good Privacy – a system devised to secure email from prying eyes by converting it into an encrypted form.

Ping A short message that says 'Are you there?'. Used to check if a remote computer is switched on or accessible before a user attempts to use it.

plan A few lines of information that are sometimes returned by finger.

POP3 (Post Office Protocol) A recent and advanced system used to copy email between a home computer and the Internet.

posting A message sent to a newsgroup or the act of sending a message to a newsgroup (*q.v.*).

postmaster The individual at a computer site who looks after email. Sometimes, but not always, the same as the sys-admin (*q.v.*).

proxy A web server installed by a service provider that keeps copies of popular web pages from around the world.

pull Applied to Internet accounts – 'pulling an account' means removing it so that a user is denied access.

Push media Information that is offered to you, as opposed to that which you actively look for.

real life Life away from the Internet.

search engine Used for tracking down useful and interesting information from the mass of links and pages on the WWW.

server An Internet computer that provides a service.

shouting WRITING SOMETHING IN CAPITALS IS CONSIDERED SHOUTING, and very rude.

sig (signature file) A standard file that is often added to the end of email and newsgroup postings and contains a witty quote, a web page reference, etc.

sign-on Connect to the Internet and/or start using one of its facilities.

site A place on the Internet which offers information, for example, a web site offers WWW pages.

smileys Minimal examples of ASCII art (*q.v.*) used to add extra emotion to text-only conversations. For example :-) means smiling or happy.

SMTP Simple mail transfer protocol – one system used to copy waiting email between the computers. See also 'POP3'.

snail-mail Mail sent the old-fashioned way with paper, ink and stamps.

spam Flooding newsgroups with copies of the same message – usually one advertising a service.

SLIP Serial Line Internet Protocol – a system used to connect modems to the Internet. Point to Point Protocol (PPP) is a better system.

surf The act of looking through pages on the WWW. Identical to browsing (*q.v.*).

Sys-admin The person responsible for maintaining a computer system.

TCP/IP Transmission Control Protocol/Internet Protocol – the system used on the Internet to move information between computers.

TCP/IP stack Part of the software which enables a PC to send or receive information using TCP/IP.

telnet An Internet service which allows you to log-on to a computer somewhere else, perhaps on another continent, via the Internet and use it as if you were sitting in front of it.

Traceroute The Internet equivalent of a homing missile. It lists all the Internet connections between a user's computer and a remote computer.

troll A newsgroup posting that looks serious but is really a practical joke intended to provoke an irate response. Often very cleverly disguised.

ukp 'UK pounds'.

Unix A long-established operating system which is frequently used on the Internet (usually by service providers and universities).

up A computer is said to be up when it is working properly.

URL (Uniform Resource Locator) The address of a web page.

Usenet The network of newsgroups.

user name (or user-id) The name you use to identify yourself to your IAP's computer system.

Uuencoding A technique developed to make it possible to send binaries (*q.v.*) across the Internet.

Veronica An extension to the Gopher service (*q.v.*) that makes it easier to navigate through keyword searches (*q.v.*).

WAIS Wide Area Information Services – an extension to Veronica (*q.v.*).

webmaster The person responsible for maintaining a web site.

web server A computer that stores web pages and passes them over the Internet whenever anyone looks at that site.

web site In the same way that a book or magazine is made up of printed pages, a web site consists of web pages which have a common theme.

web page A single page of information on the WWW.

Winsock A piece of software used by PCs running the Microsoft Windows operating system, which links the Internet connection to the rest of the software inside the PC.

World Wide Web (WWW) The most popular and most accessible way to use the Internet. The WWW is a collection of text, pictures, sounds, video clips, graphics and other information arranged in pages with links between them.

International codes in email addresses

.ac	an academic institution
.co	a company that trades in a single country
.com	a commercial organisation that trades internationally
.gov	a government department or other related facility
.nato	a NATO installation
.net	an organisation or company that provides Internet access
.org	a non-commercial organisation, such as a charity

UK-specific codes

.ltd	a UK Limited Company
.mod	anything run by the UK Ministry of Defence
.nhs	anything run by the National Health Service
.plc	a UK Public Limited Company
.police	for the police (not much used)
.sch	a school

US codes

.edu	a school or university
.k12	a school
.mil	a military base
.(state)	a two-letter state abbreviation (always followed by .us)

At the time of writing there are plans to extend these codes to include:

.arts	related to arts and culture
.firm	a business

.info   an information service
.nom   a specific private or business name
.rec   related to recreation and hobbies
.store   a trading establishment
.web   related to the WWW

Domain country codes

ad	Andorra	cg	Congo	gf	French Guyana
ae	United Arab	ch	Switzerland	gh	Ghana
	Emirates	ci	Ivory Coast (Côte	gi	Gibraltar
af	Afghanistan		d'Ivoire)	gl	Greenland
ag	Antigua and Barbuda	ck	Cook Is.	gm	Gambia
ai	Anguilla	cl	Chile	gn	Guinea
al	Albania	cm	Cameroon	gp	Guadeloupe
am	Armenia	cn	China		(French)
an	Netherlands Antilles	co	Colombia	gq	Equatorial Guinea
ao	Angola	cr	Costa Rica	gr	Greece
aq	Antarctica	cs	Former	gs	S. Georgia & S.
ar	Argentina		Czechoslovakia		Sandwich Is.
arpa	Old style Arpanet	cu	Cuba	gt	Guatemala
as	American Samoa	cv	Cape Verde	gu	Guam (USA)
at	Austria	cx	Christmas Is.	gw	Guinea Bissau
au	Australia	cy	Cyprus	gy	Guyana
aw	Aruba	cz	Czech Republic	hk	Hong Kong
az	Azerbaidjan	de	Germany	hm	Heard and
ba	Bosnia-Herzegovina	dj	Djibouti		Mcdonald Is.
bb	Barbados	dk	Denmark	hn	Honduras
bd	Bangladesh	dm	Dominica	hr	Croatia
be	Belgium	do	Dominican	ht	Haiti
bf	Burkina Faso		Republic	hu	Hungary
bg	Bulgaria	dz	Algeria	id	Indonesia
bh	Bahrain	ec	Ecuador	ie	Ireland
bi	Burundi	ee	Estonia	il	Israel
bj	Benin	eg	Egypt	in	India
bm	Bermuda	eh	Western Sahara	int	International
bn	Brunei Darussalam	es	Spain	io	British Indian
bo	Bolivia	et	Ethiopia		Ocean Terr.
br	Brazil	fi	Finland	iq	Iraq
bs	Bahamas	fj	Fiji	ir	Iran
bt	Butan	fk	Falkland Is.	is	Iceland
bv	Bouvet Is.	fm	Micronesia	it	Italy
bw	Botswana	fo	Faroe Is.	jm	Jamaica
by	Belarus	fr	France	jo	Jordan
bz	Belize	fx	France (European	jp	Japan
ca	Canada		Terr.)	ke	Kenya
cc	Cocos (Keeling)	ga	Gabon	kg	Kyrgyzstan
	Is.	gb	Great Britain	kh	Cambodia
cf	Central African	gd	Grenada	ki	Kiribati
	Republic	ge	Georgia	km	Comoros

kn	Saint Kitts & Nevis Anguilla	nl	Netherlands	sv	El Salvador
kp	North Korea	no	Norway	sy	Syria
kr	South Korea	np	Nepal	sz	Swaziland
kw	Kuwait	nr	Nauru	tc	Turks & Caicos Is.
ky	Cayman Is.	nt	Neutral Zone	td	Chad
kz	Kazakstan	nu	Niue	tf	French Southern
la	Laos	nz	New Zealand		Terr
lb	Lebanon	om	Oman	tg	Togo
lc	Saint Lucia	pa	Panama	th	Thailand
li	Liechtenstein	pe	Peru	tj	Tadjikistan
lk	Sri Lanka	pf	Polynesia (French)	tk	Tokelau
lr	Liberia	pg	Papua New	tm	Turkmenistan
ls	Lesotho		Guinea	tn	Tunisia
lt	Lithuania	ph	Philippines	to	Tonga
lu	Luxembourg	pk	Pakistan	tp	East Timor
lv	Latvia	pl	Poland	tr	Turkey
ly	Libya	pm	Saint Pierre &	tt	Trinidad and
ma	Morocco		Miquelon		Tobago
mc	Monaco	pn	Pitcairn	tv	Tuvalu
md	Moldavia	pr	Puerto Rico	tw	Taiwan
mg	Madagascar	pt	Portugal	tz	Tanzania
mh	Marshall Is.	pw	Palau	ua	Ukraine
mk	Macedonia	py	Paraguay	ug	Uganda
ml	Mali	qa	Qatar	uk	United Kingdom
mm	Myanmar	re	Réunion (French)	um	USA Minor
mn	Mongolia	ro	Romania		Outlying Is.
mo	Macau	ru	Russian Federation	us	United States
mp	Northern Mariana Is.	rw	Rwanda	uy	Uruguay
		sa	Saudi Arabia	uz	Uzbekistan
mq	Martinique (French)	sb	Solomon Is	va	Vatican City State
		sc	Seychelles	vc	Saint Vincent &
mr	Mauritania	sd	Sudan		Grenadines
ms	Montserrat	se	Sweden	ve	Venezuela
mt	Malta	sg	Singapore	vg	Virgin Is. (British)
mu	Mauritius	sh	Saint Helena	vi	Virgin Is. (US)
mv	Maldives	si	Slovenia	vn	Vietnam
mw	Malawi	sj	Svalbard & Jan	vu	Vanuatu
mx	Mexico		Mayen Is.	wf	Wallis & Futuna Is.
my	Malaysia	sk	Slovak Republic	ws	Samoa
mz	Mozambique	sl	Sierra Leone	ye	Yemen
na	Namibia	sl	Sierra Leone	yt	Mayotte
nc	New Caledonia (French)	sm	San Marino	yu	Yugoslavia
		sn	Senegal	za	South Africa
ne	Niger	so	Somalia	zm	Zambia
nf	Norfolk Is.	sr	Suriname	zr	Zaire
ng	Nigeria	st	Saint Tomé & Príncipe	zw	Zimbabwe
ni	Nicaragua	su	Former USSR		

Taken from the web site at: *http://www.december.com/html/spec/domcodes.html*

INDEX